Running to Paradise

The wind is old and still at play
While I must hurry on my way,
For I am running to Paradise;
Yet never have I lit on a friend
To take my fancy like the wind
That nobody can buy or bind:
And there the king is *but as the beggar*.

—W. B. Y.

Portrait of Yeats (1907) by Augustus John

RUNNING TO PARADISE

Yeats's Poetic Art

M. L. ROSENTHAL

New York   Oxford
OXFORD UNIVERSITY PRESS

Oxford University Press

Oxford   New York   Toronto
Delhi   Bombay   Calcutta   Madras   Karachi
Kuala Lumpur   Singapore   Hong Kong   Tokyo
Nairobi   Dar es Salaam   Cape Town
Melbourne   Auckland   Madrid
and associated companies in
Berlin   Ibadan

Copyright © 1994 by M. L. Rosenthal

Published by Oxford University Press, Inc.,
198 Madison Avenue, New York, New York 10016

First published as an Oxford University Press paperback, 1997

Oxford is a registered trademark of Oxford University Press

Library of Congress Cataloging-in-Publication Data
Rosenthal, M. L. (Macha Louis), 1917–
Running to paradise : Yeats's poetic art / M. L. Rosenthal.
p.   cm.
Includes bibliographical references and index.
ISBN 0-19-505200-5; 0-19-511391-8 (pbk)
1. Yeats, W. B. (William Butler), 1865–1939—Criticism and interpretation.
2. Modernism (Literature)—Ireland.
I. Title.
PR5907.R67   1994   821'.8—dc20   93-20178

2 4 6 8 9 7 5 3 1
Printed in the United States of America
on acid-free paper

To the memory of
David Herschel Rosenthal

Acknowledgments

Quotations from Yeats's poetry are reprinted with permission of Macmillan Publishing Company from *The Variorum Edition of the Poems of W. B. Yeats,* edited by Peter Allt and Russell K. Alspach. Copyright 1919, 1928, 1933 by Macmillan Publishing Company; copyrights renewed 1947, 1956, 1961 by Bertha Georgie Yeats. Copyright 1940 by Georgie Yeats, renewed 1968 by Bertha Georgie Yeats, Michael Butler Yeats, and Anne Yeats.

Portions of this book in their original form have appeared in *Yeats: An Annual of Critical and Textual Studies* and in *Yeats-Eliot Review.*

For other acknowledgments, see pages xv–xvi.

Contents

Illustrations

Introduction

It is now well over a half-century since the death of William Butler Yeats (1865–1939). He was arguably—although such ranking, if taken too seriously, is a game for innocents only—our greatest poet of this century writing in English. His poetry very often engages, and finds the right music for, the most difficult, intimate private and public issues: issues of love and death, of war and revolution, of Irish history and present crises. And he could be fanciful or playful, as becomes a good poet and true.

We look to the greatest poetry to give us pleasure while expressing subjective awareness and feeling almost to the point of mystical revelation. Simple as it is, this obvious double expectation needs constant restating. In addition, especially in an era that challenges the whole idea of artistic quality, it may call for a brief moment of preliminary explanation.

The "pleasure" in question—the special pleasure of art—includes much more than the sunny or voluptuous poems of un-alloyed joy that might first come to mind. It extends to work that is elegiac, tragic, bitterly witty, or even grossly disagreeable. It does not depend on the reflection of congenial attitudes. Rather, it is a matter of felicitous craftsmanship at the service of a work's inner structure of feeling and discovery. What is in itself ugly can become, in such a context, beautiful—as in these lines from the witches' chant in *Macbeth* **IV**, i:

> Scale of dragon, tooth of wolf,
> Witch's mummy, maw and gulf
> Of the ravined salt-sea shark,
> Root of hemlock digged i' th' dark,
> Liver of blaspheming Jew,
> Gall of goat and slips of yew
> Slivered in the moon's eclipse,
> Nose of Turk and Tartar's lips,
> Finger of birth-strangled babe
> Ditch-delivered by a drab,
> Make the gruel thick and slab . . .

This malicious chant adds weird notes of supernatural evil to the doom-laden tonal streams hurtling the play forward. Oddly, the viler the images become—given the brilliant fantasy and play of sound here—the more satisfying is our sense of their appropriateness. The alliterative clusters, at once melodic and harsh (as in the mixture of fluid consonants with plosives and stop-sounds), and the mouth-twisting rhymes enhance this effect. These lines breathe a morbid excitement related to the preceding horror and foreshadowing the grotesque final scene: Macbeth's gory head brandished atop a pole by Macduff, who has just killed him.

It may seem absurd to use a word like "pleasure" for effects (including notes of what we now can see as a probably unconscious racist nastiness) so contradictory to its usual meaning. But it is a peculiarly human fact that we do require such a use. We need it to identify the gratifying aspect of awareness itself, whether the aware-ness be of happy realities or cruel ones. (The sheer zest of Shake-

speare's lines makes for an almost cynical playfulness that is nevertheless a *satisfying* way of coping with images of pure revulsion.)
Yeats puts the matter drastically in his poem "Meru":

> Civilisation is hooped together, brought
> Under a rule, under the semblance of peace
> By manifold illusion; but man's life is thought,
> And he, despite his terror, cannot cease
> Ravening through century after century,
> Ravening, raging, and uprooting that he may come
> Into the desolation of reality:
> Egypt and Greece good-bye, and good-bye, Rome!
> Hermits upon Mount Meru or Everest,
> Caverned in night under the drifted snow,
> Or where the snow and winter's dreadful blast
> Beat down upon their naked bodies, know
> That day brings round the night, that before dawn
> His glory and his monuments are gone.

As these relentless lines show, human intellect is an unsentimental force. It is the original Pandora, restless to learn whatever secrets "the box"—objective reality—may hold. Art, meanwhile, is our inward, transforming mirror. In "Meru" its transforming process works by a triumphant proclamation, as it were, of the worst. Without denying "the desolation of reality," art mobilizes our psychic energies against yielding to it. The tension of this struggle is indeed a strange context for delight, but Yeats's rich, touching passage on the subject in "The Tower" perfectly reveals the consoling end in view:

> I have prepared my peace
> With learned Italian things
> And the proud stones of Greece,
> Poet's imaginings
> And memories of love,
> Memories of the words of women,

All those things whereof
Man makes a superhuman
Mirror-resembling dream.

My subject in this book is the quality of Yeats's memorable artistry in his lyrical poems and his plays, which so often resonate with grief or terror. Among the myriad studies of Yeats (as of other poets) filling the libraries, little attention is given to quality. Yet it is, precisely, quality that must be central to thinking about a great poet's work: a process of connecting with its pleasures, discoveries, and intrinsic humanity.

Yeats's artistry matured within the nineteenth-century poetic world he was born into. Blake, the Romantics, Tennyson, Arnold, and certain Irish figures (anonymous ballad-makers not least among them) were his forerunners. His technical skill grew like a second skin, enabling him at last to write brilliantly within and around the limits of traditional metrics. He taught himself to use conventional verse so naturally, with such supple variety, that in his hands it almost became a rare, highly disciplined species of free verse. Yet his virtuosity was never on display for its own sake. He subordinated it to his gift for phrasing that brings a work's emotional center into view at once—as in these lines at the start of "The Tower":

What shall I do with this absurdity—
O heart, O troubled heart—this caricature,
Decrepit age that has been tied to me
As to a dog's tail?

But I am anticipating. . . . We shall revisit "The Tower" further along. I have quoted two brief passages from it because they open a world of aesthetic pleasure that has its roots in beautiful, if not necesssarily happy, insight and phrasing. Yeats's life spanned the long interim between the last year of the American Civil War and the year World War II began. The vast struggles and changes in his own country and in the world as a whole during that period affected his poetic development to an unusual degree. At times his late work suffers artistically from his forays into militant popular verse and eccentrically angled rightist assertion. But at his frequent best he absorbed the tragic realities of our modern history, cultural and psychological as well as political, into a poetry of genuine humanity and even prophetic bearing. All in all, he too was worthy of the line in Swift's epitaph that goes (in Yeats's own translation): "He loved human liberty."

The following chapters are an essay in evaluative poetic criticism rather than a bibliographical or biographical study. I am all the more indebted, therefore, to the fine scholars and thinkers who have worked to establish accurate Yeats texts, to date and annotate them, and to set out their relevant biographical, historical, and philosophical background. I have tried to benefit from their labors (and from conversation with some of them over the years) while giving my basic attention to individual lyric poems and poetic plays and their artistry.

For information about dates of composition and publication and textual considerations, I am particularly indebted to certain well-known, established sources: most notably, Richard Ellmann's *The Identity of Yeats* (1964), Allan Wade's *A Bibliography of the Writings of W. B. Yeats* (1968), Curtis B. Bradford's *Yeats at Work* (1965) and his *Yeats's Last Poems Again* (1966), A. Norman Jeffares's *A New Commentary on the Poems of W. B. Yeats* (1984), Richard J. Finneran's "Revised" edition (1989) of *The Poems (The Collected Works of W. B. Yeats*: Volume I) and his *Editing Yeats's Poems: A Reconsideration* (1990), George Brandon Saul's *Prolegomena to the Study of Yeats's Poems* (1957) and *Prolegomena to the Study of Yeats's Plays* (1971), and Jon Stallworthy's *Between the Lines: Yeats's Poems in the Making* (1963) and *Visions and Revisions in Yeats's Last Poems* (1969).

My texts of reference are *The Variorum Edition of the Poems of*

W. B. Yeats (1957), edited by Peter Allt and Russell K. Alspach; *The Poems* (1989), edited by Richard J. Finneran; *The Variorum Edition of the Plays of W. B. Yeats* (1966), edited by Russell K. Alspach; *The Death of Cuchulain* (1982), edited by Phillip R. Marcus; and *Purgatory* (1986), edited by Sandra F. Siegel. As in my edition of *Selected Poems and Three Plays of William Butler Yeats* (1986), which contains a note on the text, I have sometimes had to make my own decisions concerning texts with rival claims to authenticity. The biographical and historical facts occasionally referred to in my discussion are readily available in any of various biographies and studies of Yeats (such as those by Thomas R. Henn, Joseph M. Hone, John Kelly, Liam Miller, William H. O'Donnell, Frank Tuohy, and F. A. C. Wilson) and surveys of Irish history. The list of extraordinary resources is a long one indeed.

Guggenheim Foundation fellowships many years ago were extremely helpful in leading to my various essays and books having to do with Yeats and with modern poetry generally—all part of the background of the present book. More recently, a sojourn at the Rockefeller Foundation's residential research center in Bellagio helped me get it started under most gracious circumstances. I am grateful, as well, to Dr. Sally M. Gall for her careful reading of the manuscript and useful suggestions.

Running to Paradise

I

Early Poems
(with Some Glances Ahead)

1. Before 1900

Yeats's earlier poems, even the love poems, are "youthful" but never quite carefree. When he was twenty, for instance, the *Dublin University Review* published his mostly unreadable pastoral play *The Island of Statues,* which did however contain some magical passages. One of them, later reprinted in revised form as the poem "The Cloak, the Boat, and the Shoes," begins:

First Voice	What do you weave so soft and bright?
Second Voice	The cloak I weave of sorrow;
	O lovely to see in all men's sight
	Shall be the cloak of sorrow—
	In all men's sight.

The easy linking of sorrow and beauty here has its sentimental side, but the gentle lyrical spell of the lines is compensation enough. And despite the vague base of the association, there are enough poetic antecedents—in Sappho and Catullus, in folk songs, in the songs in Shakespeare's plays, and in Blake and Byron and Keats among others—to have established the link as a firm convention. Yeats was drawn to it from the start, as his writings before 1900 clearly show.

One of the most delicately ardent earlier pieces, "He Wishes for the Cloths of Heaven," is touched with a charmed melancholy:

> Had I the heavens' embroidered cloths,
> Enwrought with golden and silver light,
> The blue and the dim and the dark cloths
> Of night and light and the half-light,
> I would spread the cloths under your feet:
> But I, being poor, have only my dreams;
> I have spread my dreams under your feet;
> Tread softly because you tread on my dreams.

Imagination here delights in its own ingenious design of sound and image. It is as though the poem, a single sentence that interweaves varied effects of color, vision, and mood, were itself one of "the heavens' embroidered cloths." Clearly, Yeats could have chosen to punctuate it more "logically": the first five lines making up the first sentence, and the next three each a separate one. But then the interwoven character of the whole brief piece would be lessened. The changing sky, sometimes clear and sometimes clouded, is "enwrought" with sunlight, moonlight, and starlight and is "spread" before us in the first half of this double quatrain. The fifth line—though grammatically the principal clause on which the preceding lines depend—then introduces its note of wistful gallantry, foreshadowing the language of vulnerable romantic dreaming thereafter.

"Embroidery" is certainly a pertinent term for this poem's form and phrasing. The decorative but increasingly intensified repetition of key words produces a densely overlaid pattern shot through with emotional reverberations. The end rhymes are all identical: "cloths," "light," "feet," and "dreams" each echoes itself; and the same words are also used for internal identical rhymes. The poem's successive, overlapping mood-shiftings gather around them while moving ahead toward the gentle near-pathos of the ending.

This is a love poem whose emphasis is on passive longing and on the fear of being startled into something like disillusionment. It projects a vision growing out of a state of deprivation. Yet its sadness is all but concealed by the affective resonances we have just been remarking: all the "embroidery" that constitutes an enchantment in itself even while the sadness deepens.

The mood in this poem of 1899 results from an unusually subtle balance of opposites. More characteristic is "The Pity of Love" (1892), which is fraught with images of uncertainty and of alienation from both humanity and nature. Here is the original version (marred by the comma of the first line and the awkward phrase "on flowing"—all the worse because unhyphenated—in the fifth):

> A pity beyond all telling,
> Is hid in the heart of love;
> The folk who are buying and selling,
> The stars of God where they move,
> The mouse-grey waters on flowing,
> The clouds on their journey above,
> And the cold wet winds ever blowing,
> All threaten the head that I love.

Yeats brought the poem close to its final form in his 1895 volume *Poems*. It now reads:

> A pity beyond all telling
> Is hid in the heart of love:
> The folk who are buying and selling,
> The clouds on their journey above,
> The cold wet winds ever blowing,
> And the shadowy hazel grove
> Where mouse-grey waters are flowing,
> Threaten the head that I love.

The feeling of both versions is doubtless the same; they begin and end almost identically, and the succession of images is similar though altered. But apart from rationalizing the punctuation and making small improvements of phrasing, Yeats improved the poem

measurably in other ways. Most important, he omitted the theological and possibly astrological implications of line 4 and instead began
the series of natural images with the clouds in movement "above"—
as close as this poem need be to God or the stars. The series now
moves climactically through its recital of the dangers the ceaselessly
active and indifferent real world poses to the fragile vision of an
idealized beloved.

In "He Hears the Cry of the Sedge," first published in 1898,
Yeats goes beyond the delicately fear-charged tone of "The Pity of
Love" into dire prophecy on a universal scale. Within a complex of
images of ultimate cosmic disintegration (however impossibly far off
in the future), the poet learns that love-fulfillment will never be his.
The grandeur of vision here works in a way that the isolated image
"the stars of God where they move" could not in the first draft of the
earlier poem. The result is a more painful personal expression. It
begins with an echo of Keats's line "The sedge has withered from the
lake" (in "La Belle Dame sans Merci"). But it soon moves into a
darkly eloquent epic proclamation presented as the "cry" of the wind
blowing through the sedge: a sort of wind-harp utterance—if wind-
harps could speak, and speak thunderously too—rising out of the
center of all being:

> I wander by the edge
> Of this desolate lake
> Where wind cries in the sedge:
> *Until the axle break*
> *That keeps the stars in their round,*
> *And hands hurl in the deep*
> *The banners of East and West,*
> *And the girdle of light is unbound,*
> *Your breast will not lie by the breast*
> *Of your beloved in sleep.*

The curve of this movement anticipates in miniature the dynamics of Yeats's great later poems and sequences. The opening lines
quickly imply a condition of private despair by way of the details of

landscape, with their Keatsian echo. The italicized passage thereafter bursts, with enormous force, into an entirely different realm of violent mystical vision. It is a vision of the destruction of the whole order of nature when the "axle" of the wheeling stars must "break," and space itself must collapse as dread "hands hurl in the deep / The banners of East and West," and all is plunged into blackness as "the girdle of light is unbound." And then, in the final two lines, we return to the poem's initial pressure of private despair—but now the language shares the dark prophetic exaltation of the other italicized lines.

The writer who had mastered lyrical dynamics of this quality in his early thirties needed only explore his possibilities further. The essential elements of his art were already in his grasp. "He Hears the Cry of the Sedge" stands out among Yeats's poems written before 1900 because it alone reveals his reserve of sheer power. But other pieces done at about the same time, some of which we have discussed, clearly show signs of genius as well.

For one thing—as we have in fact seen in "He Hears the Cry of the Sedge"—certain of these poems "tease us out of thought" with their mystical or prophetic edge. Yeats of course did, at various times, seriously interest himself in occultism, séances, and certain mystics and mystical groups. Although the experience enriched his writing, he did not subordinate his art to it. The poems are anything but specimens of versified arcane lore, and they should not be so read.

The body of folk-magical, Rosicrucian, cabalistic, spiritualist, and even theological lore he absorbed lies deep within subjective tradition. Without being a literal believer, Yeats could draw on its elements as emotionally magnetic realities of the imagination. They served as anodynes for the "desolation of reality"—his phrase in "Meru"—he felt early and late. As we have seen, his poem "The Tower" defiantly includes them among

> All those things whereof
> Man makes a superhuman
> Mirror-resembling dream.

The affirmation is not a matter of cheery optimism. Rather, it comes from dwelling within the long memory of human faith and imagination while remaining in touch with ordinary reality. There is always a sharp awareness of the latter, even in poems that, like "The Moods" (1893), seem sunk in ambiguous reverie:

> Time drops in decay,
> Like a candle burnt out,
> And the mountains and woods
> Have their day, have their day;
> What one in the rout
> Of the fire-born moods
> Has fallen away?

In its original version the poem's ending was more straightforward:

> Time drops in decay
> Like a candle burnt out;
> The mountains and woods
> Have their day, have their day;
> But, kindly old rout
> Of the fire-born moods,
> You pass not away.

The contrast in the version just quoted is clearly between the transitory material world, in which time itself and everything in nature must eventually burn away, and the permanent "rout / Of the fire-born moods." In this stirring if anthropocentric image, Yeats presents our thronging human states of emotion and of spirit as a part of objective universal process. The poem does not explain the paradox it presents; it simply asserts it, as a friendly exception to the general law of fatality.

The ending of the revised version changes this cheerful assertion to a riddling, perhaps troubled ambiguity. True, it *might* be read simply as a rhetorical question to which the expected answer is a happy "None." But if so, why the shift from the complacent earlier ending to the delphic question implying an ominously contrary meaning: that "the moods," too, are mortal like the rest of being and that they die off one by one? In both versions, though, the image of "a candle burnt out" connects by association with that of "fire-born moods." We are thus nudged toward the thought—again a paradox—that the fading candle of time somehow rekindles the eternal flame of spirit even as it burns out.

Visually and aurally, "The Moods" is a slight structure, just seven lines long. It is made up of short, two-stress lines (triple verse, rising rhythm) with a compact little rhyme scheme: *abcabc′a*. The metrical pattern, like the off-rhyme of the third and sixth lines, is "regular" yet hardly smooth. Stresses are placed unevenly and a kind of syncopation takes place, with hesitations in pacing and resistance to moving ahead fluidly. This slowing-down through sound-friction and sudden halts has the effect of meditative movement. One result is that each image (especially given the scale of these images: all of time, whole landscapes, the "moods" of the ages), and even each line to some degree, seems to carry vast import as the poem builds toward its mysterious ending. The tiny poem progresses like a condensed choral song in a Greek tragedy: two prophetic utterances, each a brief lament as well, and then the delphic final question.

Yeats's poetry was constantly driven by his obsession with the elusive task of combining realism with transcendent vision. Even before "The Moods," he had in poems like "The Stolen Child" (1886), "Who Goes with Fergus" (1892), and "The Man Who Dreamed of Faeryland" (1892) begun to evoke the malign seductiveness of romantic dreaming: a preoccupation of his early plays as well.

I shall add just one more early instance. First published in 1892, "Fergus and the Druid" underwent various revisions through the years, but the passage that now ends it has remained fairly constant. The situation of the poem unfolds in a dialogue between the great king Fergus and an aged, feeble Druid, "a thin grey man half lost in gathering night" who yet retains certain magical powers. Fergus wants to surrender his prowess and his throne in order to "learn the dreaming wisdom" the Druid possesses. The Druid gives him a "little bag of dreams" that fulfills his wish immediately, but—in the age-old way of such tales—at an unforeseen cost:

> *Druid.* Take, if you must, this little bag of dreams;
> Unloose the cord, and they will wrap you round.
> *Fergus.* I see my life go drifting like a river
> From change to change; I have been many things—
> A green drop in the surge, a gleam of light
> Upon a sword, a fir-tree on a hill,
> An old slave grinding at a heavy quern,
> A king sitting upon a chair of gold—
> And all these things are wonderful and great;
> But now I have grown nothing, knowing all.
> Ah! Druid, Druid, how great webs of sorrow
> Lay hidden in the small slate-coloured thing!

Fergus has been given, in the "bag of dreams" that he calls "the small slate-coloured thing," the gift of transcendence. It has enabled him, at once, to experience all forms of being and to become as omniscience-weary as the Druid (who, naturally, rues his pure dream-existence of ever-changing forms during which "No woman's loved me, no man sought my help"). Fergus's final speech is made up of long, lovely iambic pentameter lines that savor both their own sound and their succession of evocative images. It begins in melancholy reverie: "I see my life go drifting like a river / From change to change." It recalls certain states or phases of existence in sensuous flashes: "a green drop in the surge, a gleam of light / Upon a sword, a fir-tree on a hill." Then follows an archetypal contrast of strong social bearing, between an "old slave grinding at a heavy quern" and a "king sitting upon a chair of gold." Next, a moment of exultation at having "been" so many separate lives and modes of existence breaks suddenly into the dreaming catalogue: "And all these things are wonderful and great." But just as suddenly, total letdown follows: the concluding outcry at the "great webs of sorrow" woven by dreams out of everything actual life feeds into them. The whole passage has been building into the catastrophic apperception that even transcendence must exhaust itself.

That Yeats had become, potentially, a master lyric poet before the turn of the century is obvious even from these few examples. It is interesting that certain simple devices he experimented with early on remained constants of his poetic method as he moved into more complex structures and into a style of richer human immediacy. Two examples are his strategic use of dialogue and his pivotal moments of concrete description or imagery.

We have seen, in the brief passage from "The Cloak, the Boat, and the Shoes" quoted at the start of this chapter, an instance of a poem developed in dialogue form. There, of course, Yeats's model was the kind of traditional folk song built on a simple pattern of question and answer. (A ballad like "Edward" is one classic model.) But it is interesting, too, that the poem is part of a *play*. Almost from the beginning of his career, Yeats wrote plays whose structure was perhaps even more lyrical than dramatic. We shall dwell on this crucial side of his work in later chapters. Suffice it now to observe his gift for evocative dialogue, already revealed in "The Cloak, the Boat, and the Shoes."

Two later poems, "Ephemera" (1889) and "Adam's Curse" (1902), provide more-developed instances. A dialogue between lovers whose passion for each other is declining, "Ephemera" resembles "The Moods" in its fixing on cyclical change. Even the most ardent love must at last "wane," and the lovers enter new phases of love and experience. "Ephemera" lacks the cosmic sweep of "The Moods" or "He Hears the Cry of the Sedge" (although it shares the latter poem's landscape, inherited from "La Belle Dame sans Merci"). But it does present actual characters, even if their only difference— admittedly of some consequence—is that one is called "He" and the other "She." Yeats cut the original version considerably, deleting the more verbose and mawkish passages. By the time it appeared in his 1895 *Poems,* it had just about reached its present form:

"Your eyes that once were never weary of mine
Are bowed in sorrow under pendulous lids,
Because our love is waning."

                                    And then she:
"Although our love is waning, let us stand
By the lone border of the lake once more,
Together in that hour of gentleness
When the poor tired child, Passion, falls asleep:
How far away the stars seem, and how far
Is our first kiss, and ah, how old my heart!"

Pensive they paced along the faded leaves,
While slowly he whose hand held hers replied:
"Passion has often worn our wandering hearts."

The woods were round them, and the yellow leaves
Fell like meteors in the gloom, and once
A rabbit old and lame limped down the path;
Autumn was over him: and now they stood
On the lone border of the lake once more:
Turning, he saw that she had thrust dead leaves
Gathered in silence, dewy as her eyes,
In bosom and hair.

                        "Ah, do not mourn," he said,
"That we are tired, for other loves await us;
Hate on and love through unrepining hours.
Before us lies eternity; our souls
Are love, and a continual farewell."

The poem presents its essential human situation through dialogue. It begins with a mournful dramatic exchange, centered on the
lovers' helpless acknowledgment of the weariness that has overtaken
their passion. As they talk, they wander over an autumnal landscape
whose details match their feeling: a stage-setting, as it were, designed by Keats and Tennyson. But the poem ends with an effort to
repudiate brooding grief after all. In the final verse-unit, "he" argues
that love will persist in ever-renewed forms within the endless, mys-

tically conceived cycles of eternity. This turn might be deemed a "positive" one, were it not for the melancholy resonance of the key-words: "mourn," "tired," "hate," "farewell," and "unrepining"—the last of which recalls the very mood it purports to negate. The word "hate" (used idiosyncratically here, as sometimes also in Yeats's later work, to suggest a hot intensity) reinforces the darkly negative drift. So do the closing two lines, but in a gentle, more evenly balanced way. On the one hand, "our souls are love"; on the other, "a continual farewell." The dialogue form helps the poem's movement of feeling seem natural and inevitable.

One has to make allowances for some of the awkward or senti-mental phrasing (e.g., "he whose hand held hers") in "Ephemera." Yet the tone of lament for the inevitably dissolving present moment, and images like "faint meteors in the gloom" and "dead leaves/ Gathered in silence," hold fast in the memory. Yeats's implicit asso-ciation of sorrow and beauty is intensified here through such strikingly evocative effects. And the poem's use of a variously adapt-able structure—in this instance: dialogue, setting of scene, and dia-logue again—was an exceptional early discovery.

Even while stripping down "Ephemera" to its more concen-trated present text, Yeats was advancing beyond it in other poems of dialogue-centered structure. By 1902, for instance, he had published the far more compelling "Adam's Curse" in a form very close to its final redaction. Like "Ephemera," but with important differences, it laments the destruction of lovers' dreams by the workings of cyclical change. An obvious difference is that it offers no such consoling thought as that "other loves await us." Another is that it adds satire and harsh social criticism to its tonal mixture. Also, its characters—the silent, yet vividly present, beloved woman addressed as "you"; the "beautiful mild woman," her "close friend," who speaks briefly to the point that women "must labour to be beautiful"; and the poet himself—are more sharply defined than those in "Ephemera." The poet's remarks dominate the dialogue. At first he raves against the world's ignorance of his hard toil and its worth. Later, he bemoans the passing of a time when poetry, the rhetoric and rituals of courtly love, and the cultivation of womanly beauty through "labour" (in every sense of that word) were exalted and honored. A final difference between the poems is that, although the specific human situation and mood of "Ephemera" are echoed at the end of "Adam's Curse," the pitch and sense of personal loss are much more acute.

Both poems have a narrative frame; that is, both tell a story in the past tense. In "Ephemera" the story is about two lovers who, while walking along the edge of a wooded lake, sadly and sympathetically discussed the waning of their passion and its meaning. In "Adam's Curse" the story is about a conversation among three people. It begins:

> We sat together at one summer's end,
> That beautiful mild woman, your close friend,
> And you and I, and talked of poetry.

Each of the poems sustains its narrative frame; yet, since they are mainly in dialogue form, both are closer to drama than to fiction. Their passages of dialogue are nevertheless only minimally dramatic; they express little interaction between the characters. Rather, they serve a fundamentally lyrical movement, in which the successive speeches and descriptive passages build toward a poignant acceptance of irreversible loss and change. For both poems, the descriptions of natural setting contribute decisively to their affective structure. "Adam's Curse" manages this function more skillfully, from the autumnal modulation in its opening line—"We sat together at one summer's end"—to the suggestions of cosmic erosion in its penultimate verse-unit:

> We sat grown quiet at the name of love;
> We saw the last embers of daylight die,
> And in the trembling blue-green of the sky
> A moon, worn as if it had been a shell
> Washed by time's waters as they rose and fell
> About the stars and broke in days and years.

The most nearly dramatic effect in the poem comes in the confessional outcry of the succeeding verse-unit, which ends the poem. It is not a literal cry but a burning "thought" silently directed to "you," the woman who has been present without taking part in the conversation. It comes in the wake of the group's sudden hush "at the name of love" and of the successive images of unalterable change seen in the evening sky. "The name of love," in its ancient courtly sense, is in any case out of phase with the direction the modern world has taken. But in the context of those images it now seems to reach toward a personal state no longer possible to achieve. The "thought" arrives as a flash of desolate knowledge arising from all that has gone before it in the poem:

> I had a thought for no one's but your ears:
> That you were beautiful, and that I strove
> To love you in the old high way of love;
> That it had all seemed happy, and yet we'd grown
> As weary-hearted as that hollow moon.

Much farther down the road, in "The People" (1916), Yeats carried his use of dialogue to another level of structure, at once lyrical and genuinely dramatic. I shall return to "The People" later, in another context, but it is interesting to consider it just here because of its clear similarity in certain essentials to "Adam's Curse." True, it carries little trace of the earlier poem's romantic nostalgia and setting, and it is written in blank verse instead of rhyming couplets. Nevertheless, its deft alliteration and internal rhyming approach the controlled patterning of "Adam's Curse," whose skillful enjambment and natural speech rhythms, in turn, bring it close to accomplished blank verse. Also, the angrily complaining opening lines of the two poems, both presented as dialogue, are very close in spirit to one another:

> I said, "A line will take us hours maybe;
> Yet if it does not seem a moment's thought,
> Our stitching and unstitching has been naught.

> Better go down upon your marrow-bones
> And scrub a kitchen-pavement, or break stones
> Like an old pauper, in all kinds of weather;
> For to articulate sweet sounds together
> Is to work harder than all these, and yet
> Be thought an idler by the noisy set
> Of bankers, schoolmasters, and clergymen
> The martyrs call the world."
>
> ("Adam's Curse")

> "What have I earned for all that work," I said,
> "For all that I have done at my own charge?
> The daily spite of this unmannerly town,
> Where who has served the most is most defamed,
> The reputation of a lifetime lost
> Between the night and morning."
>
> ("The People")

In neither passage is the complaint simply personal—"no one appreciates my poems and my sacrifices." Rather, in both cases, it is political as well. The unappreciative philistines of "Adam's Curse" include, predictably, the traffickers in money ("bankers"). More surprisingly, they also include the supposed transmitters of culture and spirituality ("schoolmasters" and "clergymen") who are just as coarse-grained and as prone to persecute those they do not understand. "The People" picks up the attack and extends it to the whole of "this unmannerly town." (The poem does not name the town. Let us say it must be about the size of Dublin—that is, small enough for local backbiting and gossip to sting and to call forth counterattack.)

I have used the word "political" for the passages just quoted, and so far the quotations have expressed the politics of embattled artists. They show a poet striking out against a hostile commercial class, its largely unconscious lackeys, and the ignorance of the populace. But "The People" goes further. It becomes a genuine political *discussion* between the poet and a woman he calls "my phoenix," who answers him "in reproof":

"The drunkards, pilferers of public funds,
All the dishonest crowd I had driven away,
When my luck changed and they dared meet my face,
Crawled from obscurity, and set upon me
Those I had served and some that I had fed;
Yet never have I, now nor any time,
Complained of the people."

Clearly, there is a specifically autobiographical background to this exchange. There is little doubt that Yeats is referring to slanders against him because of his efforts to help raise the level of national culture—as in the struggle, for instance, for public funds to house the paintings offered to Dublin by Hugh Lane, and in the controversies over the morality or patriotism of certain plays produced by the Abbey Theatre, which Yeats helped found and direct. (John M. Synge's *The Playboy of the Western World* is perhaps the prime example.) Nor can we doubt that "my phoenix" is the great love of his life, Maud Gonne: a "phoenix" because she could endure setbacks such as her words in the poem describe and come into her own again repeatedly. Her feeling for "the people," however prejudiced and easily misled they might be, was that of a revolutionist loyal to them despite all frustrations.

We need to remember, though, that such information (even if totally accurate and relevant—dubious conditions always) doth not a poem make. Unless it enters a poem explicitly and literally, it remains only a speculative identification of a probable source, proving nothing about the poem's own vital character. What "The People" actually presents is a modern *débat* between two characters: one a man dedicated to the life of art for its own sake and as a public necessity, the other a woman dedicated to helping and fighting for the poor and the oppressed. This divergence of causes did mark Yeats's complex, awkward relationship with Maud Gonne. But "The People" precipitates out the pure essence, as it were, of an endemic inner conflict within developed modern sensibilities. Biography may be suggestive but is unnecessary for grasping the poem, and it may well be misleading.

Having observed that what the poem "actually" presents is a *"débat"* expressing counter-pressures "within developed modern sensibilities," I want to step back quickly from any suggestion that "The People" can be reduced to such an abstraction. What it "actually" presents, of course, is precisely its own language and sound and movement through all its tonal stages—from the petulant outcry at the start to the rueful confession of shame at the end:

"What have I earned for all that work," I said,
"For all that I have done at my own charge?
The daily spite of this unmannerly town,
Where who has served the most is most defamed,
The reputation of a lifetime lost
Between the night and morning. I might have lived,
And you know well how great the longing has been,
Where every day my footfall should have lit
In the green shadow of Ferrara wall;
Or climbed among the images of the past—
The unperturbed and courtly images—
Evening and morning, the steep street of Urbino
To where the Duchess and her people talked
The stately midnight through until they stood
In their great window looking at the dawn;
I might have had no friend that could not mix
Courtesy and passion into one like those
That saw the wicks grow yellow in the dawn;
I might have used the one substantial right
My trade allows: chosen my company,
And chosen what scenery had pleased me best."
Thereon my phoenix answered in reproof,
"The drunkards, pilferers of public funds,
All the dishonest crowd I had driven away,
When my luck changed and they dared meet my face,
Crawled from obscurity, and set upon me
Those that I had served and some that I had fed;

Yet never have I, now nor any time,
Complained of the people."
                            All I could reply
Was: "You, that have not lived in thought but deed,
Can have the purity of a natural force,
But I, whose virtues are the definitions
Of the analytic mind, can neither close
The eye of the mind nor keep my tongue from speech."
And yet, because my heart leaped at her words,
I was abashed, and now they come to mind
After nine years, I sink my head abashed.

The long opening verse-unit moves emphatically through three
different but interlocked states of feeling: the poet's initial burst of
angry, contemptuous complaint against modern Dublin, his dreaming counter-vision of high talk and beautiful ease such as one might
have found in the Italian Renaissance world of Castiglione's *The
Courtier,* and the quietly reproving reply of "my phoenix." Her
speech echoes his outraged sense of betrayal at the start, but without
its tone of petty resentment. She does not ask "What have I gained?"
Nor does she harp on having helped the people "at my own charge."
Also, more subtly, the quality of mind she reveals has precisely the
nobility, the mixture of "courtesy and passion into one," idealized in
the counter-vision of Urbino. That is, she embodies the supreme
aristocratic virtue of magnanimity: "Yet never have I, now nor any
time, / Complained of the people."

In the short second, and final, verse-unit, the poet—as he does
customarily—gives himself the last word. But in this instance his
response is purely defensive and in reality apologetic. His "heart
leaped at her words": a spontaneous acknowledgment of the
woman's moral superiority. She has "the purity of a natural force"
that has no need of mediation by an "analytic mind" like his. Her
words have exposed his unconscious failure of *noblesse* and the self-
pity underlying his exalted dream of Urbino. And so: "I was
abashed" at the time—and once again, remembering her words nine
years later, "I sink my head abashed."

Still, the fifteen-line passage evoking the world of Castiglione's *The Courtier* makes up almost half the poem and has its own life and force. Without it, the condensed *débat* would be *too* condensed: merely a hasty clash of opinions. With it, the woman's reproach creates a shock of moral awakening beyond any that the give and take of argument could bring about. And besides, and quite apart from the immediate issue, the dream of Urbino is seductive and endearing even if conceived during a fit of self-pity. It is a dream of an irrecoverable and indeed never-quite-existent ideal world (admittedly with no place for plebeians) without haste or ugliness or occasion for bitterness. And it enormously deepens the affective life of the poem by ranging two incommensurable worlds side by side: the empirical one of suffering and struggle and the visionary one of aesthetic and intellectual gratification.

The poem's essential structure, no longer confined within polemical limits, is thereby redirected. The mind that at first gave itself to demeaning resentment has passed through a state of transport "among . . . unperturbed and courtly images" and timeless, untroubled talk throughout enchanted nights "like those / That saw the wicks grow yellow in the dawn." When it is brought back to literal, present reality by "my phoenix," it is ennobled and ready to become abashed at the outburst that began the poem.

The word "escape" has sometimes been used for such passages in Yeats. "Attempted escape"—though still an oversimplification— might be better, for the pressure of intractable reality is always active in his poems. In "The People," that pressure takes the form of a challenge to conscience. Elsewhere it may appear as death-awareness, or as life's inevitable disillusionments, or as instinctual desire, or in some other form. In any case, "The People" well illustrates the complex psychological play enabled by the structural use of dialogue and of suddenly intruded scenes or symbolic images— methods increasingly perfected by Yeats as his work matured. The distance from "Ephemera" to "The People" is a great one, and the distance to "A Dialogue of Self and Soul" and other later poems even greater. Yet the remarkable continuity of method remains clearly discernible.

2. *1900 to 1904*

The poems of *In the Seven Woods* (1904) represent both a culmination of Yeats's early development and a deepening of his poetic maturity as he entered his fortieth year. Their heightened force and economy may owe something at least to his writing for the theater during the same period. Also, and most important artistically, their strongly defined major currents of feeling and tension—often intermingling or surfacing in altered contexts—bring the book as a whole close to the organic structure of a poetic sequence.

The first of these currents, carrying a twin struggle to control both private emotional turmoil and socially aroused anger, emerges at once in the title poem at the start of the book. It surfaces again, powerfully, in the two poems at the book's center—"Adam's Curse" and "Red Hanrahan's Song about Ireland"—and in fact generates the dominant affective strain of the volume as a whole.

The second major current, seen most directly in "The Arrow" and "The Folly of Being Comforted," is of pain at the aging of a beloved woman. It is counterpointed elsewhere by related currents of sharply felt loss or betrayal in love ("Old Memory," "Never Give All the Heart," "Under the Moon," "The Ragged Wood," "O Do Not Love Too Long"), of sadness over "women whose beauty was folded in dismay" ("Under the Moon"—a variation within the *ubi sunt* tradition), and of a tragicomic grotesquerie that anticipates the opening of "The Tower" ("The Old Men Admiring Themselves in the Water").

Finally, two closing poems distance themselves from the personal intensities and specific perspectives in the major currents, yet reinforce the tonal bearing of the volume as a whole. The first of these, "The Players Ask for a Blessing on the Psalteries and on

Themselves," has a special, encompassing poignancy in the wake of the pieces preceding it. Despite all dark knowledge, its "three voices" of performers—instrumentalists, singers, actors—assert the undying life of their arts even while offering up the humble prayers of doomed mortals:

> The proud and careless notes live on,
> But bless our hands that ebb away.

The poem thus, gently and unpretentiously, embodies the "tragic joy" implicit in all art. Yeats could easily have absorbed it into his play *The King's Threshold,* which has a kindred theme and appeared the same year as *In the Seven Woods.*

The succeeding poem, "The Happy Townland," ends the volume. In its fashion, it reprises many of Yeats's earlier poems—such as "The Man Who Dreamed of Faeryland" (1891) and "The Stolen Child" (1896)—that counterpoise the two worlds of human awareness. One is the empirical world we all know, with its ordinary satisfactions and sufferings and inevitable death. The other is the ideal world of whatever sort we may long for, whose fancied perfection can make us indifferent to life's normal joys and thus make us vulnerable to loss and remorse even beyond death. The opening stanza and refrain of "The Happy Townland" will illustrate:

> There's many a strong farmer
> Whose heart would break in two,
> If he could but see the townland
> That we are riding to;
> Boughs have their fruit and blossom
> At all times of the year;
> Rivers are running over
> With red beer and brown beer.
> An old man plays the bagpipes
> In a gold and silver wood;
> Queens, their eyes blue like the ice
> Are dancing in a crowd.

> *The little fox he murmured,*
> *"O what of the world's bane?"*
> *The sun was laughing sweetly,*
> *The moon plucked at my rein;*
> *But the little red fox murmured,*
> *"O do not pluck at his rein,*
> *He is riding to the townland*
> *That is the world's bane."*

The "happy townland" that "we" celebrate with such innocent enthusiasm at the beginning is the very region that the wise "little red fox" knows as "the world's bane." Blake's "Ah! Sun-flower" and Keats's "Ode to a Nightingale" (both far more accomplished than "The Happy Townland," it goes without saying) are among Yeats's obvious forerunners. But poems like this one and the two earlier ones I have mentioned provide a new turn in their surround of Irish folklore and landscape. They foreshadow powerful later creations like "Among School Children," the civil war sequences, and the play *Purgatory*—to say nothing of an "incidental" masterpiece like the earthily half-comic, half-elegiac "John Kinsella's Lament for Mrs. Mary Moore." In addition, they lay ominous stress on the danger— even the terror—of following the call of romantic dreams. In both these respects, they provide condensed models for his early plays.

"In the Seven Woods," the book's title poem, is a remarkable prelude to the whole stream of affective music that follows:

> I have heard the pigeons of the Seven Woods
> Make their faint thunder, and the garden bees
> Hum in the lime-tree flowers; and put away
> The unavailing outcries and the old bitterness
> That empty the heart. I have forgot awhile
> Tara uprooted, and new commonness
> Upon the throne and crying about the streets
> And hanging its paper flowers from post to post,
> Because it is alone of all things happy.
> I am contented, for I know that Quiet

Wanders laughing and eating her wild heart
Among pigeons and bees, while that Great Archer,
Who but awaits His hour to shoot, still hangs
A cloudy quiver over Pairc-na-lee.

The growth of intensity in the two opening sentences of this brief, three-sentence poem is striking. At first the quiet use of Irish place-names seems the gentlest sort of patriotism, hardly noticeable as such—a romantic tincture merely incidental to the pastoral solace of the scene. (The Seven Woods, one of which is Pairc-na-lee, were part of the estate of Lady Gregory, Yeats's friend, patron, mentor, and sometimes co-author.) But in the very first sentence, the phrase "faint thunder," although but an image for the sound of pigeons in flight, is nevertheless slightly foreboding. It is quickly followed, in the same sentence, by a barrage of desolate and outraged language: "unavailing outcries," "old bitterness," "empty the heart," and "Tara uprooted"—expressions that swarm into the poem before any impression of bucolic tranquillity can take hold.

Tara, in County Meath, was traditionally the seat of the High King and therefore a symbol, with glamorous and aristocratic associations, of Ireland as a nation. These associations have been "uprooted" by "new commonness" both upon the throne and in the spirit of the moment: an obvious allusion to British rule and, very likely, as A. Norman Jeffares has suggested, to the coronation of Edward VII in 1901 and its public celebrations. (Yeats dated the poem "August 1902.") Thus, very quickly, the poem has taken on a tone of long-cherished private resentment with emphatic political resonances.

And yet, despite the dominant philistinism—the "new commonness" that "is alone of all things happy"—the poem has claimed to "put away" the very resentment that it so strongly expresses. In the opening lines it supposedly does so in response to the pure, natural delights of the garden. And in the five closing lines, which return to the garden scene, it makes the claim again. But now we see it in the context of the political and social complaints of its middle section.

The poem ends with the image of a "Great Archer," and it becomes clear that the opening lines were in a sense a drawing of "His" bow. Although we are once more, now, in the seemingly changeless world of pigeons and bees where "Quiet" wanders "laughing," turmoil is being held at bay only for the time being. "Quiet" herself is eating away at her own "wild heart": an actively self-contradictory image that recalls but reverses the passive despair of the earlier "unavailing outcries and . . . old bitterness / That empty the heart." The garden interval is one of being "content"— i.e., holding steady—despite inward anguish because of anticipated struggle. It is a time of waiting for the "Great Archer" (presumably an epithet for the constellation Sagittarius—here symbolic of inevitable forces of retribution) to "shoot" the arrows in his "cloudy quiver" when the appointed hour arrives.

The political direction, both nationalist and aristocratic (in the special sense of despising public vulgarity, including that of the new Edwardian régime, as opposed to "Tara" and the glamour of native Irish tradition), is fairly explicit in this poem. But the subtly distributed suggestions of personal unhappiness scattered throughout it at the same time provide another dimension and give the poem its decisive emotional coloration. The desolate phrases we have noted in the first sentence are as suitable for painful private disappointment as for political or social dismay. Their tone of romantic frustration and indefinite hope softens the tendentious rhetoric that might otherwise mar the poem irreparably. They, like the final sentence, prevent the reduction of a seductive lyrical experiment with the sonnet form to a piece of obvious propaganda.

In fact, it is only the two middle poems of the volume, "Adam's Curse" and "Red Hanrahan's Song about Ireland," that return in any way to a public forum. As we have seen, the former of these fuses a tirade against the philistinism of the age with a lament for lost values of the past and, at last, with a private confession of failure in love. Like "In the Seven Woods," but more romantically and nostalgically, it begins with an evocative scene and goes on to attack current society's crass ignorance concerning the best and hardest-earned human

values. These are especially, here, the poet's art, that of the lover
when ennobled by a certain courtly formality, and that of fully cultivated womanly beauty. The ending of "Adam's Curse" is more con-
fessionally startling than that of "In the Seven Woods," but it too
shifts attention away from argument and into a realm of subjective
reverie and arousal. The result in both poems is an unusual merging
of lyrical and polemical elements: a double perspective charged with
dramatic possibility.

In simpler fashion, the highly compressed "Red Hanrahan's
Song about Ireland" presents a comparable double perspective. The
more private or subjective aspect is its tonal shifting from fearfulness
("our courage breaks") in the first stanza, through the gathering of
wrath ("Angers . . . have set our hearts abeat") in the second, to
irresistible and decisive force ("like heavy flooded waters our bodies
and our blood") in the third. The more publicly rhetorical perspective is provided by the image, repeated in the refrain, of "Cathleen
the daughter of Houlihan," emblem of Ireland and of her struggle for
independence. In the first stanza, "we" keep "hidden in our hearts"—
out of fear—the dangerous challenge she presents. In the second,
aroused by her to anger, "we have all bent low and kissed" her "quiet
feet" in devoted allegiance. In the third, she becomes a holy icon as
the revolutionary surge occurs. Even more than "In the Seven
Woods," this poem reinforces its nationalism subliminally by its Irish
place-names, landscape, religious and mythical associations, and
tradition-drenched refrain. The long seven-stress lines are subtly
varied in stress-placement to sustain their music while approaching
the colloquial vigor of folk-speech:

The old brown thorn-trees break in two high over Cummen
    Strand,
Under a bitter black wind that blows from the left hand;
Our courage breaks like an old tree in a black wind and
    dies,
But we have hidden in our hearts the flame out of the eyes
Of Cathleen, the daughter of Houlihan.

The wind has bundled up the clouds high over Knocknarea,
And thrown the thunder on the stones for all that Maeve can
    say.
Angers that are like noisy clouds have set our hearts
    abeat;
But we have all bent low and kissed the quiet feet
Of Cathleen, the daughter of Houlihan.

The yellow pool has overflowed high up on Clooth-na-
    Bare,
For the wet winds are blowing out of the clinging air;
Like heavy flooded waters our bodies and our blood;
But purer than a tall candle before the Holy Rood
Is Cathleen, the daughter of Houlihan.

Revised and reprinted under several titles from its first newspaper appearance in 1894, "Red Hanrahan's Song about Ireland"
gradually sloughed off some awkward phrasing—although, surprisingly, Yeats resorted at last to the lumpy "abeat" in line 8 after
trying other solutions. By 1897, however, he had solved an essential
structural problem by revising line 13, which originally read:
"Dark and dull and earthy our souls and bodies be." The line he
substituted—"Like heavy swollen waters are our bodies and our
blood"—is close to the improved final version: "Like heavy flooded
waters our bodies and our blood." (The improvement lay in the more
vigorous "flooded" and the better rhythmic control created by the
omission of "are," which also allows for a less abrupt pause before the
next line.)

In either case, though, whether with "swollen" or "flooded" and
with or without the verb, the basic revision gave far greater depth to
the poem. An important aspect of its emotional movement is that,
while the inner subjective state—the way "we" are said to feel—
changes with each stanza, the descriptions of external nature are
consistently violent and threatening. (Shades of "The Pity of Love,"
but with what a difference!) In the earliest version of the poem this
distinction prevails all the way through. But the change in line 13

shows the subjective "we" taking on the power of impersonal natural forces *plus* a mystical and sacramental identity: the counterpart of the Christian associations attached to Cathleen ni Houlihan in the two succeeding lines that close the poem. All in all, this poem might well have served as a choral song for Yeats's 1902 play *Cathleen ni Houlihan* had he been writing in his later dramatic style.

Together, then, at the heart of their volume, "Adam's Curse" and "Red Hanrahan's Song about Ireland" echo and develop the rhetorical motifs of the title poem despite clear differences of form and affect. Otherwise, *In the Seven Woods* revolves mainly about the sense of personal loss through the passage of time or love-disappointment or both. Such loss, vaguely hinted at in the title poem, is brought out explicitly at the end of "Adam's Curse":

> I had a thought for no one's but your ears:
> That you were beautiful, and that I strove
> To love you in the old high way of love;
> That it had all seemed happy, and yet we'd grown
> As weary-hearted as that hollow moon.

"Adam's Curse," at the center—and the heart—of *In the Seven Woods,* is the most complex effort in the volume. It is a love poem whose emotional life is inseparable from its lament for aesthetic and social values neglected in an age of philistine ascendancy. Simpler love poems precede it and provide a gathering context for its special perspective. Thus, "The Arrow," which follows the opening title poem, helps prepare the way for the book's continual brooding over time, the enemy of beauty and of sustained passion:

> I thought of your beauty, and this arrow,
> Made out of a wild thought, is in my marrow.
> There's no man may look upon her, no man,
> As when newly grown to be a woman,
> Tall and noble but with face and bosom
> Delicate in colour as apple blossom.

> This beauty's kinder, yet for a reason
> I could weep that the old is out of season.

It is interesting that Yeats placed "The Arrow" directly after "In the Seven Woods," which ends with the image of the "Great Archer" who "but awaits His hour to shoot." The very title of "The Arrow"— let alone its leading image of "this arrow, / Made of a wild thought"— would seem to connect the two poems. Despite important ways in which they are unalike, both poems share with each other and with "Adam's Curse" an embittered nostalgia for kinds of beauty— whether a woman's or a social and political world's—that are now "out of season." The whole volume, in fact, anticipates the even fiercer and more helpless sense of loss that pervades Yeats's great later sequences and that is summed up at the start of "Nineteen Hundred and Nineteen":

> Many ingenious lovely things are gone
> That seemed sheer miracle to the multitude . . . .

The little group of wry poems beginning with "The Arrow" includes, in order, "The Folly of Being Comforted," "Old Memory," "Never Give All the Heart," "The Withering of the Boughs," and— as their climax that also broadens their scope—"Adam's Curse." All brood, sadly and admiringly, on the beloved and her beauty, but each poem, in its turn, presents a subtle shift of emphasis. The impact of "The Arrow" is of a shock of realization. It arises from the contrast, envisioned in the mind's eye, between her current "kinder" appearance and manner and her suddenly remembered, dazzling very young womanhood, when she was "delicate in colour as apple blossom." Beyond this contrast, the poem hints strongly at "a reason" the poet "could weep" at this memory. What else can the "reason" be but regret for a love relationship long past?

The rueful mood continues yet is redirected in "The Folly of Being Comforted," whose rhyming couplets—despite its sonnetlike structure—echo those in "The Arrow." Here the woman's aging beauty is described a bit harshly ("threads of grey," "little shadows . . . about her eyes"), leading an "ever kind" friend to suggest that henceforth it will be "easier to be wise"—that is, to accept not being loved by her. But now it becomes clear that her aging is beside the point; indeed, it has only heightened her "nobleness":

> Heart cries, "No,
> I have not a crumb of comfort, not a grain.
> Time can but make her beauty over again:
> Because of that great nobleness of hers
> The fire that stirs about her, when she stirs,
> Burns but more clearly. O she had not these ways
> When all the wild summer was in her gaze."
>
> O heart! O heart! if she'd but turn her head,
> You'd know the folly of being comforted.

"The Folly of Being Comforted" echoes the feelings of "The Arrow" in just one line: "When all the wild summer was in her gaze." But elsewhere it corrects that poem's implication that the beloved's beauty was greater in the past than now. On the contrary, the whole quality of her "tall and noble" beauty—a matter of character and spirit rather than of physical loveliness alone—has been deepened by time. The great line "The fire that stirs about her, when she stirs" is reserved for her maturer presence.

In tracing the movement of *In the Seven Woods* from one poem to the next, we have followed the unfolding of a lyrical sequence: that is, a whole group of poems having an organic reciprocity similar to that of the parts of a single lyric poem. The individual poems can stand by themselves, but the larger structure enriches and extends their expressive reach because of their interaction. Further turns of emphasis, making explicit the disappointment in love only hinted before, come surprisingly in "Old Memory" and "Never Give All the Heart." Especially surprising in the former poem are its outright resentment and its effort to cope with that feeling without denying it.

In these respects it resembles certain of Shakespeare's most movingly reproachful love sonnets:

> O thought, fly to her when the end of day
> Awakens an old memory, and say,
> "Your strength, that is so lofty and fierce and kind,
> It might call up a new age, calling to mind
> The queens that were imagined long ago,
> Is but half yours: he kneaded in the dough
> Through the long years of youth, and who would have thought
> It all, and more than it all, would come to naught,
> And that dear words meant nothing?" But enough,
> For when we have blamed the wind we can blame love;
> Or, if there needs be more, be nothing said
> That would be harsh for children that have strayed.

The reciprocity of this poem with the three preceding it has various facets. The beauty extolled in "The Arrow" and (in an altered way) "The Folly of Being Comforted" is now seen in terms of greatness. It is not only "lofty" and "kind" but also "fierce," with a form of "strength" that is a force for potential change and the creation of a "new age." It thus takes on an almost mythical aura that makes the beloved akin to the near-divinities in "The Arrow": the allegorical, inwardly (and paradoxically) turbulent "Quiet" and the symbolic "Great Archer" poised to loose his arrows. But her beauty, redefined in these ways in "Old Memory," is not entirely a quality she was born with. Rather, it is the outcome of creative toil by the beloved woman *together with* her poet-lover who had "kneaded in the dough / Through the long years of youth."

This assertion makes for an entirely new turn in the sequence. As a result, the sense of loss conveyed in the earlier poems takes on a more intimate intensity here than before. It encompasses a feeling of betrayal by a loved comrade in arms, after years of total devotion and reciprocal strengthening of powers toward some heroic mission. He has helped make her what she is, but she has abandoned him. This complaint-laden "thought" is cleverly developed in dialogue form, as an address from his mind to her mind at some moment "when the end of day / Awakens an old memory" in her of the love they once shared. The device enables Yeats to reply to himself, as it were, in the poem's closing sentence. He can thus dismiss his own complaint as futile ("For when we have blamed the wind we can blame love") and explain away the betrayal as innocent, like the behavior of "children that have strayed." Thus the poem ends in a tone of wounded reconciliation with the inevitable.

The same tone, almost, is resumed in "Never Give All the Heart," but with the bitterness somewhat softened and distanced. At first the poem seems addressed to the world at large, but soon it becomes clear that it is intended for the *male* world in particular.

> Never give all the heart, for love
> Will hardly seem worth thinking of
> To passionate women if it seem
> Certain, and they never dream
> That it fades out from kiss to kiss;
> For everything that's lovely is
> But a brief, dreamy, kind delight.
> O never give the heart outright,
> For they, for all smooth lips can say,
> Have given their hearts up to the play.
> And who could play it well enough
> If deaf and dumb and blind with love?
> He that made this knows all the cost,
> For he gave all his heart and lost.

The first sentence has a worldly edge. In itself it might be taken as a sophisticated bit of practical advice to young men about how to deal masterfully with women. But any such impression is soon counteracted. The middle lines reverse the implied situation: it is women, not men, who exercise mastery and tire of lovers whose constant devotion is unquestionable. They are conscious actors or directors in love's rituals, while men are too immersed in their love itself to play their roles coolly enough. "Never Give All the Heart," then, continues the mood of complaint but in a somewhat more generalized perspective. The emotional distancing is carried a step farther in "The Withering of the Boughs," a poem no less melancholy but removed from any reference to a literal personal relationship. In the succession of poems we have been considering, this one reclaims for the poet himself all responsibility for the disappointments previously attributed to a woman's indifference or changing attitudes or outright betrayal. He has paid the price for spelling out the impossible dreams of magical happiness in which he has lost himself. The refrain is both a cry of remorse for his inability to conceal his innermost feelings and a surrender to defeat:

No boughs have withered because of the wintry wind;
The boughs have withered because I have told them my dreams.

It is at this point that "Adam's Curse" enters the volume. It draws all the previous poems into its orbit by giving their motifs heightened dramatic focus. It does so through its evocative description and characterization, the emotional dynamics of its dialogue and its whole movement, and its final private confession—all discussed earlier in this chapter. To its blazing historical and cultural indignation and personal poignancy, "Red Hanrahan's Song about Ireland" then adds its Irish nationalist and religious flames. These are the climactic poems within the sequence, followed by the touchingly comic "The Old Men Admiring Themselves in the Water." The charm of this piece lies in its simple humanity and its whimsical parody of all the book's brooding over the aging of beautiful women. The lament of old *men* over the loss of *their* "beauty" is both natural and, in context ("hands like claws," "knees . . . like the old thorntrees") grotesque. The poem is a marvelous instance of the emotional power a deceptively facetious bit of art can exert:

I heard the old, old men say,
"Everything alters,
And one by one we drop away."

> They had hands like claws, and their knees
> Were twisted like the old thorn-trees
> By the waters.
> I heard the old, old men say,
> "All that's beautiful drifts away
> Like the waters."

This is the lovely start of the fading-out movement of the sequence. It is followed by three relatively simple poems—"Under the Moon," "The Ragged Wood," and "O Do Not Love Too Long"—that bring to the surface again three main streams of feeling often joined in the book. These are the "burden" of "the dream of women whose beauty was folded in dismay," the unachievable desire for unchallenged love ("Would that none had ever loved but you and I!"), and the pain of loving "too long" and growing "out of fashion / Like an old song." The sequence is easing off musically and emotionally, and now it comes to its end in the two closing poems noted earlier: poems detached from its literal concerns, yet in harmony with its overall elegiac character and tempered by an elusive affirmation.

II

Early Drama
(with Some Glances Ahead)

1. Before 1900—vis-à-vis The Hour-Glass *and* Calvary

Yeats began writing plays in the late 1890's. Although a few were fairly successful as theater pieces, or because they were politically stirring, he was not a dramatist in the same full sense as Shaw, O'Casey, Wilde, or even Synge. But he did have an instinct for a kind of dramatic dialogue, sometimes in the form of an inward debate of the self. As we have seen, this instinct helped him cultivate a powerful, flexible technique in handling contradictory elements in his poems. Writing plays, and his serious involvement with theatrical production—which began in 1898 and intensified after he helped found the Abbey Theatre in 1904—brought his structural mastery to new levels.

Still, he was a lyric poet first and foremost. His plays, at their best, are remarkable for their striking poetic passages and for something more elusive: their lyrical dynamics—that is, their affective shiftings toward a balancing of the emotional pressures at work. These shiftings occur primarily in the *language* of successive passages, rather than in the action or unfolding of character.

One of the subtlest aspects of the plays is the way they relate an

ultimate skepticism to religious and mystical feeling and to the
"magic" and grotesquerie of folk superstition. Yeats's early plays
plunge vigorously into this ambiguity-riddled, politics-saturated,
and (*circa* 1900 in Ireland more than in most Western countries)
danger-ridden realm. Essentially, despite his fascination with the
realms of faerie and visionary occultism, his thinking was that of an
aesthete in love with what he could no longer believe. Like many
other writers of his generation and later, he exalted artistic integrity
over the authority of priests, politicians, ideologues, and "the mob."
"I believe," he wrote in 1901,

> that literature is the principal voice of the conscience, and that it is its
> duty age after age to affirm its morality against the special moralities of
> clergymen and churches, and of kings and parliaments and peo-
> ples. . . . I have no doubt that a wise ecclesiastic, if his courage
> equalled his wisdom, would be a better censor than the mob, but I
> think it better to fight the mob alone than to seek for a support one
> could only get by what would seem to me a compromise of principle.

This declaration was part of a letter to the *Freeman's Journal* (13
November 1901) against ecclesiastical censorship of plays. Richard
Ellmann, in *Yeats: The Man and the Masks* (1979), characterized it as
a specifically Irish program of mystical symbolism:

> Ireland was to be a holy land full of holy symbols, not in the orthodox
> clergyman's sense but in the poet's sense, which was also the mystic's
> sense; here alone in a degenerate Europe would spiritual realities be
> understood.

Ellmann's characterization was accurate. I would only add that
Yeats, in taking this direction, enabled himself to accommodate a
cultural *atmosphere* of religiosity while improvising a sphere of imaginative independence within which he could test the limits of his
daring. From his dramatic pieces written before 1900, Yeats chose to
reprint only *The Countess Cathleen* and *The Land of Heart's Desire* in
The Collected Plays (1934). On the surface, both these pieces assume
a pious Irish Catholic outlook alien alike to the poet's Protestant
background and his experimentally cultivated mystical sensibility.
Their seemingly devout centers met Irish theatrical expectations of

the time, as well as the presumed mental set of the peasant world that is the scene of the plays. Meanwhile, a non-Christian preoccupation slowly makes itself felt.

The process is especially clear in *The Countess Cathleen,* first produced in 1892. In this play, famine rages through the land and the devil's agents find many needy folk only too willing to sell their souls cheap to buy food for their families. The devout, humble Mary Rua keeps the faith, but—more typically—her loutish husband Shemus and son Teigue do not. It is left to the selfless Countess Cathleen to save "her" people from damnation. She does so by using all her wealth to buy back their souls and then by selling her own soul to gain more money toward that end. Divine justice declares the sale null and void, of course, and she ascends to eternal joy. —But as we shall see, this summary needs qualifying.

A parallel conflict takes place in *The Land of Heart's Desire* (1894). There a young bride, Mary Bruin, is tempted to leave hearth and loving husband for the realm of unsanctified ecstasy promised by a honey-tongued "Faery Child." Good old Father Hart struggles—as do her husband and his family—to prevent the forbidden super-natural powers from succeeding. Torn between the two worlds, she trembles on the verge of unholy choice; but the agony of her predica-ment kills her at the crucial moment. (We should note that the good Father Hart might have saved her for a life of virtuous wifehood and motherhood had he shown more presence of mind. To placate the protesting Faery Child, he benignly agrees to remove the family's protective crucifix from the room just when they need it most. Yeats himself, I am afraid, must be blamed for this bit of mischief that keeps the Church from winning a hands-down victory over the eerie un-known. He obviously preferred killing off his dreaming heroine to leaving her in the humdrum bosom of the Bruin family.)

Such are the overt motifs and plot lines of the two plays. Clearly, they honor a certain religious conventionality and are also indebted, in their imaginative range, to deeply entrenched archaic beliefs in weird supernatural beings and forces. But at the same time, Yeats interwove various contrary perspectives with these motifs and plot

Playbill of The Land of Heart's Desire, *designed by Aubrey Beardsley (1894)*

lines, creating a sort of internal quarreling within each play. The process parallels his handling of mystically and supernaturally charged elements in his early poetry.

An obvious and important instance is the way, in the course of revising *The Countess Cathleen* over the years, he developed the engaging romantic character Aleel the poet. Aleel plays a crucial role, not only as a non-Christian celebrant of primal joy but also as Cathleen's would-be lover. He begs her to go off with him

> and live in the hills
> Among the sounds of music and the light
> Of waters, till the evil days are done.
> For here some terrible death is waiting you,
> Some unimagined evil, some great darkness
> That fable has not dreamt of, nor sun nor moon
> Scattered.

Indeed, Cathleen is drawn, albeit without yielding, toward Aleel much as the heroine is drawn toward forbidden joy in *The Land of Heart's Desire*. Aleel, however, is not sinister but a force for life and freedom. Like Father Hart, he wishes to save the heroine from destroying herself. Although a pagan, he is inspired by "angelical" beings:

> *Aleel.* I have come to bid you leave this castle and fly
>   Out of these woods.
> *Cathleen.*   What evil is there here
>   That is not everywhere from this to the sea?
> *Aleel.* They who have sent me walk invisible.
> *Cathleen.* So it is true what I have heard men say,
>   That you have seen and heard what others cannot.
> *Aleel.* I was asleep in my bed, and while I slept
>   My dream became a fire; and in the fire
>   One walked and he had birds about his head.
> *Cathleen.* I have heard that one of the old gods walked so.
> *Aleel.* It may be that he is angelical;
>   And, lady, he bids me call you from these woods . . .

The passage is a relatively early instance of Yeats's delight in turning pious thought inside out. The god with "birds about his head" who appeared to Aleel is Aengus, described by Yeats elsewhere as the ancient Celtic "master of love" and god of youth, beauty, and poetry. He "reigned in Tir-Nan-Oge, the country of the young," the pre-Christian paradise whither Aleel wishes Cathleen to fly with him.

Now, while the play shows gentle respect for the faithful and devout peasant Mary Rua, and chivalric adoration for the saintly and magnanimous Countess Cathleen, it gives its heart to Aleel. When he speaks or sings, his visionary dreaming—sometimes sad, sometimes buoyant—reveals the work's true spirit. His paganism, as we see in his epiphanic account of Aengus, is neither grossly physical nor a form of diabolism. When Aleel is persuaded that Cathleen's soul has been consigned to damnation, his dismay is like that of any true Christian believer; and he pictures her supposed future state in blank verse modeled on (but hardly up to) Milton's description of Hell in *Paradise Lost*.

At the same time, Aleel puts his Christian model to the service of un-Christian thought: a type of co-option Yeats was to become ever more adept at. The underworld Aleel speaks of is peopled by ancient Irish mythical personages superficially like Milton's demonized deities. But it exists without reference to anything like Lucifer's revolt against heaven, or original sin. It is a hell without theological implications. Its heavy atmosphere is syrupy-thick with exotic evil. If not for the dragging metric and diction, we might call the passage an ingenious mixture of Keatsian dream and Miltonic vision:

> The brazen door stands wide, and Balor comes
> Borne in his heavy car, and demons have lifted
> The age-weary eyelids from the eyes that of old
> Turned gods to stone; Barach, the traitor, comes
> And the lascivious race, Cailitin,
> That cast a Druid weakness and decay
> Over Sualtim's and old Dectora's child;

> And that great king Hell first took hold upon
> When he killed Naoise and broke Deirdre's heart;
> And all their heads are twisted to one side,
> For when they lived they warred on beauty or peace
> With obstinate, crafty, sidelong bitterness.

Aleel, his dismayed imagination thus aroused, goes on to describe Cathleen's female companions-to-be in this anticipated underworld. The passage is livelier than the one given Balor and his crew; indeed, until the final line, it is seductively erotic in tone. It again has little to do with theology, let alone the *dramatic* movement of the play:

> First, Orchil, her pale, beautiful head alive,
> Her body shadowy as vapour drifting
> Under the dawn, for she who awoke desire
> Has but a heart of blood when others die;
> About her is a vapoury multitude
> Of women alluring devils with soft laughter;
> Behind her a host heat of the blood made sin,
> But all the little pink-white nails have grown
> To be great talons.

Yeats's indulgence here and elsewhere in voluptuously suggestive language for its own sake also serves quietly as a form of detachment from the play's conventionally pious surface. Such detachment becomes more emphatic in his later writing—with the ambivalent exception of *The Hour-Glass: A Morality* (prose version, 1903; mixed verse and prose, 1913).

The Hour-Glass is in part didactic; in part, especially in the mixed "New Version," movingly troubled; and in part, because of the character called Teigue the Fool, joyously playful. It centers on a brilliant teacher, the Wise Man, who has persuaded all the world except the Fool to renounce religious faith in favor of "the seven sciences" of secular rationalism. A boastful passage in the prose ver-

sion sums up his teachings with a mystical fervor that seems out of
character:

> With Philosophy that was made from the lonely star, I have taught
> them to forget Theology; with Architecture, I have hidden the ram-
> parts of their cloudy Heaven; with Music, the fierce planets' daughter
> whose hair is always on fire, and with Grammar that is the moon's
> daughter, I have shut their ears to the imaginary harpings and speech
> of the angels; and I have made formations of battle with Arithmetic
> that have put the hosts of Heaven to the rout. But, Rhetoric and
> Dialectic, that have been born out of the light star and out of the
> amorous star, you have been my spearmen and my catapult! O! my
> swift horsemen! O! my keen darting arguments, it is because of you
> that I have overthrown the hosts of foolishness!

Yeats dropped this eloquent yet inappropriate speech from his
much improved "New Version." In both texts the Wise Man has
been teasing the Fool about his superstition. Teigue claims he has
"seen plenty of angels" and that he goes "out on the hills every
morning" with his shears to cut the "great black nets," which men
"dressed in black" have laid to "catch the feet of angels." Indeed, he
says, he has just now seen one who, surprisingly, was "not laughing"
in the usual manner of angels. The Wise Man (apparently he has not
read his Blake) dismisses these tales teasingly and then, in the "New
Version," muses with just a hint of self-doubt:

> What were they all but fools before I came?
> What are they now but mirrors that seem men
> Because of my image? Fool, hold up your head.
> > [*The fool does so.*]
> What foolish stories they have told of the ghosts
> That fumbled with the clothes upon the bed,
> Or creaked and shuffled in the corridor,
> Or else, if they were pious bred,
> Of angels from the skies,
> That coming through the door,
> Or, it may be, standing there,
> Would solidly out-stare

> The steadiest eyes with their unnatural eyes,
> Aye, on a man's own floor. . . .
> Yet it is strange, the strangest thing I have known,
> That I should still be haunted by the notion
> That there's a crisis of the spirit wherein
> We get new sight, and that they know some trick
> To turn our thoughts for their own needs to frenzy.

Alas for the Wise Man's boasts, blatant in one version, subtler in the other, they are given the lie at once by the sudden appearance before him of the dour angel the Fool has already seen. Moreover, the angel brings him the news that he must die within the hour and be damned forever because "no souls have passed over the Threshold of Heaven since you came into this country." His only hope for salvation is to find just "one soul, / Before the sands have fallen, that still believes." In that case he may eventually, "the purgatorial fire being passed, / Spring to . . . peace."

But the poor Wise Man has taught everyone—including his pupils, his wife, and his children—much too successfully. All are certain he is merely testing them. Only the Fool, innocently in touch with the supernatural, knows better, and he fears to reveal what he knows lest the Wise Man reprove him or "steal away my thoughts."

In the earliest version, he finally does give the saving word after the Wise Man goes down on his knees and begs him to do so. But, wrote Yeats in his preface to the "New Version,"

> I took the plot . . . from an Irish Folk tale but tried to put my own philosophy into the words. An action on the stage, however, is so much stronger than a word that when the Wise Man abased himself before the Fool I was always ashamed. My own meanings had vanished and I saw before me a cowardly person who seemed to cry out "the wisdom of this world is foolishness" and to understand the words not as may a scholar and a gentleman but as do ignorant preachers.
>
> I began a revision of the words from the moment when the play converted a music hall singer and sent him to mass and to confession; but no revision of words could change the effect of the Wise Man

down on his knees before the Fool; so last year I changed action and all.

I made a new play of it and when I had finished discovered how I might have taken the offence out of the old by a change of action so slight that a reader would hardly have noticed it. I shall let "our second company" go on playing the old version thus amended in Irish provincial towns but think the new one better for myself and my friends.

The "change of action" was to drop the offending scene and, instead, have the Wise Man refuse the Fool's delayed offer to say what he knows and take the great risk of heroic humility: "I know enough, that know God's will prevails." This revision could hardly offend either a typical Irish audience or the clergy. At the same time, it allowed the Wise Man to retain both dignity and, in a certain sense, the intellectual authority of his original position. He was, after all, refuted only by the visible presence of the Angel; and the psychological force of the passage about the notion of "a crisis of the spirit" comes close to the actual secular, yet undogmatic, working of the modern mind.

In the dramatic structure of a much later play like *Calvary* (1921), the detachment from orthodox piety is a decisive active pressure. Here both the natural world and certain key New Testament figures—Judas, Lazarus, and the Roman soldiers present at the Crucifixion—either oppose or are indifferent to the authority of Jesus. "God," as the Chorus repeats, "has not died for the birds." Judas' defense is that betraying Christ was his only recourse if he wished to remain free and independent. Lazarus' argument is similar: he resents having been dragged back into life without his consent. And the soldiers, good-natured roughnecks, do not care one way or another. (One of them observes: "They say you're good and that you made the world, / But it's no matter.") When toward the end of the play Jesus cries out, "My Father, why hast Thou forsaken me?" his words mean something very unlike their Gospel import. He is not speaking in his character as a sacrificed *man* but as a failed divinity, rejected by humanity and disregarded by the animal world:

> The ger-eagle has chosen his part
> In deep blue of the upper air
> Where one-eyed day can meet his stare;
> He is content with his savage heart.

The most striking passages in *Calvary,* it should be noted, are the songs of the three Musicians that begin and end the play and also appear at two points within it. All these songs are centered on bird figures and bird imagery, and press the point of the total irrelevance of Jesus' sacrifice to nature's creatures. The beautiful opening song will illustrate:

First Musician.
> Motionless under the moon-beam,
> Up to his feathers in the stream;
> Although fish leap, the white heron
> Shivers in a dumbfounded dream.

Second Musician.
> God has not died for the white heron.

Third Musician.
> Although half famished he'll not dare
> Dip or do anything but stare
> Upon the glittering image of a heron,
> That now is lost and now is there.

Second Musician.
> God has not died for the white heron.

First Musician.
> But that the full is shortly gone
> And after that is crescent moon,
> It's certain that the moon-crazed heron
> Would be but fishes' diet soon.

Second Musician.
> God has not died for the white heron.

Even before the play's explicit subject is revealed, this song starts things off with a double detachment from traditional Christian emphasis. The tone of the refrain ("God has not died for the white heron") insinuates itself at once, an overture to Christ's unhappy agons with Lazarus, Judas, and the Roman soldiers. The refrain aside, however, the song is totally independent of the religious context of the main plot. Paralyzed by his own "glittering image" in the water under the full moon, liberated only by the fading of his reflection as the moon changes, the heron is totally self-absorbed and is subject only to impersonal natural process.

The force of this initial vision of the isolated ecstasy of individual creatures is intensified in the speech of the First Musician immediately after the song. He describes the "mocking crowd" surrounding Christ on the road to Calvary, then interrupts himself abruptly with a brief, terrified second song that seems to speak for Christ. It is as though Christ, stung by the crowd's mockery, had a sudden premonition of futility and saw his own self-entranced dream mirrored in that of the heron "crazed by the moon":

> O, but the mockers' cry
> Makes my heart afraid,
> As though a flute of bone
> Taken from a heron's thigh,
> A heron crazed by the moon,
> Were cleverly, softly played.

To return now to *The Countess Cathleen*: the Musicians' songs in *Calvary* are dramatically better placed and lyrically more concentrated than the poet Aleel's speeches and songs in the earlier play. They have a comparable role, however, in implying a world of thought free of established religion and morality. Aleel does so halfplayfully at first when, to distract Cathleen's mind from "the evil of the times," he reminds her of ancient tales about "Maeve the Queen of all the invisible host" and about the faery dancers who served her. Some of his phrasing, when he dwells on the full moon's effect on the dancers, foreshadows that of the songs in *Calvary* about the "heron crazed by the moon." Maeve, he says,

sleeps high up on wintry Knocknarea
In an old cairn of stones; while her poor women
Must lie and jog in the wave if they would sleep—
Being water-born—yet if she cry their names
They run up on the land and dance in the moon
Till they are giddy and would love as men do,
And be as patient and as pitiful.
But there is nothing that will stop in their heads,
They've such poor memories, though they weep for it.
O yes, they weep; that's when the moon is full.

A bit farther along in the dialogue, Cathleen's devoted and devout old foster-mother, Oona, tries to protect her from Aleel's profane thoughts. He has been wondering

What Queen Maeve thinks on when the moon is pinched;
And whether now—as in the old days—the dancers
Set their brief love on men.

"These are no thoughts," Oona protests, "for any Christian ear."
But Aleel ignores her, picks up his lute, and sings a song to Cathleen
inviting her to forget her moral burdens and emulate Maeve's
dancers:

Lift up the white knee;
Hear what they sing,
Those young dancers
That in a ring
Raved but now
Of the hearts that broke
Long, long ago
For their sake.

But the dance changes,
Lift up the gown,
All that sorrow
Is trodden down.

It is of some interest that, in the play's 1892 version, in which "Cathleen" was spelled with an initial "K" and her poet friend was named "Kevin," Oona was better inclined toward the world of Maeve and ancient legendry. So too was Kathleen, far more than in the final version. ("I hear the horn of Fergus in my heart," she says longingly.) When Kathleen grieves over the famine and the marketing of souls, it is Oona who seeks to distract her with talk of that other world. In the early version she has a warm sympathy with the poet Kevin's dreams, something very different from her sharp distrust of his successor, Aleel:

> I have lived now nearly ninety winters, child,
> And I have known three things no doctor cures—
> Love, loneliness, and famine—nor found refuge
> Other than growing old and full of sleep.
> See you where Oisin and young Niam ride
> Wrapped in each other's arms, and where the Finians
> Follow their hounds along the fields of tapestry,
> How merry they lived once, yet men died then.
> I'll sing the ballad young bard Kevin sang
> By the great door, the light about his head,
> When he bid you cast off this cloud of care.

The ballad she sings—eventually reprinted separately as "Who Goes with Fergus?"—is one of Yeats's loveliest early poems. Nevertheless, Yeats removed the song from the text after a number of printings. He did so in the process of simplifying Kathleen's and Oona's roles while also clearing the play of its welter of allusions to mythical Irish history. He might well have kept such a finely resonant moment, putting the words in Aleel's mouth instead of Oona's. Perhaps he felt that their foreboding tone contradicted the joy Aleel has been promising Cathleen if she runs off with him to the forbidden realm. More to the point, the omission was part of the stripping-down needed to make *The Countess Cathleen* a more actable play. Here, at any rate, is the song as originally printed:

Who will go drive with Fergus now,
And pierce the deep wood's woven shade,
And dance upon the level shore?
Young man, lift up your russet brow,
And lift your tender eyelids, maid,
And brood on hopes and fears no more.
And no more turn aside and brood
Upon love's bitter mystery;
For Fergus rules the brazen cars,
And rules the shadows of the wood,
And the white breast of the dim sea
And all dishevelled wandering stars.

These lines suggest eternal unfulfillment. But their mood is matched by another song, more closely related to the love plot, inserted in later versions. This is Aleel's forlorn song at the end of Scene IV of the final version. It is very much of a piece with such poems of the same period as "He Wishes for the Cloths of Heaven" and "He Hears the Cry of the Sedge":

Impetuous heart be still, be still,
Your sorrowful love can never be told,
Cover it up with a lonely tune.
He who could bend all things to His Will
Has covered the door of the infinite fold
With the pale stars and the wandering moon.

A note by Yeats (reprinted in the *Variorum Edition* of his plays) on his revisions of *The Countess Cathleen* is illuminating. It clarifies both his dramatic reasoning and the political and religious considerations involved:

. . . Some of the characters . . . have dropped out of the play during revision. The players had to face a very vehement opposition stirred up by a politician and a newspaper, the one accusing me in a pamphlet, the other in long articles day after day, of blasphemy be-

cause of the language of the demons or of Shemus Rua, and because I
made a woman sell her soul and yet escape damnation, and of a lack of
patriotism because I made Irish men and women, who, it seems, never
did such a thing, sell theirs. The politician or the newspaper persuaded some forty Catholic students to sign a protest against the play,
and a Cardinal, who avowed that he had not read it, to make another,
and both politician and newspaper made such obvious appeals to the
audience to break the peace, that a score or so of police were sent to
the theatre to see that they did not. I had, however, no reason to regret
the result, for the stalls, containing almost all that was distinguished in
Dublin, and a gallery of artisans alike insisted on the freedom of
literature.

   After the performance in 1899 I added the love scene between
Aleel and the Countess. . . . Now at last I have made a complete
revision to make it suitable for performance in the Abbey Theatre.
The first two scenes are almost wholly new, and throughout the play I
have added or left out such passages as a stage experience of some
years showed me encumbered the action; the play in its first form
having been written before I knew anything of the theatre.

The Cardinal who "avowed he had not read" the play might
have found one saving grace if he somehow saw the later version.
Aleel is so caught up by the momentum of the ending that, in his
concern lest Cathleen's soul be borne to Hell, he absents himself from
pagan felicity for the moment at least and experiences religious con-
version. After she dies, warrior angels battle the demons sent to
collect her soul and hurtle them back down to Hell. As the victors
gaze "downward with stern faces," Aleel calls to them:

Aleel. Look no more on the half-closed gates of Hell,
   But speak to me, whose mind is smitten of God,
   That it may be no more with mortal things,
   And tell of her who lies there. [*He seizes one of the angels.*]
                                        Till you speak
   You shall not drift into eternity.
The Angel. The light beats down; the gates of pearl are wide;
   And she is passing to the floor of peace,
   And Mary of the seven times wounded heart
   Has kissed her lips, and the long blessed hair

Has fallen on her face; The Light of Lights
Looks always on the motive, not the deed,
The Shadow of Shadows on the deed alone.
                    [*Aleel releases the Angel and kneels.*]

Without digressing into matters of influence, I think it fair to say
that the passage—like others in Yeats's work and in his corre-
spondence—reflects an affinity with Goethe. One of his letters, in
fact, refers to *Faust* as perhaps one of "our sacred books, man self-
sufficing and eternal." Cathleen, like Goethe's Gretchen, has sinned
yet is saved. The "Shadow of Shadows" would prefer to possess her
precious soul in Hell, but "The Light of Lights / Looks always on the
motive, not the deed." This exactly matches the balance of divine
judgment in *Faust* when, at Gretchen's death, Mephistopheles cries
out triumphantly, "She is judged!" but a voice from Heaven replies,
"She is saved!"

In another, subtler context, it matches the salvation of Faust
himself in Part II. Despite his terrible lapses, Faust has discovered
the happiness of serving others. More important, however, is the way
he embodies the process of what Yeats was to call "man self-sufficing
and eternal." This becomes the effort to respond to "*das Ewig-
weibliche*"—the divine, loving, "eternally feminine" force that draws
him into the realm of exaltation at the end of Part II.

Obviously, *The Countess Cathleen* lacks anything like the complex structure and intellectual depth of *Faust*. Yet it has its plain
affinities as an early attempt at seriously interweaving conflicting
perspectives, moods, and moral pressures. This may be seen, most
simply, in the play's unusual range of tonalities. I have so far stressed
passages of pure lyricism to show how, while Yeats was certainly
interested in dramatic values, he wrote primarily as a poet. As he
noted in *Plays and Controversies* (1923), his first plays had been
lyrically driven:

> Somebody . . . had said in my hearing that dramatic poetry
> must be oratorical, and I think that I wrote partly to prove that false;

but every now and then I lose courage, as it seems, and remembering that I had some reputation as a lyric poet wrote for the reader of lyrics.

Earlier on, in his preface to *Plays for an Irish Theatre* (1911), he had argued:

> In poetical drama there is, it is held, an antithesis between drama and lyric poetry, for lyric poetry however much it move you when read out of a book can, as these critics think, but encumber the action. Yet when we go back a few centuries and enter the great periods of drama, character grows less and sometimes disappears, and there is much lyric feeling, and at times a lyric measure will be wrought into the dialogue, a flowing measure that had well befitted music, or that more lumbering one of the sonnet.

But this primacy of the lyrical has its protean possibilities and is compatible with dramatic action and character, however much it may "encumber" them. In *The Countess Cathleen* we have scenes dominated by the coarse, inhumane Shemus and Teigue, or by the smoothly ruthless merchant-demons from Hell, in direct conflict with the humbly devout Mary. Others center on the aristocratically benign but equally devout Cathleen (who nevertheless, surprisingly, yearns for a pagan existence she cannot permit herself to indulge in); or on the romantically free-spirited poet Aleel; or on the crowd of panic-stricken peasants; or on the triumphant angel announcing Cathleen's apotheosis. Around these figures, as the play progresses, scenes and units of dialogue are built that counterpoise tones ranging from crude, thoughtless cruelty to glowing selflessness. The play's dynamics depend far more on this structure of tonal effects than on dramatic probability.

Sometimes, too, the effects are purely visual. For instance, after the army of angels has defeated malign Balor and his forces, the stage-direction reads:

> *The darkness is broken by a visionary light. The Peasants seem to be kneeling upon the rocky slope of a mountain, and vapour full of storm and ever-changing light is sweeping above them and behind them. Half in the light, half in the shadow, stand armed angels. Their armour is old*

and worn, and their drawn swords dim and dinted. They stand as if
upon the air in formation of battle and look downward with stern faces.
The peasants cast themselves on the ground.

Sometimes, too, a flash of Yeatsian wit intrudes itself suddenly,
as in this innocent, generous-spirited utterance of Mary's:

> God's pity on the rich!
> Had we been through as many doors, and seen
> The dishes standing on the polished wood
> In the wax candle light, we'd be as hard,
> And there's the needle's eye at the end of all.

And in the brief closing speech of the play, Oona takes over the
stage. In her first two, highly compressed lines, she speaks of her
passionate yearning to die so that she may rejoin Cathleen "upon the
floor of peace." Her three succeeding lines then present a powerful
and tragic image, deeply of the elemental peasant world. They culmi-
nate in the simplest possible expression of personal loss and heart-
break:

> Tell them who walk upon the floor of peace
> That I would die and go to her I love;
> The years like great black oxen tread the world,
> And God the herdsman goads them on behind,
> And I am broken by their passing feet.

Oona's speech staves off any temptation to let the play end in a
fireworks display of facile celebratory sentiments. Cathleen is saved,
but for the world at large—where famine, panic, and evil were the
order earlier on—the heavy march of fatality continues.

2. The Land of Heart's Desire *and Plays of 1900 to 1908*

A clear bohemian current, in the Romantic anti-bourgeois, half-
anarchist sense, runs through Yeats's early plays and never quite

disappears. In *The Countess Cathleen,* we see it in Aleel's attitudes until the very end, and in Cathleen's sacrificial devotion to the common folk. Often it is accompanied by a *frisson* of terror at what success in winning freedom may really mean. In *The Land of Heart's Desire,* the newly married Mary Bruin's indifference to conventional domesticity, and her vulnerability to the perilous call of the forbidden, provide an instance of this ambivalence. She courts disaster by appealing directly to the world of the faeries:

> *Mary.* Come, faeries, take me out of this dull house!
>   Let me have all the freedom I have lost;
>   Work when I will and idle when I will!
>   Faeries, come take me out of this dull world,
>   For I would ride with you upon the wind,
>   Run on the top of the dishevelled tide,
>   And dance upon the mountains like a flame.

She is answered by the world that she yearns for and yet—as she confesses to her husband—fears. The answer, sung by a lovely "Faery Child," is both an invitation and a warning:

> The wind blows out of the gates of the day,
> The wind blows over the lonely of heart,
> And the lonely of heart is withered away.
> While the faeries dance in a place apart,
> Shaking their milk-white feet in a ring,
> Tossing their milk-white arms in the air;
> For they hear the wind laugh and murmur and sing
> Of a land where even the old are fair,
> And even the wise are merry of tongue;
> But I heard a reed of Coolaney say,
> "When the wind has laughed and murmured and sung
> The lonely of heart is withered away!"

From a conventional religious standpoint, perhaps, the play might be taken as a parable teaching the virtue and *safety* of pious conformity. But from the standpoint of its affective movement, it resonates a fear-tinged longing for just the opposite state. The ro-

"*Mr. W. B. Yeats presenting Mr. George Moore to the Queen of the Fairies*" (*cartoon by Max Beerbohm*)

mantic pull of unknown and anathematized powers is also seen as the pull of death; and it is interesting that the play's epigraph, "O Rose, thou art sick" (from Blake's "The Sick Rose"), stresses the negative side of this predicament. This emphasis is especially interesting because some of Yeats's most powerful work—for instance, his "Nineteen Hundred and Nineteen"—celebrates the opposite:

> Some moralist or mythological poet
> Compares the solitary soul to a swan;
> I am satisfied with that,
> Satisfied if a troubled mirror show it,
> Before that brief gleam of its life be gone,
> An image of its state;
> The wings half spread for flight,
> The breast thrust out in pride
> Whether to play, or to ride
> Those winds that clamour of approaching night.

Nevertheless, *The Land of Heart's Desire*—like much of Yeats's other work, from a very early poem like "The Stolen Child" to a very late one like "Cuchulain Comforted"—appears both to glorify and to shy away from the daring life of imaginative adventure. Winning through to a climax of depressive transcendence like the passage just quoted (written over a quarter-century later than the play) amounted to a difficult triumph of poetic resolution.

In a different if ultimately related context, it is also of some interest that, in *The Land of Heart's Desire,* Mary (to everyone's dismayed amazement that she should be reading anything at all) buries herself in a book she happens to find in the Bruin household. It is the myth of Edain, who—as Mary is tempted to do—followed "a voice singing on a May Eve like this" into "The Land of Faery." Edain's tale is partly pathetic, endlessly fanciful, and elusively romantic. Taken as a second wife by Midhir, a king in the supernatural world of the Sidhe, she was changed by the jealous first wife into a purple fly. The wind carried her to the dwelling of Aengus, the god of love, who temporarily restored her original form. This was hardly the end of her adventures and metamorphoses, but in some of his early writing Yeats simplified her story as an embodiment, however vague, of the glamorous but disastrous course of love in the treacherous dreamland of supernatural fulfillment.

Edain and Aengus are important figures of reference in his poetic drama *The Shadowy Waters,* written and much revised between 1900 and 1911. In early versions, they are described as appearing when the hero, the sea-voyaging Forgael, who is making his way to an undefined land of heart's desire, plays his magic-making harp. One of the sailors says:

> The other night, while he was playing it,
> A beautiful young man and girl came up
> In a white breaking wave; they had the look
> Of those that are alive for ever and ever.

The sailor identifies them as "Aengus and Edain, the wandering lovers, / To whom all lovers pray." Delightful. But he also warns that "there is not one / Of the Ever-living half so dangerous / As that wild Aengus." These "wandering lovers" of Irish myth prefigure the passionate, doomed voyage of Forgael and Dectora. (Dectora is the queen whose husband Forgael kills in sea-battle. He then woos and wins her because—if the word "because" could be of much use in this crowded jumble of a plot—they recognize each other as eternal lovers, recurring incarnations of their past selves.)

In his later "acting version" of *The Shadowy Waters* (1911), Yeats mercifully dropped all mention of Aengus and Edain. He seems to have realized along the way that the story of Forgael and Dectora was confusing enough. He did not need to plant hazy allusions to Aengus and Edain in order to prefigure it. They had served his imagination primarily as a bridge to his future work linking terror or death to passionate desire and the search for eternal ecstasy.

Despite its hopeless clutter, *The Shadowy Waters* itself is a comparable bridge to Yeats's future writing, and also a bridge for him between pure poetry and the demands of the theater. Its main charm still lies in its evocative and singing passages, its visions of Aengus and Edain rising from the waves like dolphins and disappearing, its mystical talk of "man-headed" birds that fly westward singing of "happiness beyond measure, happiness where the sun dies," and other such marvels of dreaming fantasy. At the same time it reflects Yeats's struggles for dramatic mastery during the first decade of the 1900's, especially in plays centered on a usually tragic struggle between pressure to conform and pressure to take mortal (and moral) risks of defiance. The risks are in pursuit of an ideal, a vision, or free experience of the forbidden. Yeats's chief plays of the period— *Cathleen ni Houlihan* (1902), *The King's Threshold* (1904), *On Baile's Strand* (1904), and *Deirdre* (1907)—all are instances.

In the first of these, *Cathleen ni Houlihan,* the initial scene—a comfortably domestic one in the interior of a rural cottage—is virtually identical with those of *The Countess Cathleen* and *The Land of Heart's Desire*. Its dramatic situation, too, is a curious variation on that of the latter play. Michael Gillane, the hero, is snugly and contentedly at home with his family and on the verge of a happy marriage to Delia Cahel. He is looking forward to the fine new suit he will wear at the wedding and the generous dowry he will receive, and of course to life with the "nice comely girl" who will be his bride. But suddenly a "strange woman" comes up the path to the house, and the feelings she conveys and the songs she sings drive those expectations quite out of his mind.

Thus Michael, like Mary Bruin, is lured from life's sweet normal comforts by a death-fraught summons. His story is almost the same as Mary's—except, of course, that what he is being called to is the recurring bloody battle for Irish freedom. The "strange woman" is Cathleen ni Houlihan, the soul of Ireland roaming the land to summon the young men to that battle once more. Through most of the play she appears as the "Old Woman"; but at the very end she is seen to be—as Michael's younger brother Patrick puts it—"a young girl, and she had the walk of a queen." The gratification she promises is immortal glory for the suffering that must be endured.

Instead, then, of the Faery Child's seductively sinister appeal to the "lonely of heart" to come to the place where faeries dance and laugh endlessly, Cathleen ni Houlihan's songs celebrate men who have died for love of her and those who will dare to do so in the future. In form they resemble the many heroic keenings of Irish folk-tradition. Cathleen's first song begins:

> I will go cry with the woman,
> For yellow-haired Donough is dead,
> With a hempen rope for a neckcloth,
> And a white cloth upon his head.

This is the promise Cathleen offers, instead of bliss as we ordinarily think of it. And yet, as the history she draws on shows, the risk of almost certain death has lured as many to its flame as has the dream of joy unconfined. Part of the promise—like that of Aleel when he woos the countess, and that of the Faery Child singing to Mary—is of immortality, this time to be gained by giving oneself to the great cause. Cathleen ni Houlihan spells it out to Michael:

It is a hard service they take that help me. Many that are red-cheeked now will be pale-cheeked; many that have been free to walk the hills and the bogs and rushes will be sent to walk hard streets in far countries; many a good plan will be broken; many that have gathered money will not stay to spend it; many a child will be born and there will be no father at its christening to give it a name. They that have red cheeks will have pale cheeks for my sake, and for all that, they will think they are well paid.

> [*She goes out; her voice is heard outside singing.*]
> They shall be remembered for ever,
> They shall be alive for ever,
> They shall be speaking for ever,
> The people shall hear them for ever.

The cause is political, and is rooted in actual tragic history. The appeal is to undo the wrongs of the past at whatever cost: an appeal, farfetched as it may seem, not altogether unlike the faery world's summons to a magical realm where the tedium of ordinary mortal life will be forever left behind. But for patriotic young Irish people, what Cathleen tells Michael and his parents Bridget and Peter must have been thrilling indeed:

> *Bridget* [*to the Old Woman*]. Will you have a drink of milk, ma'am?
> *Old Woman.* It is not food or drink that I want.
> *Peter* [*offering shilling*]. Here is something for you.
> *Old Woman.* This is not what I want. It is not silver I want.
> *Peter.* What is it you would be asking for?
> *Old Woman.* If anyone would give me help he must give me himself, he must give me all.
> [*Peter goes over to the table staring at the shilling in his hand in a bewildered way, and stands whispering to Bridget.*]
> *Michael.* Have you no one to care you in your age, ma'am?
> *Old Woman.* I have not. With all the lovers that brought me their love I never set out the bed for any.
> *Michael.* Are you lonely going the roads, ma'am?
> *Old Woman.* I have my thoughts and I have my hopes.
> *Michael.* What hopes have you to hold to?
> *Old Woman.* The hope of getting my beautiful fields back again; the hope of putting the strangers out of my house.
> *Michael.* What way will you do that, ma'am?
> *Old Woman.* I have good friends that will help me. They are gathering to help me now. I am not afraid. If they are put down to-day they will get the upper hand to-morrow. [*She gets up.*] I must be going to meet my friends. They are coming to help me and I must be there to welcome them. I must call the neighbours together to welcome them.
> *Michael.* I will go with you.

Yeats's note about the play in *The United Irishman* of 5 May 1902 succinctly explained its kinship with *The Land of Heart's Desire:*

> My subject is Ireland and its struggle for independence. The scene is laid in Ireland at the time of the French landing. . . . It is the perpetual struggle of the cause of Ireland and every other ideal cause against private hopes and dreams, against all that we mean when we

say the world. I have put into the mouth of Kathleen ni Houlihan verses about those who have died or are about to die for her, and these verses are the key of the rest. She sings of one yellow-haired Donough in stanzas that were suggested to me by some old Gaelic folk-song . . . I have written the whole play in the English of the West of Ireland, the English of people who think in Irish. My play, "The Land of Heart's Desire," was, in a sense, the call of the heart, the heart seeking its own dream; this play is the call of country. . . .

In *The King's Threshold,* first produced in 1903, the "ideal cause" the hero sacrifices himself for is the right of the poets to be represented on the king's council. "I took the plot of it," Yeats wrote, "from a Middle Irish story about the demands of the poets at the court of King Guaire, but twisted it about and revised its moral that the poet might have the best of it." At the same time, he noted, the play was related to the modern "hard fight" the National Theatre Society had waged "for the recognition of pure art in a community of which one half was buried in the practical affairs of life, and the other half in politics and a propagandist patriotism."

Yeats might well have aimed that second barb—"politics and a propagandist patriotism"—against his own *Cathleen ni Houlihan.* Its saving grace as "pure art," however, lies partly in its unforced, melodic speech-rhythms: "the English of people who think in Irish." The dialogue in the opening movement of this brief play is that of an ordinary family comfortably at home with one another. They are anticipating Michael's wedding and their related good prospects with pleasure, although Michael is hardly burning with excitement. Sounds of cheering, heard in the distance, stimulate only a mild, unconcerned curiosity. Not until the Old Woman comes to the door and is invited to enter does the play begin to gain intensity. At first she only arouses pity, but soon she emerges as the carrier of a perilous wisdom, speaking in political riddles while the dialogue takes on the staccato heightening of stichomythia:

Bridget. What was it put you wandering?
Old Woman. Too many strangers in the house.

Bridget. Indeed, you look as if you'd had your share of trouble.
Old Woman. I have had trouble indeed.
Bridget. What was it put the trouble on you?
Old Woman. My land that was taken from me.
Peter. Was it much land they took from you?
Old Woman. My four beautiful green fields.

Shortly after this exchange she begins to sing her challenging songs. First comes the lament for Donough. Then, a bit further on, comes the superficially puzzling admonition *not* to mourn, albeit the language seems to suggest every reason to do so. It does, however, shift from the tone of grief shared with "the woman"—presumably Donough's widow or beloved—of the previous song to one of dire yet dauntless death-anticipation:

> Do not make a great keening
> When the graves have been dug to-morrow.
> Do not call the white-scarfed riders
> To the burying that shall be to-morrow.
> Do not spread food to call strangers
> To the wakes that shall be to-morrow;
> Do not give money for prayers
> For the dead that shall die to-morrow. . . .

Here the song breaks off abruptly, and Cathleen offers, still a bit ambiguously, an explanation in incantatory prose: "They will have no need of prayers, they will have no need of prayers." The obvious implication, whose shadow has of course hovered over the play right along, is that the martyrs of Irish nationalism are already sanctified by their actions. Implication is replaced by outright assertion when Cathleen, after she leaves the house, is heard singing their immortal renown:

> They shall be remembered for ever,
> They shall be alive for ever,
> They shall be speaking for ever,
> The people shall hear them for ever.

At this point Michael becomes so entranced that he entirely forgets his coming wedding and all the pleasures attendant on it. His dismayed mother cries out that "he has the look of a man that has got the touch." Young Patrick rushes in to shout that "There are ships in the Bay; the French are landing at Killala!"—and Michael breaks away from Delia's arms and follows Cathleen's inspiring voice. He is off to join the French, who have come to help the Irish rebellion against England. The play's patriotic pulse is now pounding wildly, death's finality has been denied, and the result must be one of the most effective recruiting plays ever performed. Even at the very end, a single electrifying touch magically transforms Cathleen into a romantic dream-figure whose ardent admirers must eagerly follow her into war's charnel realm:

> Peter [*to Patrick, laying a hand on his arm*]. Did you see an old woman going down the path?
> Patrick. I did not, but I saw a young girl, and she had the walk of a queen.

It is all a striking variation on "La Belle Dame sans Merci" and, by the same token, on *The Land of Heart's Desire*—but given a powerful political coloration this time around. The ambiguity of the play's emotional bearing lies in its death-obsession on one hand and its overlay of self-sacrificial idealism on the other. One needs to be totally caught up in its spirit of revolutionary struggle, or a comparable one, not to feel the cold touch of the propagandist's hand in Michael's choice and, consequently, to cast a cold eye on what the play is up to—as Yeats himself did, ruefully, many years later in his poem "Man and the Echo":

> All that I have said and done,
> Now that I am old and ill,
> Turns into a question till
> I lie awake night after night
> And never get the answers right.
> Did that play of mine send out
> Certain men the English shot?

The King's Threshold is equally partisan, but is hardly a direct
appeal for new volunteers in the ranks of death. True, its protagonist,
the legendary poet Seanchan, chooses for the sake of a principle to
fast until death on the steps before the royal palace. We see him lying
there as the play begins, in protest against the king's annulment of
the poets' ancient right to sit in his council of state. But this play
reaches back into a mythical, archaic past. If its underlying pressure
is the modern need to oppose the demeaning of the arts, its literal
situation is far enough removed from our own world to prevent any
sense of it as ordinary propaganda. It does attack the arrogance of
rulers and the alliance of church and state. And also it affirms Yeats's
characteristically half bohemian and anarchistic, half feudal or aristocratic, regard for the common people. Its main preoccupation, however, is with restoring "the ancient right of the poets"—not exactly a
demand that will rouse young militants to arm themselves and take
to the streets. The political resonances of *The King's Threshold* are
akin to those of any serious literary work having to do with power
and injustice without itself being an instrument of direct activism.

Although built on a series of agons, the play works like a sophisticated poetic counting-out game. The agons are absorbing but more
or less static dramatically. They do not grow out of one another in the
classic manner of, say, *Oedipus Tyrannos,* so that each step would
seem to necessitate the next and limit the choices open to characters
and creator alike. Rather, they resemble a series of related major
images, or larger affective units, in a lyric poem.

At the start of the play (it is also the start of the first agon), the
king addresses Seanchan's disciples. He wishes them to persuade
their master to yield, but one would never think so from his eloquent
speech, which seems to place him completely on the side of the poets.
"I welcome you," he says—

> Both you that understand stringed instruments,
> And how to mingle words and notes together
> So artfully that all the Art's but Speech
> Delighted with its own music; and you that carry

> The twisted horn, and understand the notes
> That lacking words escape Time's chariot;
> For the high angels that drive the horse of Time—
> The golden one by day, by night the silver—
> Are not more welcome to one that loves the world
> For some fair woman's sake.
> > I have called you hither
> To save the life of your great master, Seanchan,
> For all day long it has flamed up or flickered
> To the fast-cooling hearth.

At first this all-too-cunning speech, with its flattery and its air of kindly concern for Seanchan, confuses the disciples. Their spokesman, the "Oldest Pupil," expresses natural bewilderment:

> I owe you all obedience, and yet
> How can I give it, when the man I have loved
> More than all others, thinks that he is wronged . . . ?

But then, not quite believably, he is won over for the moment, even though the king accuses Seanchan of malice and asserts his own arbitrary, overriding prerogatives and those of

> > my courtiers—
> Bishops, Soldiers, and Makers of the Law—
> Who long had thought it against their dignity
> For a mere man of words to sit amongst them
> At the great Council of the State and share
> In their authority. I bade him go,
> Though at the first with kind and courteous words,
> But when he pleaded for the poets' right,
> Established at the establishment of the world,
> I said that I was King, and that all rights
> Had their original fountain in some king,
> And that it was the men who ruled the world,
> And not the men who sang to it, who should sit
> Where there was the most honour.

Overawed, the Oldest Pupil grants the point gratefully:

> I can breathe again.
> You have taken a great burden from my mind,
> For that old custom's not worth dying for.

And he begins (in an image that recurs later in *Calvary*) to urge
Seanchan to "waken out of your dream" and to be more practical, for

> The hunger of the crane, that starves himself
> At the full moon because he is afraid
> Of his own shadow and the glittering water,
> Seems to be little more fantastical
> Than this of yours.

However striking this image, the Oldest Pupil's abrupt turn-
about is dramatically awkward and creaky. Nevertheless, his sudden effort to move Seanchan, even if so weakly motivated, does serve
its structural purpose. It begins the play's *major* series of agons,
in which the oldest pupil, the youngest one, the mayor (together
with assorted characters), the chamberlain, a monk, two princesses,
Seanchan's sweetheart, and the king all try to sway the great poet.
They fail—though at the cost of Seanchan's death—and so the punishment the king fears for himself will indeed follow in time. His
own knowledge, in his own prophetic words, should have warned
him:

> there is a custom,
> An old and foolish custom, that if a man
> Be wronged, or think that he is wrong, and starve
> Upon another's threshold till he die,
> The common people, for all time to come,
> Will raise a heavy cry against that threshold,
> Even though it be the King's.

Seanchan's triumph-to-come is a desolate one, however. It parallels both the dénouement of *Cathleen ni Houlihan* and the tragic

vision of Yeats's later years. By the end of *The King's Threshold,* all the pupils—including the oldest one, who has now become, as it were, Seanchan reborn—share that vision. It is the Oldest Pupil who, in the emotional register that defines the whole set of the play, utters the final brooding prophecy:

> nor song nor trumpet-blast
> Can call up races from the worsening world
> To mend the wrong and mar the solitude
> Of the great soul we follow to the tomb.

The *lyrical* structure of the play lies in its affective movement between its two extremes: on the one hand, the sheer delight of poetry, so hypocritically described by the king at the very start; on the other, the tragic exaltation, reflected in the Oldest Pupil's closing speech, of great art's confrontation of death, defeat, and the soul's basic solitude. The stilted *dramatic* structure resembles a series of operatic arias and duets that serve this movement mainly through their varied emphases and intensities. It seems clever of Yeats to have opened the play by having a royal figure pay tribute, however hypo-critical, to poetry in images suggesting its appeal to lovers and its kinship with immortal energies: the "high angels that drive the horse of Time." When, shortly afterwards, we learn that the man seen lying on the palace steps in protest is, ironically, the very person who embodies everything the king has been praising, the issue of the play has been drawn. The "action" lies, first, in Seanchan's resistance to the attempts to lure or argue him into submission and, second, in his death. But its affective progression, more than its dramatic move-ment, is what gives this play its life.

Thus, Seanchan's agon with his oldest pupil is hardly dramatic conflict at all. He simply asks him to repeat what he has learned over the years about the monstrous thing existence would be without the arts, and to recall the special reason poetry must be guarded with one's life. "One of the fragile, mighty things of God, / That die at an insult," it must be defended because, long ago,

>   the poets hung
> Images of the life that was in Eden
> About the child-bed of the world, that it,
> Looking upon those images, might bear
> Triumphant children.

The Oldest Pupil, thus reminded through his own words of poetry's bright mission and the rightness of Seanchan's cause, ceases his misguided effort forthwith. At the end of the play, he defies the king and supports his master wholeheartedly, leading the other pupils in their tragic chant: "Die, Seanchan, and proclaim the right of the poets." His dialogue with Seanchan has been a lyrical reinforcement of the king's initial praise of poetry, but has also conveyed a superior sense of the art's character. The king had seen it purely as the lovely source of a kind of voluptuous spirituality. Now, though, it has emerged as something far more as well—something comparable to all the "venerable things / God gave to men before He gave them wheat." It is first of all the carrier of the glorious images that have created humanity's visions of its best and happiest possibilities. But also, it can inspire bitter sacrifice when necessary, for the sake of the rights and integrity of art in the face of gross, philistine power.

That sacrifice and confrontation are sometimes incumbent on the poet is of course symbolized (though not yet articulated) at the very start of the play, when we see the starving Seanchan prone on the palace steps. His dialogue with the Oldest Pupil then brings this symbolic action more clearly into emotional and intellectual focus. And the next agon, between the Youngest Pupil and Seanchan, concentrates on its hard meaning explicitly as the central driving force of the play. When the boy asks plaintively how he can survive without his master and how he will be able to "sing verses or make music / With none to praise me, and a broken heart," he receives the same kind of ruthlessly decisive reply that Cathleen ni Houlihan might have given a young disciple. Her terms would have been political rather than poetic, but the romantically passionate, suicidal ardor of revolutionary Irish tradition flames as fiercely in Seanchan's words:

What was it that the poets promised you
If it was not their sorrow? Do not speak.
Have I not opened school on these bare steps,
And are you not the youngest of my scholars?
And I would have all know that when all falls
In ruin, poetry calls out in joy,
Being the scattering hand, the bursting pod,
The victim's joy among the holy flame,
God's laughter at the shattering of the world.
And now that joy laughs out, and weeps and burns
On these bare steps.

Here the play hits a high note of elegiac ecstasy. But now a largely farcical prose interlude (though interspersed with serious notes), with some Punch-and-Judy elements, follows. The mayor of Kinvara, Seanchan's town, has arrived to do his bit for the king. He is a little like some of the official bumpkins in Shakespeare, but also has a touch of the pompous cliché-spewing Flaubert loved to satirize. Seanchan, scornful of all who would intrude on his chosen tragic purpose, replies witheringly. And because the stupidly servile mayor defends the king's right to be as cruel as he chooses, he is ridiculed and humiliated by three Seanchan supporters from the ranks of the Irish poor who arrive with him: Brian, a loyal old servant of Seanchan's family, and two crippled beggars of wildly anarchistic temperament who are masters of invective and of the ancient art of incantatory cursing. All three, uneducated and comically literal-minded though they be, are spirited men altogether unlike the mayor, who is the essence of a cringing, small-souled type often decried in Yeats's writings.

In both his poems and his plays, Yeats often enough leavened his normally serious poetic eloquence with quietly humorous or whimsical effects. He liked to introduce colorful folk idioms and, sometimes, passages of boisterous vaudeville. If he could never have achieved the convincingly racy realism of an O'Casey, he was at least able to give to the romantic, poet-centered *The King's Threshold* a comic satirical range that helped buoy it up theatrically. Caricatures of self-im-

portant personages, gifted jeering by the crew of anti-authoritar-
ian cripples, and the uncompromisingly savage insults Seanchan
aims at the king and all who do his bidding are all welcome seasoning
in a play that might otherwise have become overly didactic. (Incidentally, instances of Yeats's use of comedy in other plays include the
slight but delightful *The Pot of Broth,* with its rogue-tramp-poet
protagonist and its sly feminist bearing; the robustly deglamorizing
The Green Helmet, with its cavalier treatment of the mythical heroes
of Ireland and their wives; and two adventurous experiments in early
absurdism: *The Player Queen* and *The Herne's Egg.*)

But to return to the long interlude in *The King's Threshold* that
begins with the mayor's arrival alongside Brian and the cripples.
This interlude, by allowing common life and speech to swarm onto
the scene, saves the play from reaching a premature climax. It breaks
the spell of the self-enclosed dialogue between Seanchan and his
pupils, which had already reached desolate resolution in the manner
of a lyric poem. Without the dramatic ritual—as in a morality play—
of having one character after another try to reason with or tempt
Seanchan from his purpose, the play could hardly have gained further momentum. Also, the opportunity would have been lost for the
broad range of satirical tones just noted. One example—centrally
relevant, as it happens, to Yeats's struggle with the clergy for freedom of artistic expression—is Seanchan's exchange with an intolerant monk:

Monk.   The pride of the poets!
   Dancing, hurling, the country full of noise,
   And King and Church neglected. Seanchan,
   I'll take my leave, for you are perishing
   Like all that let the wanton imagination
   Carry them where they will, and it's not likely
   I'll look upon your living face again.
Seanchan. Come nearer, nearer!
Monk.   Have you some last wish?
Seanchan. Stoop down, for I would whisper it in your ear.

> Has that wild God of yours, that was so wild
> When you'd but lately taken the King's pay,
> Grown any tamer? He gave you all much trouble.

Monk. Let go my habit!

Seanchan.   Have you persuaded him
> To chirp between two dishes when the King
> Sits down to table?

Monk.   Let go my habit, sir!

> > *[Crosses to centre of stage.]*

Seanchan. And maybe he has learned to sing quite softly
> Because loud singing would disturb the King,
> Who is sitting drowsily among his friends
> After the table has been cleared. Not yet!

[Seanchan has been dragged some feet clinging to the Monk's habit.]

> You did not think that hands so full of hunger
> Could hold you tightly. They are not civil yet.
> I'd know if you have taught him to eat bread
> From the King's hand, and perch upon his finger.
> I think he perches on the King's strong hand,
> But it may be that he is still too wild.
> You must not weary in your work; a king
> Is often weary, and he needs a God
> To be a comfort to him.

[The Monk plucks his habit away and goes into palace. Seanchan holds up his hand as if a bird perched upon it. He pretends to stroke the bird.]

> > A little God,
> With comfortable feathers, and bright eyes.

From this point onward, most of the play is dominated by Seanchan's anger against all, even his sweetheart Fedelm, who try to weaken his resolution. Fedelm's plea is both loving and seductive, and Seanchan drifts into forgetting—almost long enough to end his fast. But he remembers in time, turns abusively against her, and then is seized with remorse and apologizes but remains steadfast. For her part, she steels herself to accept his death as necessary—as do his pupils, who defy the king's threat to hang them all if they do not persuade Seanchan to live. And so the play ends, with Seanchan dying triumphantly amid a chorus of support for the ancient right of the poets and for the immortal glory of seeking out death in such a cause.

I have lingered over this play, which has its flaws: namely, some high-flown rhetoric and an overloaded, stop-and-go dramatic progression. Nevertheless, it has absorbing *reading* appeal, in good part because of its emotionally varied lyrical passages. Sometimes these are indeed dramatic but too subtly so for strong theatrical impact. An example is the passage in which Seanchan temporarily forgets his mission and responds to Fedelm's urging that he return home with her. She has in mind an earthly if innocent refuge she will share with him. But her talk of a "smooth lawn" and an "apple-tree" at once conjures up, for him, the Garden of Eden—a visionary place that he, as the archetypal poet, invented in "a poem I made long ago." Their dialogue here is a subtle, almost undetectable pursuit of two central motifs in Yeats's early plays. One—which had been set forth blatantly in *Cathleen ni Houlihan*—is that of sanctification through sacrificing oneself for a great cause. The other is that of the tragic magnetism of an unattainable ideal.

Seanchan. It's certain that there is some trouble here,
       Although it's gone out of my memory.
       And I would get away from it. Give me your help.
                                        [*Trying to rise.*]
       But why are not my pupils here to help me?
       Go, call my pupils, for I need their help.
Fedelm. Come with me now, and I will send for them,
       For I have a great room that's full of beds
       I can make ready; and there is a smooth lawn
       Where they can play at hurley and sing poems
       Under an apple-tree.
Seanchan.   I know that place:
       An apple-tree, and a smooth level lawn
       Where the young men can sway their hurley sticks.

[*Sings*]
> The four rivers that run there,
> Through well-mown level ground,
> Have come out of a blessed well
> That is all bound and wound
> By the great roots of an apple
> And all the fowls of the air
> Have gathered in the wide branches
> And keep singing there.

[*Fedelm, troubled, has covered her eyes with her hands.*]

Fedelm. No, there are not four rivers, and those rhymes
> Praise Adam's paradise.

Seanchan.   I can remember now,
> It's out of a poem I made long ago
> About the Garden in the East of the World,
> And how spirits in the images of birds
> Crowd in the branches of old Adam's crab-tree.
> They come before me now, and dig in the fruit
> With so much gluttony, and are so drunk
> With that harsh wholesome savour, that their feathers
> Are clinging one to another with the juice.

Another, equally strong appeal of *The King's Threshold* is its passionate defense of the sheer human importance of poetry. We have seen Seanchan's glowing metaphors for the way the poets shape a people's vision and values. But the play also presents grimmer metaphors for what happens to our lives when the arts are held in contempt. Thus, Seanchan's final speech amounts to an early, presurrealist gesture of cultural disgust and despair—the equally true bearing of this paradoxical play along with all its brave affirmations:

> O, look upon the moon that's standing there
> In the blue daylight—take note of the complexion,
> Because it is the white of leprosy
> And the contagion that afflicts mankind
> Falls from the moon. When I and these are dead
> We should be carried to some windy hill

> To lie there with uncovered face awhile
> That mankind and that leper there may know
> Dead faces laugh.

As we have noted, *The King's Threshold* resembles Yeats's other early plays that embody what he called "the perpetual struggle of the cause of Ireland and every other ideal cause against . . . all that we mean when we say the world." It is unique among them, however, for its inspired defense of poetry: a defense that makes it at once a primary statement of modern Romantic criticism and its richest poetic expression. It is unique among them, too, as his outstanding effort to write a play perfectly straightforward on its surface but elusively many-sided in its deeper lyrical structure.

The variety of Yeats's theatrical experiments during the years from 1900 to 1908 is striking. If *The King's Threshold* is arguably his purest dramatic work of the period, *Where There Is Nothing* (1902)—a prose collaboration with Lady Gregory and Douglas Hyde—certainly lives down to its title. Its omission from the collected volume (it can be found in Russell K. Alspach's *The Variorum Edition of the Plays*) was certainly justified, and yet was almost regrettable.

The play's chief value for Yeats, and also for us, was that in it he tried to give dramatic life to major dissident and "shocking" attitudes he had been entertaining—his "clear bohemian current" of thought mentioned earlier on. Its hero, Paul Rutledge, is a wealthy country gentlemen who is "dead sick of this life" of genteel, privileged respectability but has done little beyond clipping his hedges into shapes that satirize his complacent family and local social peers. Quite suddenly, he joins a company of itinerant tinkers, masters their jargon and their tin-mending trade, marries one of their women, and lives a full life of cockfighting, wild drinking, and brawling. In addition, he treats the common folk of the whole area to an endless round of drunken celebration. When his former male companions—all propertied gentry and therefore local magistrates as well—come to put a stop to the carousing and get the people back to work, Paul holds a mock trial and exposes the self-deception of their professed Christian piety.

The next abrupt shift in the play shows Paul becoming a friar and outdoing all his brethren in ecstatic saintliness. He then leads them to act out their holy joy of life through singing and dancing and letting go generally while he himself practices extreme asceticism. He and his new followers are suspected of witchcraft, and indeed he betrays a certain yearning to penetrate the realm of death and be welcomed by the chthonic powers of destruction:

> . . . take me up in your brazen claws. But no—no—I will not go out beyond Saturn into the dark. Take me down—down to that field under the earth, under the roots of that grave.

Thus Paul Rutledge in the moments before he dies, when he has grown mortally feeble through bodily self-denial and while an angry mob is attacking his half-diabolical crew of inspired friars. He anticipates Seanchan, though to less specific purpose, both in his self-willed death and in his final terror-filled vision. (In the wake of that vision he has one more utterance—"where there is nothing there is God"—which is either an ambiguous mystical affirmation or the ultimate negation.)

Strongly anti-bourgeois and somewhat influenced by William Morris's aesthetic socialism, *Where There Is Nothing* shows an appealing love of common speech and sympathy with the rural Irish poor: "the old kingdom of the people of the roads, the houseless people" who must endure seeing "their young sons dying by the roadside in a little kennel of straw under the ass-cart." Nevertheless, except for a few pathetic or bacchanalian moments, it adds up to hardly more than a somewhat eccentric and diffuse tract for the stage. A basic dramatic weakness hampers the play's impact: namely, its dependence on the intrinsically undistinguished central character, Paul Rutledge. He attempts to give his life meaning by exploring alternative social worlds and moral roles, but not even successive blood transfusions—life with the tinkers, life with the friars, and a

final injection of satanism mixed with pure, aimless martyrdom—
clarify very much for himself or for the play. He lacks the compelling
presence and energy that would sustain either the Tolstoyan purity
he sometimes seems to be after or his supposedly Faustian purpose.

Five years later an almost unrecognizable revision of *Where
There Is Nothing,* renamed *The Unicorn from the Stars,* was produced
in the Abbey Theatre. Much of it was the work of Lady Gregory,
whose contribution provided a sometimes amusing, sometimes tire-
some linguistic low comedy. "She had generally some part wherever
there is dialect," Yeats tells us in his preface to *The Collected Plays,*
"and often where there is not."

For this reason, and because it remains so largely a sprawling
prose work, *The Unicorn from the Stars* seems of little importance in
Yeats's growth as a poetic playwright. It does, nevertheless, carry a
bit further his effort to clarify dramatically—for himself at least—his
highly individual if confused sort of mystical anarchism. The new
version lacks the feeling for the miseries of the poor shown in *Where
There is Nothing.* Its hostility to established institutions and the demeaning calculations of tradespeople has little to do with the ideas of
Marx or Bakunin or even William Morris. Its source is eccentrically
private: the visionary experience of its new protagonist, Martin
Hearne. He is driven to try to impose the ideal, supernaturally
charged, primally free order of that experience on the empirical
world—or at least on Ireland (the world of the play)—at whatever
cost: "Once men fought with their desires and their fears, with all
that they call their sins, unhelped, and their souls became hard and
strong. When we have brought back the clean earth and destroyed
the Law and the Church, all life will become a flame of fire, like a
burning eye." Martin is a a far cry from the wealthy Paul Rutledge of
Where There Is Nothing, bored by his ambience of meaningless privilege into dilettante-radicalism and a hunt for interesting new life-
roles. Yet he shares with Paul, and with Seanchan and with Cuchulain and other heroes out of Irish legend who appear in Yeats's
plays, the doom that must attend an unconforming spirit.

Martin is subject to coma-like trances during which he inhabits a pagan paradise of Celtic pre-Christian life and energy: the realm that he feels is the true reality we have been cut off from. Trained at first in the art of coachmaking by his uncle Thomas Hearne, the essential practical, extroverted businessman, he almost completes a wondrous gilded coach that the English king will purchase on his coming visit to Ireland. But he loses interest in this effort and focuses on his imagined true mission. His revolutionary rhetoric is of course misunderstood by would-be followers at every step.

Thus another uncle, Andrew, enthusiastically interprets Martin's rejection of the gospel of unremitting labor in search of profit as a new gospel of simple self-gratification. A true believer in the pleasure principle, Andrew leads the local working people into drunken revelry. Other enthusiasts take Martin to be the popular patriotic terrorist Johnny Gibbons in disguise; and he, not recognizing the difference between their aims and his, encourages them in an orgy of violence and burning. He dies, finally, by gunshot amid accusations of betrayal. In suggesting Yeats's own distrust of the murderous side of political militancy, the play foreshadows the subtler and more complex probings of such later work as "Easter, 1916" and the Civil War sequences.

On Baile's Strand (1904) and *Deirdre* (1907), two other plays centered on conflict between the free, idealistic spirit and rigid, manipulative power, are far more concentrated than *Where There Is Nothing* and *The Unicorn from the Stars*. In them, Yeats draws on tales—based on Lady Gregory's translations of Irish sagas that led to her *Cuchulain of Muirthemne* (1902)—of how the archetypal cunning monarch, Conchubar, tragically deceived two nobly honorable heroes. The plots have the classic simplicity, inevitability, and distancing from the present moment of their mythic origins: an enormous structural advantage.

In *Deirdre,* the heroine's beloved husband, Naoise, who years earlier had thwarted the elderly king's plan to marry her himself, is fatally tricked. After years of wandering in other lands, he has taken at face value—it is a matter of principle not to yield to fear—a message from Conchubar pardoning him and Deirdre and inviting them to a feast of reconciliation. His death and Deirdre's suicide are the inevitable double outcome. Indeed, the whole play, in a slightly stilted blank verse that yet maintains a vaguely antique dignity, moves in the spirit of an elegiac tale:

> *Naoise*.   You would have known,
>   Had they not bred you in that mountainous place,
>   That when we give a word and take a word
>   Sorrow is put away, past wrong forgotten.
> *Deirdre*. Though death may come of it?
> *Naoise*.   Though death may come.
> *Deirdre*. When first we came into this empty house
>   You had foreknowledge of our death, and even
>   When speaking of the paleness of my cheek
>   Your own cheek blanched.

The chorus of Musicians, three women who play an important role in the dialogue, speaks with prophetic foreboding throughout and also sings two elegiac songs of love and death. The first is a sadly exultant ballad about the doomed Edain (again!—Yeats was still reworking *The Shadowy Waters*) and "her goodman." The other is a lament for the transience of love itself. The latter song accompanies the quiet chess match that Deirdre and Naoise, after the model of the legendary Lugaidh Redstripe and "his lady" who "had a seamew's body half the year," play while awaiting death. Both songs strongly reinforce the lyrical movement that defines this play.

On Baile's Strand, though complicated by a lively subplot, is in essence equally uncluttered in its movement. It enacts the tale of how the archetypal hero Cuchulain, because he had graciously surrendered his high-spirited independence for the supposed good of the state (as embodied in the authority of Conchubar), unwittingly killed his own son. The tale has the irreversible momentum and tragic irony—though not the compelling execution—of *Oedipus* or *The Pardoner's Tale.*

It is clear that, despite the fact that he was always to remain primarily a poet even in his best plays, Yeats had learned much about writing for the stage during the first decade of the century. In *On*

Baile's Strand he was able to hew to his source's fundamental elements while adding a comic subplot with prophetic overtones. Meanwhile, too, he explored a conflict of values, like that in *The King's Threshold,* which is crucial both within the play and in human history generally. He had begun writing about the father-son incident in the Cuchulain legend a dozen years earlier, in his poem "Cuchulain's Fight with the Sea" (originally named "The Death of Cuchulain"), basing his version there on Jeremiah Curtin's *Myths and Folk-Lore of Ireland* (1890). —But it seems best to delay further consideration of *On Baile's Strand* and other works centered on Cuchulain to a later chapter.

III

Poetry of Transition I
(1910-1914)

1. *The Green Helmet and Other Poems*

The Green Helmet and Other Poems (1910), Yeats's first completely new collection in seven years, was a thin volume that nevertheless showed a new kind of strength: a tougher-minded and more literally confessional expression than he had dared before. Its relative slightness, like its delayed creation—the poems in it had come to birth only recently—was the direct result of his theatrical commitments during the preceding decade. Not only had he written some nine plays of his own, but he was also enmeshed in the founding and managing of the Abbey Theatre and in fighting its political and financial battles. Or, as he put it in "The Fascination of What's Difficult" (1909),

> The fascination of what's difficult
> Has dried the sap out of my veins, and rent
> Spontaneous joy and natural content
> Out of my heart. There's something ails our colt
> That must, as if it had not holy blood
> Nor on Olympus leaped from cloud to cloud,

Shiver under the lash, strain, sweat and jolt
As though it dragged road metal. My curse on plays
That have to be set up in fifty ways,
On the day's war with every knave and dolt,
Theatre business, management of men.
I swear before the dawn comes round again
I'll find the stable and pull out the bolt.

The word "fascination" here is of course at war with the overall
burden of complaint. For the time being, Yeats was giving his primary energies—zestfully, yet the situation troubled him—to something else than his verse. A certain ambiguity, related to his divided
feeling, attends the thought that "There's something ails our colt." In
context, the primary meaning is doubtless that Pegasus, the mythical
winged horse of poetic inspiration—unnamed in the poem but the
only "holy" steed ever known on Olympus—has had hard and sweaty
going of late because he must compete with the pull of the theater.
Hence the speaker's loss of "spontaneous joy" in conceiving and
writing his poems.

On the other hand, a colt is a *young* horse—and so the image
may also, if a bit awkwardly, have to do with the still youthful Abbey
Theatre itself: the combined excitement of helping create a new,
truly Irish drama and frustration at having to cope with all the practical problems. If so, the reference to "our" colt and the closing vow to
free the balky, suffering Pegasus Jr. from confinement become
clearer. Also, the vow does anticipate Yeats's decision in 1909, the
year he wrote this poem, to give up much of his administrative
responsibility. Opening the poem to this risky split reading hardly
undid the knotty little ambiguity Yeats had fallen into. It did,
though, wrench and reorient the traditional Pegasus symbol away
from being a facile cliché, and thus reinforced the gathering affect of
exhaustion and exasperation.

The personal vehemence of "The Fascination of What's Difficult" foreshadowed future developments in Yeats's poetry. Almost a
sonnet but a line short, and rhyming *abbaccaddaeea* (with an

initial off-rhyme and one other), the poem is typical of his growing virtuosity in formal improvisation without resort to free verse. Its movement is rapid and intense from the start. It gathers new force repeatedly from the harsh, monosyllabic *olt*-rhymes and from the skillful turns, twice after caesuras, in lines 4, 8, and 12. The turns are lively shifts of direction. After the lament for lost artistic buoyancy, the graphic evocation of the "colt's" predicament thrusts into the foreground. Then the heartfelt "curse" breaks in, and then the impatient closing vow.

All this adds up to a new down-to-earth immediacy in Yeats's writing. It is enhanced by the sharp contrast between the lines on Pegasus' rightful glorious freedom "on Olympus" and those on his entrapment in the workaday world of "lash, strain, sweat and jolt." The poem is a soliloquy by a modern man dissatisfied with the pressures of a profession he has chosen. Its whole character shows the result of years of shaping plays and thinking about the kind of speech that helps make effective theater.

Some bibliographical information, whose relevance will soon become evident, is in order at this point. In its first printings (1910 and 1911), *The Green Helmet and Other Poems* was divided into two sections of verse and the play that gave the book its title. The first verse-section had the heading "Raymond Lully and His Wife Pernella," but an erratum slip by Yeats corrected "Raymond Lully" to "the later alchemist Nicolas Flamel." It was an organically related sequence of eight poems, all but the first of which are centered on a difficult love relationship. The second section, whose opening poem was "The Fascination of What's Difficult," was called "Momentary Thoughts." It contained a miscellaneous though variously lively and moving series of pieces to which we shall return. In the later editions of *The Green Helmet,* the poems follow the same order as at first, with a few poems added at the end of "Momentary Thoughts," but are no longer printed as separate groups with separate headings.

The poems of the original opening sequence often show the same degree of intimate expression, despite very different preoccupations, that marks "The Fascination of What's Difficult." Before looking at them more closely, one might for a moment consider their curious original heading in itself and in relation to its strangely surreal opening poem.

All three of the figures named in the title and its correction—Lully, Flamel, and Pernella—had appeared years before in Yeats's prose fantasy *Rosa Alchemica* (1897). Partly through the mind of his invented character Michael Robartes, he centered that Poe-like, death-haunted, almost incense-redolent spiritualist work on the medieval world of mystical alchemy. Yeats's chief motive in reviving Flamel and Pernella without explanation, and only in the title, must have been to gain some distance, however slight, from his emotional self-exposure in most of the eight poems. Naming those figures lost in the mists of the past somehow suggests that they, and not Yeats and an actual woman he loved, are the cross-purpose couple of the poems. Perhaps, too, he meant to recall the whole atmosphere of the earlier work as the context for "His Dream," the poem that so strangely starts off the book and professes, as did *Rosa Alchemica,* to celebrate the desirability of death:

> I swayed upon the gaudy stern
> The butt-end of a steering-oar,
> And saw wherever I could turn
> A crowd upon a shore.
>
> And though I would have hushed the crowd,
> There was no mother's son but said,
> "What is the figure in a shroud
> Upon a gaudy bed?"
>
> And after running at the brim
> Cried out upon that thing beneath
> —It had such dignity of limb—
> By the sweet name of Death.
>
> Though I'd my finger on my lip,
> What could I but take up the song?
> And running crowd and gaudy ship
> Cried out the whole night long,

> Crying amid the glittering sea,
> Naming it with ecstatic breath,
> Because it had such dignity,
> By the sweet name of Death.

The tone and key phrasing of this poem parallel those of the moment of transcendent exaltation in *Rosa Alchemica* in which the protagonist

> felt my memories, my hopes, my thoughts, my will, everything I held to be myself, melting away; then I seemed to rise through numberless companies of beings who were . . . each wrapped in his eternal moment. . . . And then I passed beyond these forms . . . into that Death which is Beauty herself, and into that Loneliness which all the multitudes desire without ceasing.

Not to force the point, the prose passage has a certain clear affinity with the poem. True, the speaker in "His Dream" does not *explain* his role as steersman on the ship carrying a shrouded figure given "the sweet name of Death." But he shares the mystically rhapsodic sense of "that Death which is Beauty herself." And the poem's "crowd upon a shore" matches the "multitudes" in the prose who "desire" the "Loneliness" of death's supernal state. In the poem, not only the "running crowd" but the steersman and the "gaudy ship" itself—and, in all earlier printings from 1908 through 1921, even "fishes bubbling to the brim" of the "glittering sea"—join in the universal acclaim "with ecstatic breath."

A celebration of death with suicidal overtones, "His Dream" serves as a morbidly exultant prelude to the poems of misery in love that follow it. Its ambiguities, of a sort unusual for Yeats, present undeciphered dream-imagery. When it first appeared in *The Nation* of 11 July 1908, Yeats's introductory note said as much:

> A few days ago I dreamed that I was steering a very gay and elaborate ship upon some narrow water with many people upon its banks, and that there was a figure upon a bed in the middle of the ship. The people were pointing to the figure and questioning, and in my dream I sang verses which faded as I awoke, all but this fragmentary thought, "We call it, it has such dignity of limb, by the sweet name of

Death." I have made my poem out of my dream and the sentiment of my dream, and can almost say, as Blake did, "The authors are in Eternity."

It is interesting to speculate—one could hardly *prove* it—that somehow the "figure in a shroud" called "Death" is also to be associated with the lost female beloved of the succeeding poems. In "His Dream," this figure dominates and is celebrated by everything that exists, the whole of "brimming" and "glittering" creation. And yet, the poem says, it is only every *"mother's son"* (my italics) in the "crowd" that takes part in the celebration. Were there no women in that crowd? The question is irrelevant if the shroud-hidden figure at the poem's center is their very embodiment. In that case it is Woman—as source, as mother of beauty and life—who is being called upon by the "sweet name of Death."

This profound and paradoxical identification, in various guises, was already familiar both in myth and in literary tradition, from *Oedipus at Colonus* to Whitman's "When Lilacs Last in the Dooryard Bloom'd"—to say nothing of the eponymous heroine, at once an elderly mother-figure and a lovely young woman, in *Cathleen ni Houlihan*. Yeats, by the way, deeply admired Whitman, whom he described in one letter (11 March 1887) as "the greatest teacher of these decades" and in another (10 November 1894) as "the most National" of America's poets despite being "so neglected and persecuted that he had, perhaps, fallen silent but for the admiration and help of a little group of Irish and English artists and men of letters." So perhaps it is no exaggeration to suspect a current of influence—that is, of transmission of qualities of insight—from Whitman to Yeats. For instance, there seems to be a strong affinity between "His Dream" and the song of the hermit thrush in Whitman's elegy for Lincoln. A few stanzas from the elegy will illustrate:

Come lovely and soothing death,
Undulate round the world, serenely arriving, arriving,
In the day, in the night, to all, to each,
Sooner or later delicate death.

Prais'd be the fathomless universe,
For life and joy, and for objects and knowledge curious,
And for love, sweet love—but praise! praise! praise!
For the sure-enwinding arms of cool-enfolding death.

Dark mother always gliding near with soft feet,
Have none chanted for thee a chant of fullest welcome?
Then I chant it for thee, I glorify thee above all,
I bring thee a song that when thou must indeed come, come
    unfalteringly.

Approach strong deliveress,
When it is so, when thou hast taken them I joyously sing the dead,
Lost in the loving floating ocean of thee,
Laved in the flood of thy bliss O death.

If a brief digression that is not really one may be permitted here, we know surprisingly little about Yeats's own mother. She is a suppressed presence in his work and memory. She was reportedly not very communicative (although a good storyteller) and essentially incompatible with his highly articulate, brilliant, irascible father. Circumstances—among them her possibly pathological condition (he described her as usually "feeble as to nervous power and memory"), the boy's hypersensitivity, and their frequent physical separation—prevented a normally evolving relationship between mother and son. Very possibly as a result, he was awkward in his youthful contacts with women. The lost beloved of the poems may well have merged psychologically with the lost, because unknown mother. (Yeats's late play *Purgatory,* to be discussed further on, provides a final turn on this possibility.) Without pressing such speculation as a key to interpretation, we may still find in it an elusive relevance to the seven poems of difficult love that follow "His Dream."

The first of those poems, "A Woman Homer Sung," begins by recalling two opposite sources of youthful unhappiness in love:

> If any man drew near
> When I was young,
> I thought, "He holds her dear,"
> And shook with hate and fear.
> But O! 'twas bitter wrong
> If he could pass her by
> With an indifferent eye.

The vivid memory of mingled jealousy and touchy pride is the opening confessional touch of the poem, with perhaps an edge of wry middle-aged self-irony at the contradictory torments that once had been at work. The next stanza quickly distances itself from the anguish of that past time by describing the artistic result of having coped with it. The sense of accomplishment might seem complacent, were it not for the contrary indications in the phrasing: a lifetime of labor has been involved, and what has been created is but a mirror-image (the word "shadowed" matches the "grey" of the second line) of something that, however beautiful, no longer exists. The shaping of this complex evocation is exquisite not only in its strategic turns of line-length and enjambment and its handling of emphatic rhyme as though it were incidental to natural speech, but also in its light movement from narrative to vision to climactic dialogue:

> Whereon I wrote and wrought,
> And now, being grey,
> I dream that I have brought
> To such a pitch my thought
> That coming time can say,
> "He shadowed in a glass
> What thing her body was."

The final stanza, still harking back to an irrecoverable past (in comparison with which all later accomplishment and experience seem "but an heroic dream"), dwells entirely on "her" as she was then. Or more precisely it dwells on her youthful self as mirrored in the poet's art. The stanza unfolds as pure music, all but deifying her image. She "had fiery blood" and, goddess-like, walked "as 'twere upon a cloud"; indeed, she was Helen herself, the "woman Homer sung":

> For she had fiery blood
> When I was young,
> And trod so sweetly proud
> As 'twere upon a cloud,
> A woman Homer sung,
> That life and letters seem
> But an heroic dream.

The next poem, "Words" (originally called "The Consolation"), is a sort of reprise of "A Woman Homer Sung" albeit in a very different key. It, too, begins by summoning up unhappy memories but then moves into a mood of reconciliation earned by the creative triumph wrested from psychic turmoil. It has none of the preceding poem's bittersweet idealization of the beloved, however, nor does it rise to so poignantly melodic a pitch of feeling. Instead, it is consistently introspective and literal in its statement. At first the speaker recalls, realistically, his acute disappointment at "my darling's" inability to grasp the import of his poetry:

> I had this thought a while ago,
> "My darling cannot understand
> What I have done, or what would do
> In this blind bitter land."

Then comes the reconciliation with that hard truth, in the form of an odd yet convincing thought: that it was her very lack of sympathetic response that had led him to perfect his poetry. His greatest motive had been "to make it plain" to her. The final stanza sums up the result of his long, unsuccessful struggle to do so. Although he can report a genuine artistic triumph wrung from that failure, the poem ends in desolation as he reminds himself that the effort has cost him nothing less than the chance "to live." He has mastered "words": that is, taught himself to write a poetry that he hoped would lead "her" to respond both to its import and to his love. No such luck. He concludes with a melancholy, self-mocking pleasantry:

> . . . had she done so who can say
> What would have shaken from the sieve?
> I might have thrown poor words away
> And been content to live.

Yeats's incompletely reciprocated passion for the beautiful Maud Gonne surely affected the emotional life of this sequence. They had early on formed an intimate yet platonic relationship. Her presence as an actress and as a political force (despite his disapproval of her committed activism) enthralled him. She, for her part, recognized his genius and had played the title role in his *Cathleen ni Houlihan*. It has been suggested, reasonably, that the original title of the sequence may have had something to do with their once-shared mysticism, as if they were "Pernella" and the "late alchemist" reborn. Also, Maud Gonne felt that, in general, Yeats's poems were too distant from the people's lives and needs—a view perhaps reflected in the complaint of "Words" that "my darling" just did not understand. She is not named in this sequence, any more than she is named in comparable poems like "Adam's Curse" and "The People." But the identification seems obvious, one important context for the psychological pressures at work in the poems.

At the same time, however, the "she" of the poems remains a created figure: not a literal portrait of Maud Gonne in rhyme, but an imagined energizing source of desire, regret, and a whole complex of feeling. She has been molded from fantasy, literary and mythical tradition, and memories of other women, as well as from Yeats's version of his relationship with Maud Gonne. A clear instance occurs in "No Second Troy," the next poem of the sequence. There "she" certainly resembles Maud Gonne, both as the cause of the poet's private unhappiness and as a political revolutionary, seen by Yeats through sharply critical eyes. Yet she is also modeled on Helen of Troy; and moreover the poem, which has the form of a Shakespearean sonnet without the final couplet, resembles in spirit the sonnets in which the despairing speaker both bemoans the wretchedness his friend has caused him and finds ways to excuse the betrayal or to reconcile himself to it:

> Why should I blame her that she filled my days
> With misery, or that she would of late
> Have taught to ignorant men most violent ways,
> Or hurled the little streets upon the great,
> Had they but courage equal to desire?
> What could have made her peaceful with a mind
> That nobleness made simple as a fire,
> With beauty like a tightened bow, a kind
> That is not natural in an age like this,
> Being high and solitary and most stern?
> Why, what could she have done, being what she is?
> Was there another Troy for her to burn?

Viewed not as autobiography but as verse, these lines move rapidly from the music of private emotional hurt to that of political outrage and then to that of moral contempt—all in the first five lines. Then comes the turn to the hymn of praise in the next five lines, echoing but also heightening the pure romantic transport of "A Woman Homer Sung." Their soaring eloquence reverses the preceding resentful tone, which had already been partly negated by being couched in a self-questioning manner. The reversal is a leap into awed recognition: she exists on a more rigorous, exalted, and committed plane than the meanness of our present historical moment allows for.

The poem's scorn now focuses on that unworthy existential moment, rather than on the destructive aspects of her goddess-like heroism. The similes "nobleness made simple as a fire" and "beauty like a tightened bow" match and exalt her antique virtues of being "high and solitary and most stern." The shift of focus carries over to the two closing lines, which reprise all the mood tonalities that have so far entered the poem, including the altered emphasis. In them, the poem's clashing emotions—its distress at the personal and social turmoil left in her wake, its forgiving apology for her as a modern Helen bereft of epic challenge, and its celebration of her intrinsic splendor—are brought into a single vision of glory in an inglorious world. By this point, the vision can have little to do with the empirical Maud Gonne. Rather, we may well associate it with the key metaphor in "Nineteen Hundred and Nineteen" (to be examined further on). There the poet is "content" to compare "the solitary soul," facing an impersonal universe, to a swan poised for flight into "desolate heaven" against buffeting winds.

The remaining four poems of the sequence pick up this note of tragic reconciliation that has been emerging throughout the sequence. "His Dream," its first poem, can now be seen as an all-embracing prelude to a symphony of depressive transcendence, in which loss is met straightforwardly, accepted, and then restated with a fey exaltation. The loss of the beloved, equated in "Words" with the loss of the opportunity "to live," is a symbolic death like that allegorized in "His Dream" and weirdly celebrated there on a universal scale.

That is to say, reconciliation—even, in this context, a joyous reconciliation—with the idea of death itself is by definition an acceptance, in some respect triumphant, of the surrender of one's dearest hopes in life. The final group of four poems begins, in fact, with one called "Reconciliation," in which the parted lovers are described as having reunited: a literal reconciliation, marked understandably by a "laughing, weeping fit." For the space of this one poem at least, it would seem that hope is no longer a thing of the past. All is well once more. But still the cold memory of abandonment hovers starkly over the poem's plaintive ending, which has the ring of the closing plea in "Dover Beach":

> But, dear, cling close to me; since you were gone,
> My barren thoughts have chilled me to the bone.

The remaining three poems diminish in intensity. The passionate close of the previous poem, still charged with remembered
anguish, has disappeared. One gathers that the marvelous reunion
did not hold, and so the sequence returns to the wry reconciliation to
loss reached in "Words." Now, however, it is tempered by nostalgia
and sweet-spirited distancing.

The shift of tone reveals itself slowly in the next poem, "King
and No King." Its title was borrowed, along with its opening line,
from Beaumont and Fletcher's drama of the same name, which is
centered on a confusion of identity that, when resolved, allows two
lovers to marry without fear of incest. For Yeats, the title would seem
to be a play on the illusion of recovered joy in "Reconciliation." His
poem begins: "'Would it were anything but merely voice!' / The No
King cried who after that was King." The obstacle in the Eliz-
abethan work is the pair of words "brother and sister," which the
hero calls "merely voice." In Yeats's poem it is "a pledge you gave / In
momentary anger long ago"—presumably the beloved's resolve
never to marry or live with the poet.

The sixteen-line "King and No King" winds its way rather
tortuously through its allusion-pocked landscape until the ninth line.
There its essential feeling, a sad bafflement in the face of happy
memory, finally thrusts itself into the light. The lovers, the poem
grieves,

> Have been defeated by that pledge you gave
> In momentary anger long ago;
> And I that have not your faith, how shall I know
> That in the blinding light beyond the grave
> We'll find so good a thing as that we have lost?
> The hourly kindness, the day's common speech,
> The habitual content of each with each
> When neither soul nor body has been crossed.

The nostalgia is for a condition of normal love-relationship, apparently experienced in the past if only very briefly. The grief in
the passage is expressed so gently that almost no trace of former

bitterness—not even the rhetorical question "Why should I blame her?"—remains. The poem that follows, "Peace," is even more gently nostalgic. It harks back to "A Woman Homer Sung" but without any of that poem's tension. Rather, it adds a new tonal element: a lament for the beloved's aging, something that has relaxed the lover's urgency if not his sense of loss. Landor might have written the first lines of this poem:

> Ah, that time could touch a form
> That could show what Homer's age
> Bred to be a hero's wage.

The sequence ends with "Against Unworthy Praise." This poem, too, is linked with "A Woman Homer Sung," but it both completes and emphatically reorients the movement of reconciliation. In it, any thought of reproaching the beloved or of mourning unfulfilled passion is left far behind. It dwells, instead, on the subtle, wringing struggle of a lifetime reported in "A Woman Homer Sung": the poet's struggle to have his writing mirror "what thing her body was"—a thought we should take to refer to the whole body of her nature or what he was later, in "The Tower," to call "the labyrinth of another's being." His life and hers, his work and hers, have been parallel labors against the odds, with the great difference that she has been the stronger figure on whom his effort has depended:

> O heart, be at peace, because
> Nor knave nor dolt can break
> What's not for their applause,
> Being for a woman's sake.
> Enough if the work has seemed,
> So did she your strength renew,
> A dream that a lion had dreamed
> Till the wilderness cried aloud,
> A secret between you two,
> Between the proud and the proud.

Bereft of its original title that set it off from the rest of *The Green Helmet and Other Poems,* this striking little sequence—let us call it the "Pernella" sequence—no longer attracts attention immediately as a unit. One wishes Yeats had found a better title and kept the group separate and intact. On the other hand, though, the slightness of the volume as a whole became less obvious without the former division into two groups. The second group's title, "Momentary Thoughts," was as perfunctory as the first was cumbersome; and the poems in the section, however alive enough in themselves, had none of the organic interaction of a sequence.

The most memorable of them, in addition to "The Fascination of What's Difficult," are the six-line love poem "A Drinking Song"; the aristocratically idealistic "Upon a House Shaken by the Land Agitation," "These Are the Clouds," and "At Galway Races"; the gloomily self-analytical "All Things Can Tempt Me"; and the whimsically dreamy dialogue with a coin, "Brown Penny," about trying to find out "if I might love." (Several of these poems had different titles in earlier printings.)

As its title suggested, the original "Momentary Thoughts" group was basically a miscellaneous collection that helped make *The Green Helmet* large enough to form a book. Yet the poems are by no means negligible in themselves and often reveal a certain kinship of feeling with the "Pernella" sequence. The three semi-political poems that I have described as "aristocratically idealistic" are interesting instances. These poems equate the most inspired aesthetic and moral values with those of rich social heritage. Although that particular assumption is as eroded in our later days as the faded names on ancient tombstones, the celebratory language it is couched in has much in common with the praise of the beloved in the opening sequence.

The similarity of phrasing is most obvious in "Upon a House Shaken by the Land Agitation," whose images of high culture and *noblesse* cast an aura of glamour over the landowning classes. It combines elegiac notes on their behalf (out of fear that egalitarianism may soon prevail) with a paean to their supposed almost divinely endowed greatness. The poem's eloquence would have an impact like that of "No Second Troy" were it not for its question-begging tendentiousness. The typical possessor of a great country house, threatened by the movement toward land reform, is said to embody—like Rose Aylmer in Landor's poem—every virtue and every grace:

> How should the world be luckier if this house,
> Where passion and precision have been one
> Time out of mind, became too ruinous
> To breed the lidless eye that loves the sun?
> And the sweet laughing eagle thoughts that grow
> Where wings have memory of wings, and all
> That comes of the best knit to the best? . . .

The verse form is the same as in "No Second Troy": a truncated Shakespearean sonnet whose emotional dynamics depend on a series of rhetorical questions. And the soaring imagery in the opening lines just quoted makes for another similarity. But an incantation against elementary democratic reforms—even though it grants "mean roof-trees" would become "sturdier" as a result—is hardly as irresistible an expression as the generous tribute to a heroic woman's greatness by her heartbroken lover in "No Second Troy."

"At Galway Races" is lighter-weight, an almost cheerful complaint about the way "the merchant and the clerk" have "breathed on the world with timid breath" and displaced the gallant older culture of hard-riding country gentry. It takes hope from the crowd's delight at "the riders upon the galloping horses" at the race-track. Perhaps that old world will come again, and with it a fit audience for artists of "hearers and hearteners of the work."

"These Are the Clouds" is a heavier lament, for losses already borne. It purports to console a friend who, having "made greatness your companion," is now enduring both personal unhappiness and grief over the discordant breakdown and leveling in society generally. The poem's language of consolation has the ring of the stoical reconciliation with disaster in the "Pernella" poems:

These are the clouds about the fallen sun,
The majesty that shuts his burning eye.

The closing poems in the 1910 *Green Helmet* were "All Things Can Tempt Me" and "Brown Penny" (called "The Young Man's Song" in the 1910 edition). The former piece is remotely akin to "The Fascination of What's Difficult" in its complaint about the demands of artistic commitment. But what wearies the poet in "All Things Can Tempt Me" is not theater management but the ease with which he can be distracted from writing poems:

> All things can tempt me from this craft of verse:
> One time it was a woman's face, or worse—
> The seeming needs of my fool-driven land;
> Now nothing but comes readier to the hand
> Than this accustomed toil. When I was young,
> I had not given a penny for a song
> Did not the poet sing it with such airs
> That one believed he had a sword upstairs;
> Yet would be now, could I but have my wish
> Colder and dumber and deafer than a fish.

So much of Yeats's poetry has to do with "a woman's face" and with his "fool-driven land"—witness the "Pernella" sequence and "Upon a House Shaken by the Land Agitation" in this volume alone—that the thought in the opening sentence might appear simply forgetful. Still, it is a common complaint of writers that they are always being lured by this or that away from their "accustomed toil" at their desks. So the half-serious daydream of being cut off finally from all distractions, especially the virtually unavoidable ones of love and politics, is familiar enough.

Translated into a theory of art, though, the daydream becomes the ideal of total surface impersonality. To be "colder and dumber and deafer than a fish" is not to obliterate all the intensely inward personal pressures that set a work going. On the contrary, it is to find a means of coping with them aesthetically. If only one could, simultaneously, be dead (i.e., more impervious to human life and emotion "than a fish") and yet at the same time totally alive inwardly! One could then also, through a process of distancing aesthetic transformation, make one's poems more purely and without being "tempted" by "all things." The oxymoronic wish, and the image that projects it, balance the celebration of death and the shrouded figure with its beautiful "dignity of limb" at the start of the book.

Thus, near the end of *The Green Helmet,* "All Things Can Tempt Me" makes its gesture toward turning away from the very pressures that have given shape to the "Pernella" poems and the poems rooted in Ireland's political and cultural life. Pressures like these are inescapable, however. They reappear in certain poems added to *The Green Helmet* in its 1912 edition but then transferred to *Responsibilities* (1914). One poem, "Friends," returns to "a woman's face, or worse"—to *three* unidentified women, in fact, who in their several ways "have wrought / What joy is in my days." Another, the lapidary "That the Night Come," dwells on the tormenting yet passionately loved "she" we have come to know in many other poems. This poem speaks of her totally in the past tense, as though she were already dead. It presents her as one who abandoned the need to "live" in the ordinary, satisfying sense used in the poem "Words." Instead, we are told,

> She lived in storm and strife,
> Her soul had such desire
> For what proud death may bring
> That it could not endure
> The common good of life . . . .

This poem offers one more turn on the motif of reconciliation with the realities of "her" nature, which have deprived both her and the poet of so much they might have shared. But it also exalts her political dedication as having carried her into an orbit beyond ordinary considerations. She had, in that orbit, achieved the state the poet longs to reach in "All Things Can Tempt Me": that state in which one can (in the words of Yeats's elegy for himself many years later) *"cast a cold eye / On life, on death."*

One other poem among those added temporarily to *The Green Helmet* in 1912 should be mentioned here. "The Cold Heaven" dives directly into the contradictory states of feeling—unforgettable inner turbulence and, at the same time, the "cold" wish to subdue and transcend it—that have dominated the whole volume. Here the emphasis is on the ultimate terror of the "injustice" of the uncaring, unconscious natural world:

> Suddenly I saw the cold and rook-delighting heaven
> That seemed as though ice burned and was but the more ice,
> And thereupon imagination and heart were driven
> So wild that every casual thought of that and this
> Vanished, and left but memories, that should be out of season
> With the hot blood of youth, of love crossed long ago;
> And I took all the blame out of all sense and reason,
> Until I cried and trembled and rocked to and fro,
> Riddled with light. Ah! when the ghost begins to quicken,
> Confusion of the death-bed over, is it sent
> Out naked on the roads, as the books say, and stricken
> By the injustice of the skies for punishment?

The momentarily exhilarating image of the first line quickly becomes forbidding in the second, a simile for a universe alien to humanity. The chilling realization drives all trivial concerns out of mind, leaving only bitter, irrationally self-reproachful memories of thwarted love. (The reconciliation to loss so painfully won in the "Pernella" sequence is forgotten in this stripped-down vision of things.) An ecstasy of misery follows, brilliantly spotlighted by the dire revelation of "heaven" as ice that "burned and was but the more ice." The final, questioning sentence of the poem is a leap into ultimate desolation. It envisions the afterlife as "punishment": an endless, lonely wandering by the "naked" soul "on the roads" of unreciprocated need. Yeats's skillful use of his long, six-stress lines and simple but unmechanical rhyme scheme is notable here. Although the movement is swift between the successive affective units just described, it is deliberately drawn out within each one. More than half the lines are enjambed and without caesuras; not until the final sentence, with its anguished cry of dread, do we have a quickening of tempo to match the imagined awakening to ultimate terror "when the ghost begins to quicken."

Not all of *The Green Helmet* is as troubled as the poems leading up to "The Cold Heaven." Yeats leavened its pages with some pieces of considerable wit and charm that float free of the book's major directions. The 1912 edition, for instance, included the boisterously satirical quatrain "On Hearing That the Students of Our New University Have Joined the Agitation against Immoral Literature":

> Where, where but here have Pride and Truth,
> That long to give themselves for wage,
> To shake their wicked sides at youth
> Restraining reckless middle-age?

And the 1910 volume included two memorable pieces that are almost totally free of the deep melancholy permeating the "Pernella" sequence and the poems of love in its wake. "A Drinking Song" is a classic instance of the traditional romantic lyric so often set to music:

> Wine comes in at the mouth
> And love comes in at the eye;
> That's all we shall know for truth
> Before we grow old and die.
> I lift the glass to my mouth,
> I look at you, and I sigh.

Part of the classic appeal of this "song," as of others in the great European repertoire of such *Lieder,* lies in its blend of feelings. It mingles a lover's happy improvisation with a momentary reflection mildly tinged with sadness. The formal elements reinforcing this music of playful longing are simple, unmechanical, and harmonious. They include the dominant liquid consonants; the mixture of exact with slant and identical rhymes, and of the long breath-sweeps in the four opening lines with the ever-decreasing ones at the end; the parallel yet varied syntax; and the skillful distribution of elementally evocative words and phrases ("wine," "mouth," "love," "eye," "all we shall know," "old," "die," "lift the glass," "look at you," "sigh").

Finally, we have the equally ravishing "Brown Penny," which ends the volume on a note even more distanced from the obsessions of the "Pernella" poems. It is as if the poet has wished all that pain and remorse away and is starting the risky adventure of youthful love—epitomized in the impulsive refrain—all over again. The poem's original title, in fact, was "The Young Man's Song." It takes the form of a dialogue between the "young man" and a wise penny, whose advice about love he solicits and receives. The dialogue is like the beginning of a folktale, but the only "story" is that the youth becomes his own oracle. He replies to the penny with an ingenious, magically haunting set of images to rationalize his impatience, which nevertheless bursts forth at the very end:

> I whispered, "I am too young."
> And then, "I am old enough";
> Wherefore I threw a penny
> To find out if I might love.
> "Go and love, go and love, young man,
> If the lady be young and fair."
> Ah, penny, brown penny, brown penny,
> I am looped in the loops of her hair.
>
> O, love is the crooked thing,
> There is nobody wise enough
> To find out all that is in it,
> For he would be thinking of love
> Till the stars had run away
> And the shadows eaten the moon.
> Ah, penny, brown penny, brown penny,
> One cannot begin it too soon.

What is retained here from the spirit of the sequence is the magnetic force of passion, and even the sense of its cosmic dimensions. There is a mild tonal echo of the earliest love poems, but the colloquial ease and humor are of a different order. Also, the poem's character suggests a readiness to turn to "fresh woods, and pastures new," in the next volume.

2. *Responsibilities*

Published in 1914, just before Yeats turned fifty, *Responsibilities* was enriched by the half-dozen poems it annexed from the 1912 edition of *The Green Helmet*. Chief among these were "Friends," "That the Night Come," and "The Cold Heaven." These poems, we have seen, altered the already complex emotional set of the "Pernella" poems. But they also began to free themselves of its spell and were a segue to new motifs in *Responsibilities*—for instance, disgust with Irish parochialism and dramatically symbolic challenges to its moral and religious certainties; earthy parables of greed, lust, and ecstasy; and even attention to other women besides "her."

"Friends," for instance, ends by reprising the earlier motif of reconciliation and continuing enthrallment by "her" despite bitter memories. That ending, however, is preceded by praise of two other women: one for the unsullied friendship of "mind and delighted mind" she has shared with the poet; the other for their love relationship, in which she "so changed me that I live / Labouring in ecstasy." In "That the Night Come," the elegiac form and past tense suggest an admiring, even adoring, yet definite farewell. And "The Cold Heaven" is a profoundly depressed self-elegy, centered on irreparable loss, with no pretense of having come to endurable terms with the situation.

To these transitional poems having to do with the torment inflicted on him by the great love of his life, Yeats added two more in *Responsibilities*: "A Memory of Youth" and "Fallen Majesty." The first of these recalls the moment in their youth when, for all their mutual regard and pleasure in praising and being praised by one another, it became clear that "even the best of love must die" and that

> . . . we, for all that praise, could find
> Nothing but darkness overhead.

The second of these added poems, following directly after the first, is full of nostalgia for her past beauty and majesty of bearing. But "although crowds gathered once if she but showed her face," that moment is over: "I record what's gone." Now, years later, time has won its victory over what had seemed immortal. The day has come when "a crowd"—*unbelievably,* and yet it is true—

> Will gather, and not know it walks the very street
> Whereon a thing once walked that seemed a burning cloud.

These five poems form an isolated near-sequence toward the end of *Responsibilities.* "A Memory of Youth" and "Fallen Majesty" now introduce the group with their notes of painful recollection and sad change. Then comes "Friends," with its gracious tributes, its quiet reference to the joy of a new love, and its retracing of both the anguish and the undiminished strength of the old love. "The Cold Heaven" follows, with its imagery of emotional disaster. And "That the Night Come," the elegiac celebration of "her" self-destructive heroism, rounds off the brilliantly confessional little unit. The contagious intensity of these poems deepens the whole volume emotionally and lends urgency to its new preoccupations.

One of those preoccupations emerges in certain poems of self-liberation from the world of bitter experience, reaching out toward the sheer delight of moral freedom. Their serious implications are countered by a surface playfulness that is a value in its own right. The buoyant poem "Running to Paradise" is a happy example:

> As I came over Windy Gap
> They threw a halfpenny into my cap,

For I am running to Paradise;
And all I need do is to wish
And somebody puts his hand in the dish
To throw me a bit of salty fish:
And there the king is *but as the beggar.*

My brother Mourteen is worn out
With skelping his big brawling lout,
And I am running to Paradise;
A poor life, do what he can,
And though he keep a dog and a gun,
A serving-maid and a serving-man:
And there the king is *but as the beggar.*

Poor men have grown to be rich men,
And rich men grown to be poor again,
And I am running to Paradise;
And many a darling wit's grown dull
That tossed a bare heel when at school,
Now it has filled an old sock full:
And there the king is *but as the beggar.*

The wind is old and still at play
While I must hurry upon my way,
For I am running to Paradise;
Yet never have I lit on a friend
To take my fancy like the wind
That nobody can buy or bind:
And there the king is *but as the beggar.*

The charm of "Running to Paradise" resides in its pure lyricism
of form, its easy folk speech, and its contradictory devil-may-care
profundity. It assumes, half-comically, the character of a beggar who
also speaks like one of the so-called fools so important to many of
Yeats's plays. They have the innocently amoral wisdom of the supernatural world they are in touch with—as opposed to bourgeois calculation and dogmatic puritanism. (The character Teigue in *The Hour-*

Glass, the play Yeats included in his *Responsibilities* volume, is just such a figure.)

As the title and mid-stanza refrain suggest, the poem expresses an ecstatically free and transcendent spirit. I would connect it with the real right, even bohemian, spirit of art itself. And the major refrain of each stanza—"*And there the king* is *but as the beggar*"—is in the poignant mode of prayer as assertion. At the same time, the verbal fun of following the King James Bible's italicizing of copulatives (when omitted from the Hebrew) leavens the pathos of that effect. Here as elsewhere, Yeats anticipates, say, the tragicomic mixture in such later work as Beckett's *Waiting for Godot* and Pinter's *The Caretaker.* We are "running to Paradise," but we scarcely believe we shall actually get there. Yet perhaps we can, *without caring,* see our beggarly lot—our "bit of salted fish" and our lives in the free-blowing wind "that nobody can buy or bind"—as the closest to Paradise we shall ever come.

The "beggar" motif runs through five consecutive poems in *Responsibilities*: "The Three Beggars," "The Three Hermits," "Beggar to Beggar Cried," "Running to Paradise," and "The Hour before Dawn." In part, this series acts as an allegorical mirror of the disillusioned and accusatory pieces on current Irish mentality that precede it. In the wake of those forceful pieces (which we shall return to), it is hard to avoid the feeling that the allegorical series is meant to project the human race—all of us—as little more than wretched beggars. Like the shopkeepers, politicians, philistine persons of wealth, and betrayed nobler figures of the immediately preceding poems, the beggarly rest of us, too, cope with our existential squalor in our various limited ways.

Thus, some of us—like the inspired speaker in "Running to Paradise," the singer "giddy with his hundredth year" in "The Three Hermits," and the "cursing rogue" of "The Hour before Dawn"—come merrily to terms with our condition. Others, like the eponymous characters in "The Three Beggars," are defeated by our own squalid greed. The complex figure who screams his way ("*being frenzy-struck*") through "Beggar to Beggar Cried" is a special case.

In his driven anxiety, social attitudes, love of "a humorous happy speech," and spiritual and sexual restlessness, he sounds very much like a self-caricature of the poet himself. Other self-reflections, though only in profile, as it were, emerge in the humorously secular thinker and in the foiled mystic who (with the "giddy" ancient already mentioned) round out the cast of "The Three Hermits."

These three figures do not literally belong to Yeats's wonderful gang, in both poems and plays, of rather philosophical beggars. But they do bear a strong family resemblance to them, especially in their apparent penury and their exposure to the elements. The kinship is clearest in the memorably half-comic opening lines:

> Three old hermits took the air
> By a cold and desolate sea,
> First was muttering a prayer,
> Second rummaged for a flea;
> On a windy stone, the third,
> Giddy with his hundredth year,
> Sang unnoticed like a bird . . .

However, their conversation—most of the poem consists of dialogue—is *essentially* that of holy men. It concerns prayer, the afterlife, and the transmigration of souls. The third hermit, the centenarian, has transcended both human pain and debate. He is one variety of saint; in his condition of pitiable yet glorious transport (the nearest we can come to supernal bliss), he has already finished "running to Paradise" and now is singing there. He at once embodies both the beggarly and the blessed. The last two lines just quoted are repeated at the very end of the poem as well: a refrain that serves as a paean to his sheer mindless joy.

As opposed to this happy state, the first hermit is cursed with too much consciousness. Lost in prayer, he is one of many pathetic characters in Yeats's writing who sacrifice their lives vainly to the pursuit of revelation or an ideal state of existence. Never in any case ready for the great moment if and when it arrives, they always fail. Thus this poor hermit's lament:

"Though the Door of Death is near
And what waits behind the door,
Three times in a single day
I, though upright on the shore,
Fall asleep when I should pray."

The second, flea-rummaging hermit, replies unsympathetically. The "shades of holy men / Who have failed, being weak of will," he says, are doomed to be reborn after death and then be "plagued by crowds, until / They've the passion to escape." The rebirth may return them to their previous miserable state. Or they may be lucky enough to become "a poet or a king / Or a witty lovely lady": that is, to reach a condition second only to eternal grace. If they are so exalted, however, they will be subjected to endless, unbearable demands of one sort or another. This argument, a blend of secular teasing with an existential weighing of psychic values, carries the deepest burden of the poem. But it does so side by side with a low-life closeup of its worldly and humorous, yet mystical speaker. While advancing his eloquent thoughts, he had "rummaged rags and hair" and "caught and cracked his flea" as well. —And of course, that sort of beggar's triumph, *faute de mieux,* is in its way as close to bliss as life allows.

All the "beggar" pieces are enlivened by their clever, unmechanical handling of simple prosodic patterns. Yeats deploys them unobtrusively, like skillful stage-lighting, to help focus a given tone—joking, gravely formal, offhandedly colloquial, or whatever. The scene-setting opening lines of "The Three Hermits," already quoted, provide a lovely instance. They are four-stress lines, but their surface is constantly ruffled in all sorts of ways. These include the variations of stress placement, so that some lines *can* be read as three-stress; the shift from enjambment at the start to a series of end-stops; the syntactic jolt, combined with a caesura, in the fifth line; the movement into telegraphese (dropping the articles) in lines three and four, and then the departure from it; and the deft mixture of exact and off-rhymes. By such means, the formal pattern is sufficiently loosened to allow the poem to move like natural speech, with surprising turns of emphasis and feeling.

The "beggar" pieces, with their raffishly humorous flavor and occasional sexual boldness, reinforce the seven anti-philistine poems that precede them: "To a Wealthy Man Who Promised a Second Subscription to the Dublin Municipal Gallery If It Were Proved the People Wanted Pictures," "September 1913," "To a Friend Whose Work Has Come to Nothing," "Paudeen," "To a Shade," "When Helen Lived," and "On Those That Hated 'The Playboy of the Western World,' 1907" (all composed in 1913 except the last, which has been dated 1909).

The first of these poems begins satirically. It reads like an early form of fund-raising by inducing guilt:

> You gave, but will not give again
> Until enough of Paudeen's pence
> By Biddy's halfpennies have lain
> To be "some sort of evidence,"
> Before you'll put your guineas down,
> That things it were a pride to give
> Are what the blind and ignorant town
> Imagines best to make it thrive.

The rest of the poem, however, abandons the sardonic tack almost entirely. It appeals to the "wealthy man" to be guided by the idealized standards of Renaissance Italian nobility:

> What cared Duke Ercole, that bid
> His mummers to the market-place,
> What th'onion-sellers thought or did
> So that his Plautus set the pace
> For the Italian comedies?
> And Guidobaldo, when he made
> That grammar school of courtesies
> Where wit and beauty learned their trade
> Upon Urbino's windy hill,

Had sent no runners to and fro
That he might learn the shepherds' will. . . .

The elegant argument here is followed by a highflown exhorta-
tion to "Look up in the sun's eye and give / What the exultant heart
calls good." The poem has become a skillful foray in public relations,
insulting at first and then implicitly flattering. As all Dublin was
aware, the "wealthy man" was William Martin Murphy, publisher of
popular newspapers and leader of the employers' lockout of striking
workers in an important labor struggle. He was a fierce opponent of
the proposal that the Dublin Corporation see to proper housing in
the Municipal Gallery for the collection of paintings offered to the
city by Hugh Lane, Lady Gregory's nephew. Yeats's detestation of
Murphy, the "old foul mouth" of "To a Shade," was well known in
Dublin. The poem's first readers (it appeared originally in the *Irish
Times*) would have seen it as both a direct attack on Murphy's meanness of spirit and an effort to attract other, higher-minded donors.
Later readers, if unaware of the tissue of circumstances around the
poem, may well misread it as self-contradictory and even compromised.

The next poem, "September 1913," is free of any such ambiguity. Together with "To a Shade," it stands out in this group of
seven embittered pieces for its emotional concentration and force. In
a sense it is a belated elegy for the Fenian leader John O'Leary
(1830–1907), who had endured five years of penal servitude and
fifteen of exile for his devotion to the nationalist struggle. He is seen
here as an heir to earlier idealistically patriotic figures: the martyred
revolutionists the poem names and the "wild geese" of the seven-
teenth and eighteenth centuries, who had to flee Ireland because of
the Treaty of Limerick and the Penal Laws but planned to return
and fight at a later date. In a larger sense, though, the poem is an
elegy for the "romantic Ireland" whose people aspired to the fulfillment of dreams far beyond the calculating and slavish mentality of
the present. It begins with mock approval, until the refrain replaces
disgusted irony with lamentation:

> What need you, being come to sense,
> But fumble in a greasy till
> And add the halfpence to the pence
> And prayer to shivering prayer, until
> You have dried the marrow from the bone?
> For men were born to pray and save:
> Romantic Ireland's dead and gone,
> It's with O'Leary in the grave.

After this the next stanza recalls the thrilled sacrificial spirit of *Cathleen ni Houlihan*—now, however, darkened by the feeling that all the heroic effort of the past has come to naught:

> Yet they were of a different kind,
> The names that stilled your childish play,
> They have gone about the world like wind,
> But little time had they to pray
> For whom the hangman's rope was spun,
> And what, God help us, could they save?
> Romantic Ireland's dead and gone,
> It's with O'Leary in the grave.

These lines, written by a man of forty-eight remembering his own youthful dreams and loyalties, foreshadow the political despair and tragic view of history that mark much of his subsequent work— especially perhaps, but hardly exclusively, the civil war sequences in *The Tower* (1928). "September 1913" does not probe deeper into the stark mood of the lines just quoted, although the start of the next stanza sustains the mood rhetorically:

> Was it for this the wild geese spread
> The grey wing upon every tide;
> For this that all that blood was shed . . .

And the fourth stanza returns to the painful letdown in the nation's spirit. If, it tells the Irish people, "those exiles as they were / In all their loneliness and pain" could be brought back to life, it would mean nothing to you. You would dismiss them as madmen, for they gave no thought to personal reward and advancement:

> They weighed so lightly what they gave.
> But let them be, they're dead and gone,
> They're with O'Leary in the grave.

The poem is remarkable for its colloquial immediacy and direct emotional appeal. It is charged with a political passion that takes the form of reproach shot through with nostalgia and helpless outrage. The basically rapid movement, with its alternately rhyming tetrameter lines and infectious refrain, has folksong qualities. But the rhythmic speed is braked by strategic enjambment, by intellectual subtleties, and by the sudden expressions of stricken memory or realization: "names that stilled your childish play"; "Was it for this the wild geese spread / The grey wing upon every tide?"; "They weighed so lightly what they gave."

"To a Shade" parallels "September 1913" in its caustic allusions to the petty commercialism Yeats saw as the ruling demon of the day. It is a much quieter yet equally intense poem, imagining that the shade of Parnell (1846–1891), Ireland's great spokesman, has returned to enjoy his old haunts. The shade is advised not to linger in this still ignoble land, whose parochialism had brought Parnell down less than a quarter-century earlier. The beginning is classically restrained yet razor-sharp:

> If you have revisited the town, thin Shade,
> Whether to look upon your monument
> (I wonder if the builder has been paid)
> Or happier-thoughted when the day is spent
> To drink of that salt breath out of the sea
> When grey gulls flit about instead of men,
> And the gaunt houses put on majesty:
> Let these content you and be gone again;
> For they are at their old tricks yet. . . .

Yeats connects the poem's three verse-units gracefully, by a simple visual device. Each of the first two units is a single sentence, ending before the unit's closing line is completed. The rest of that line, metrically speaking, drops to a shorter line that introduces the next unit and sustains the five-stress pattern and the rhyme scheme. The partial lines replace conventional stanza breaks:

> For they are at their old tricks yet.
>   A man
> Of your own passionate serving kind who had brought
> In his full hands what, had they only known,
> Had given their children's children loftier thought,
> Sweeter emotion, working in their veins
> Like gentle blood, has been driven from the place,
> And insult heaped upon him for his pains
> And for his open-handedness, disgrace;
> Your enemy, an old foul mouth, had set
> The pack upon him.
>   Go, unquiet wanderer . . .

The "man" referred to is Hugh Lane, whose rejected offer had been the subject of "To a Wealthy Man . . . ," the poem addressed to William Martin Murphy. By way of Murphy, the "enemy" of both Parnell and Lane, Yeats links the causes of artistic and political freedom. The association arises naturally, and the touch of vituperation that accompanies it adds an overlay of anger to the gently mournful tone otherwise dominating the poem.

A certain helpless feeling—of a free, open mind confronting adamant, ignorant prejudice and impersonal historic tides—pervades this anti-philistine group. The personal issue, the crisis of the individual creative mind isolated by these forces, is epitomized in "To a Friend Whose Work Has Come to Nothing":

> For how can you compete,
> Being honour bred, with one

> Who, were it proved he lies,
> Were neither shamed in his own
> Nor in his neighbours' eyes?

The solution the poem proposes, for the friend who has been "Bred to a harder thing / Than Triumph," is to shun the unequal battle and go one's own way. It is a program for survival with integrity:

> Be secret and exult,
> Because of all things known
> That is most difficult.

The little poem "Paudeen," printed immediately after "To a Friend Whose Work Has Come to Nothing," acts on this proposal to "be secret and exult." At least temporarily, it turns quietly away from endless social confrontation to the natural world. There, instead of the "obscure spite" of money-centered minds, one finds pure "morning light" and the sound of curlews crying to one another "in the luminous wind"—and with these comes release into an ecstatic thought foreshadowing the "giddy" centenarian's song in "The Three Hermits":

> Indignant at the fumbling wits, the obscure spite
> Of our old Paudeen in his shop, I stumbled blind
> Among the stones and thorn-trees, under morning light;
> Until a curlew cried and in the luminous wind
> A curlew answered; and suddenly thereupon I thought
> That on the lonely height where all are in God's eye,
> There cannot be, confusion of our sound forgot,
> A single soul that lacks a sweet crystalline cry.

The next three poems return sharply to the unresolved obstacles of Paudeen-mentality and human limitations in general. As we have seen, "To a Shade" does so with a vengeance when Parnell's poor ghost is warned that nothing has changed in Dublin. The poem ends:

The time for you to taste of that salt breath
And listen at the corners has not come;
You had enough of sorrow before death—
Away, away! You are safer in the tomb.

"When Helen Lived" broadens the sense of the philistine enemy to include a perverse demon within all of us: our stubborn, innate resistance to giving "Beauty that we have won / From bitterest hours" the full honor and attention it merits. "We" ourselves, the very persons who have most deplored this inner barrier (the soul's erratic attention-span, as it were) in others, have the same failing. For despite our pretensions, we too,

> . . . had we walked within
> Those topless towers
> Where Helen walked with her boy,
> Had given but as the rest
> Of the men and women of Troy,
> A word and a jest.

The shift here to introspection and self-reproach serves as a mild corrective to the sometimes *ad hominem,* sometimes question-begging rhetoric that attends this otherwise beautiful group of troubled poems. For one aesthetic instant, "When Helen Lived" holds back the gathering flood of disdain. Then the flood resumes, powerfully but in a new form, in "On Those That Hated 'The Playboy of the Western World,' 1907."

This title refers, of course, to the original vilifying of John Synge's masterpiece. The poem's literal scene is not Dublin but Hell. And the characters in that scene are not Synge and his provincial assailants but the ultra-virile Don Juan and the envious eunuchs who—"even like these": i.e., like Paudeen and Co.—"rail and sweat / Staring upon his sinewy thigh." But the symbolism is obvious. The viewers' shock and anger at Synge's play derived from their spiritual impotence: their inability, even at the level of half-comic dramatic fantasy (admittedly intermixed with realism), to entertain unconventional and uninhibited dialogue and images.

The figure of "great Juan" riding jauntily through Hell prepares the way for the allegorical "beggar" poems of self-liberation and contempt for genteel concerns that come next. These poems, in turn, are followed by "A Song from 'The Player Queen'"—a lovely ballad with exquisite rhythmic variations in its first and last stanzas. Charged with ambiguous melancholy and magic, it also distantly echoes the tensions between worldliness and the pursuit of beauty in the poems that have gone before. Its major connection with those poems lies in the way it reflects our human bafflement over our unresolvable tangle of ambitions and dreams:

> My mother dandled me and sang,
> "How young it is, how young!"
> And made a golden cradle
> That on a willow swung.
>
> "He went away," my mother sang,
> "When I was brought to bed,"
> And all the while her needle pulled
> The gold and silver thread.
>
> She pulled the thread and bit the thread
> And made a golden gown,
> And wept because she had dreamt that I
> Was born to wear a crown.
>
> "When she was got," my mother sang,
> "I heard a sea-mew cry,
> And saw a flake of the yellow foam
> That dropped upon my thigh."
>
> How therefore could she help but braid
> The gold into my hair,
> And dream that I should carry
> The golden top of care?

Six poems now follow: "The Realists," the linked and numbered pair called "The Witch" and "The Peacock," "The Mountain Tomb," and another linked and numbered pair called "To a Child Dancing in the Wind" and "Two Years Later." In the wake of the lyric purity of "A Song from 'The Player Queen,'" they introduce tonalities more personal than any since the "Pernella" poems.

Indeed, they contain muted echoes of those poems; and by the same token they prepare us for the complex little group of five poems, beginning with "A Memory of Youth," to follow. We have already reviewed that group because of its retrospective preoccupation with the obsessive love defined in the "Pernella" poems. The six pieces after "A Song from 'The Player Queen,'" however, are personal in a different sense. Thus, "The Realists" is a defense, though obliquely and a trifle awkwardly couched, of Yeats's symbolic method. It justifies the use of myth-informed fantasy in the art of a censorious country ("a dragon-guarded land"), for such fantasy is the only means a writer or painter has to "awake a hope to live / That had gone / With the dragons." The punning play on "dragons," and the metaphoric character of the poem's argument, leaven this essentially serious reply to advocates of a shallow and doubtless sentimental "realism."

The linked pair called "I—The Witch" and "II—The Peacock" are far more intense than "The Realists" both in the negative passion of the first and in the affirmative force of the second. These pieces return to the anti-philistine fray, but their phrasing has an introspective cast. The former poem imagines, at first in metaphors of sexual disgust, what it must be like to live obsessed with money. Then, its final turn, a surprising outburst—really, a sudden cry of the heart— echoes the darker "Pernella" poems for a moment:

> Toil and grow rich,
> What's that but to lie
> With a foul witch
> And after, drained dry,
> To be brought

To the chamber where
Lies one long sought
With despair?

"The Peacock" picks up the theme of money and property—but only to disdain it at once, in favor of the abundant wealth of the poet's creative powers. However adverse his circumstances, "the pride of his eye" far surpasses the merchant class's pride of literal "riches." The poem has its splendor despite its too-easy implied dismissal of the impact of real suffering. In its joyously boastful defense of the poet's symbol-making art, it is certainly far more exuberant and alive than "The Realists." The "great peacock" he has envisioned is too dazzling to need detailed description; it is the very embodiment of an artist's pride in his work. Also, the poet's imagination—called his "ghost" here for obvious reasons—can keep adding new "feathers" at whim to the peacock it has made even after his death:

What's riches to him
That has made a great peacock
With the pride of his eye?
The wind-beaten, stone-grey,
And desolate Three Rock
Would nourish his whim.
Live he or die
Amid wet rocks and heather,
His ghost will be gay
Adding feather to feather
For the pride of his eye.

The conceit here of a poet's spirit gaily continuing to create after he dies made it natural for Yeats to place "The Mountain Tomb" directly after "The Peacock." It is an elegiac celebration—or a celebratory elegy—for Father Christian Rosenkreuz, the medieval founder of Rosicrucianism whose undecayed body is said to have been discovered in its tomb. As in the far more brilliant "The Peacock," we find a mixture of zest and pathos in this poem too. Its call to devotees to dedicate an orgy to the memory of "our Father Rosicross," who still holds "all wisdom shut into his onyx eyes," is not as vividly compelling as it might be. Yet it anticipates a whole line of moving if sardonically edged poetic lamentations: Wallace Stevens's "The Emperor of Ice-Cream," for one.

The final pair of numbered poems, "I. To a Child Dancing in the Wind" and "II. Two Years Later," brings us very near the realm of passionate intensity the next five poems return to. They are addressed, in a spirit of anxious pity, to a girl whose innocent daring makes her vulnerable to life's betrayals; she will "suffer as your mother suffered." Neither mother nor daughter is identified by name in these poems, but the general assumption is that they must be Maud and Iseult Gonne. If so, the poems carry a new sort of buried reproach for the "she" who brought the poet such misery and whose endearing but willful nature has been passed down to her child.

The despairing and aggrieved protectiveness of their *tone,* however, rather than any biographical identification, is what defines these poems. In "To a Child Dancing in the Wind," that tone catches, precisely, the wounded concern of an unheeded elder:

> Being young you have not known
> The fool's triumph, nor yet
> Love lost as soon as won,
> Nor the best labourer dead
> And all the sheaves to bind.

The feeling here is poignantly akin to the portion of Wordsworth's "Tintern Abbey" in which the poet expresses his loving concern for Dorothy, his "dear, dear Sister." Despite his self-comforting assertion that "Nature never did betray / The heart that loved her," Dorothy's immature "wild ecstasies" troubled Wordsworth as the "dancing" child's indifference to his advice troubled Yeats. What we read can be as deeply formative an experience as any other; thus, the girl of Yeats's pair of poems is very possibly a conflation of Iseult and Dorothy, just as her mother is at least a conflation of Maud Gonne and Helen of Troy.

Of course, the feeling in Yeats's linked pair of poems is hardly identical with the far more intimately involved one toward Dorothy in "Tintern Abbey." Wordsworth copes with the pressure of an anxious special personal responsibility, complicated by an overwhelming relationship of affection. Yeats, acutely frustrated by his inability to connect across the generations, is at least as ironically scolding as he is tender: "But I am old and you are young, / And I speak a barbarous tongue." Nevertheless, the affective streams these poets are following in the instances under discussion do converge momentarily. In Yeats's case, the stream carries him swiftly toward the five poems of intensely reconsidered passion that follow.

After those five poems (the post-"Pernella" group), we are very near the close of *Responsibilities*. In the book's final pages, two short poems—"The Magi" and "The Dolls"—stand out. Sharp departures from traditional assumptions of Christian thought and sexual morality, they point the way to Yeats's future wide-ranging and radically unconventional symbolism. Underlying both is the vast implication that divine power and its supposed inalterable laws of right and wrong are human inventions to which we have attributed an independent life. In "The Magi," the New Testament figures of the title are seen both as iconic figures and as living beings hovering over the earth. They stare downward at us to discover the revelations the biblical account is supposed to embody. The long six-stress lines of this poem make up a single periodic sentence of great visionary gravity, and the incantatory parallelism and repetition of key words also deployed in the simple rhyming pattern give the lines the authority of a sacred (i.e., a sacred-secular) text of heretical force:

> Now as at all times I can see in the mind's eye,
> In their stiff, painted clothes, the pale unsatisfied ones
> Appear and disappear in the blue depth of the sky
> With all their ancient faces like rain-beaten stones,
> And all their helms of silver hovering side by side,
> And all their eyes still fixed, hoping to find once more,
> Being by Calvary's turbulence unsatisfied,
> The uncontrollable mystery on the bestial floor.

"The Dolls," less austere but scathingly anti-puritanical, is an allegorical parable. The dolls of the poem tyrannize over the household of the dollmaker who created them. They are indignant because his wife has given birth to a living baby: "'The man and the woman bring / Hither, to our disgrace, / A noisy and filthy thing.'" At this outcry, the mother is reduced to abject shame and apologizes to her husband: "'My dear, my dear, O dear, / It was an accident.'" The story, as such, is simultaneously absurd and touching. Allegorically, the dolls, mere artifacts, symbolize the obsolete moral strictures— also mere artifacts—that compel people to think of the body and its natural sexuality as gross and evil. In this context, the screaming anti-humanity of the dolls represents a cruel existential reality of Yeats's Ireland.

With "The Magi" and "The Dolls," then, Yeats gives notice that he will henceforth deal as freely and uninhibitedly with the largest issues of thought and behavior as he has done with his private intensities and his public denunciations of philistine antagonism to the arts. The days of partially accommodating parochial assumptions are over, in very much the sense of Stephen's decisions at the end of Joyce's *A Portrait of the Artist as a Young Man*. The frank wrestlings with a difficult love relationship, the assaults on petty local prejudice and the empty lives and nasty politics it thrives on, the buoyantly anti-bourgeois poems featuring free-spirited beggars—all these are united in the reoriented perspectives of "The Magi" and "The Dolls" toward the close of *Responsibilities*. Then, in "A Coat," Yeats bids his former imitators and the mannerisms they have stolen a Whitman-like farewell. He lets them keep the "coat / Covered with embroideries / Out of old mythologies" that they have snatched away from him. He no longer needs it:

> Song, let them take it,
> For there's more enterprise
> In walking naked.

IV

Drama of Transition and the Cuchulain Cycle

1. The Dreaming of the Bones *and Plays of the 1920s*

We have seen, in Yeats's *Responsibilities* (1914), the flaring up of painful introspection together with a new, self-liberating, and icono-clastic freedom. Two or three years later, his theatrical work revealed similar changes, limited only by the difficulty of making a stage production directly confessional. Two of the plays thus influenced, *At the Hawk's Well* (1917) and *The Only Jealousy of Emer* (1919), belong to his gradually unfolding Cuchulain cycle and will therefore be discussed in the next section of this chapter. His other plays of the period are *The Dreaming of the Bones* (1919), *Calvary* (1921), *The Player Queen* (1922), and *The Cat and the Moon* (1924).

All these pieces are strikingly different from the "new" version of *The Hour-Glass,* the play that immediately preceded them. Printed at the end of *Responsibilities,* it allegorizes the conflict between scien-tific rationalism and mystical folk-religiosity. It does so, essentially, in the good, set, oversimplified terms of familiar debate—despite the whimsically tinctured character of Teigue the "fool," an inspired innocent in touch with the supernatural world, and the unintentionally amusing onstage presence of a dour angel *ex machina*. And it ends, thumpingly, on the orthodox doctrinal side of the argument—a denouement that Yeats rued and tried to soften. But once he had put a "real" angel in view of an audience, it rather cramped any secularist rebuttal.

One of his purposes in adding this play to the *Responsibilities* volume may well have been to balance its compromised character against the uninhibited imaginative boldness and dynamics of the poetry: "The Magi" and "The Dolls" especially. Those poems, like the plays of 1917 to 1924, challenge conventional assumptions by reorienting traditional symbols and by inventing new ones that take on a mythlike glow of their own. At the same time, though, *The Hour-Glass* does "connect" with the character of the poems in one way: it is faintly confessional. That is, the predicament of the Wise Man, its protagonist, reflects one of Yeats's crucial quarrels with himself. Always opposed to mechanical rationalism, he nevertheless maintained a certain sceptical and "experimental" distance from the very mysticism that so engaged him. In this particular respect, the intimate self-questioning in many poems of *Responsibilities* provides a deep personal surround for the play.

Yeats's theatrical writing of the decade after 1917 sometimes reflects the confusions and chaos of the times—of World War I and after, and of the "troubles" in Ireland. Paradoxically, its intellectual courage resides partly in its resolute ambivalence despite the pressure in such times to choose an ideological side and stick with it inflexibly. *The Dreaming of the Bones* (1919) is a most interesting instance. The time is 1916, after the Easter Rebellion. A militant rebel (the "Young Man") from the Aran Islands, fleeing the victorious British after fighting them in Dublin, has reached County Clare during the night. He is seeking a hiding place until morning, when rescuers will return him home by boat. Two revenants (the "Stranger" and the "Young Girl") who he assumes are living persons come upon him and guide him to such a place on a mountain-top, which they remember from seven centuries earlier.

But they need his help far more than he needs theirs. They are

the shades of Queen Dervorgilla and Diarmuid, her "king and lover."
Without revealing their identities or the fact that they are ghostly
beings, Dervorgilla tells their story and explains that, when they
were alive, her lover had been

> overthrown in battle by her husband,
> And for her sake and for his own, being blind
> And bitter and bitterly in love, he brought
> A foreign army from across the sea.

The Young Man knows the story, which is part of Irish semi-
historical legendry. The next bit of dialogue presents the gist of the
play's moral tension:

Young Man. You speak of Diarmuid and Dervorgilla
    Who brought the Norman in?
Young Girl.   Yes, yes, I spoke
    Of that most miserable, most accursed pair
    Who sold their country into slavery; and yet
    They were not wholly miserable and accursed
    If somebody of their race at last would say,
    "I have forgiven them."
Young Man.   O, never, never
    Shall Diarmuid and Dervorgilla be forgiven.

The crime that led to the unresolved guilt they carry with them
was not their adultery. "If that were all," we are told, they would
soon have been forgiven; all humanity would cherish and shelter
them because of their great love. Rather, it is their act of treason that
has made them unpardonable. Unless forgiven by one of their own
people, they must always turn away in shame whenever they are
about to touch. They would, says Dervorgilla (still masking her
account in the third person),

> be blessed could their lips
> A moment meet; but when he has bent his head
> Close to her head, or hand would slip in hand,

The memory of their crime flows up between
And drives them apart.

So it has been through the centuries. They have never found forgiveness from anyone among their own people. The intransigently patriotic Young Man is strongly moved by the plight, so touchingly described, of those ancient lovers. But as he has said earlier on:

> In the late Rising
> I think there was no man of us but hated
> To fire at soldiers who but did their duty
> And were not of our race, but when a man
> Is born in Ireland and of Irish stock,
> When he takes part against us—

The conclusion of his unfinished sentence is obvious. And toward the end of the play, as dawn breaks after their long climb and dialogue, he looks eastward and observes:

> So here we're on the summit. I can see
> The Aran Islands, Connemara Hills,
> The Galway in the breaking light; there too
> The enemy has toppled roof and gable,
> And torn the panelling from ancient rooms;
> What generations of old men had known
> Like their own hands, and children wondered at,
> Has boiled a trooper's porridge. That town had lain,
> But for the pair that you would have me pardon,
> Amid its gables and its battlements
> Like any old admired Italian town;
> For though we have neither coal, nor iron ore,
> To make us wealthy and corrupt the air,
> Our country, if that crime were uncommitted,
> Had been most beautiful.

Here is the essential nationalist accusation against the English and, even more, against all the Irish who have ever collaborated with them. But as the Young Man speaks, the disappointed revenants are performing a dance of pain. His speech shifts abruptly as the dialogue takes a revelatory turn—

> Why do you gaze, and with so passionate eyes,
> One on the other; and then turn away,
> Covering your eyes, and weave it in a dance?
> Who are you? what are you? you are not natural.
> *Young Girl.* Seven hundred years our lips have never met.
> *Young Man.* Why do you look so strangely at one another,
> So strangely and so sweetly?
> *Young Girl.*   Seven hundred years.
> *Young Man.* So strangely and so sweetly. All the ruin,
> All, all their handiwork is blown away
> As though the mountain air had blown it away
> Because their eyes have met. They cannot hear,
> Being folded up and hidden in their dance.
> The dance is changing now. They have dropped their
> eyes,
> They have covered up their eyes as though their hearts
> Had suddenly been broken—never, never
> Shall Diarmuid and Dervorgilla be forgiven.

The lovers disappear, and the Young Man—he now realizes who they were—exclaims: "I had almost yielded and forgiven it all— / Terrible the temptation and the place!" But he has not necessarily been "right." The play has juxtaposed the immediate world of political warfare, with its demand for unwavering loyalty to a chosen cause, and the world of humanity's long memory, with its tales of ecstatic love and tragic loss, and of the perils of violating accepted taboos. The pathos of the two shades has an appeal certainly rivaling that of the Young Man's unflinching political ardor, which the play puts in a context transcending local history.

An important aspect of this dual emotional emphasis on both the Young Man's sturdy political integrity and the pity of irredeemable *and* unavoidable past choices is that it is one way, artistically, for the play to remain independent of ideological weighting. The chorus of Musicians—not mentioned hitherto because they are not part of the dramatic action—is crucial to this independence. Its songs and descriptive dialogue build an atmosphere of sad, uncanny universal awareness that goes counter to the Young Man's heroic and undeviating activism. Thus, the opening lines of the first song:

> Why does my heart beat so?
> Did not a shadow pass?
> It passed but a moment ago.
> Who can have trod in the grass?
> What rogue is night-wandering?
> Have not old writers said
> That dizzy dreams can spring
> From the dry bones of the dead?

And again, the Musicians' final song brings the play to a pitch of melancholy much of whose idiom seems to have been borrowed in Eliot's "The Hollow Men." The song begins:

> At the grey round of the hill
> Music of a lost kingdom
> Runs, runs and is suddenly still.
> The winds out of Clare-Galway
> Carry it: suddenly it is still.
>
> I have heard in the night air
> A wandering airy music;
> And moidered in that snare
> A man is lost of a sudden,
> In that sweet wandering snare.
>
> What finger first began
> Music of a lost kingdom?
> They dream that laughed in the sun.
> Dry bones that dream are bitter,
> They dream and darken our sun.

The Musicians do top off their song with an enthusiastic apostrophe to "the strong March birds a-crow" at dawn: an image of the sort that inevitably suggests some sort of annunciation. Here it might be taken—but probably should not—as a token of renewed Irish political hopes after the crushed 1916 Rising. More likely it serves the same purpose as the image of the white heron in *Calvary* (1921) that "God has not died for." There the whole drift is away from religious rather than political orthodoxy. Lazarus and the other biblical figures resent Christ's power, the Roman soldiers dismiss its importance, and the Musicians' songs center on nature's indifference to him. (See the extended comparison of *Calvary* with *The Hour-Glass* in Chapter II.) In *The Dreaming of the Bones,* the closing apostrophe seems to serve as the Musicians' humbling yet happy acceptance of the irrelevance of human ideals and desires to the larger natural scheme of things. As a momentary relief from the pressure to make apparently crucial choices, it expresses a universal yearning:

> I have heard from far below
> The strong March birds a-crow.
> Stretch neck and clap the wing,
> Red cocks, and crow!

The Dreaming of the Bones, like *Calvary,* is essentially a beautiful and moving lyrical drama that projects an inward resistance to powerful demands on belief. The amount of exposition the story of Diarmuid and Dervorgilla calls for sometimes makes it a bit clumsy in execution; so does the complex confrontation of two rival worlds of passionate allegiance in so compressed a work. But *The Dreaming of the Bones* holds a special place in Yeats's drama because of the way each of those self-absorbed worlds illuminates the limitations of the other. While the pull of contradictory sympathies is a recurrent motif in his work, it becomes unusually vivid here. The tragic effort of the chthonic lovers creates a pessimistic hope like that of the myth of Orpheus and Eurydice, and the sturdily militant Aran fisherman's resistance to his instinctive compassion betrays his nobler self in the name of patriotism. The lovers and the fisherman—all three of whom are deeply appealing to Yeats's imagination—evoke the existential pity of having to sacrifice one cherished, life-defining meaning for another. Also, their meeting in a place where historical memory, modern struggle, and the restless ghosts of the long-buried dead converge gives the play an eerily transcendent time-dimension.

Yeats's next piece to be performed, *The Player Queen,* (1922) was some fifteen years or so in the making. Nevertheless, it seems sprawling and improvisational when compared to his other, close-knit plays of the period between 1917 and the late 1920's. All of those plays, too, with the single exception of *The Cat and the Moon,* are centrally tragic in their bearing, while *The Player Queen* is so only marginally and by implication. In the main, it is a prose potpourri combining farcical satire, broad comedy, and romantic self-mockery (in the character of Septimus the poet). The mixture is seasoned with harsh cynicism about political action and the motives of government, sexual proclivities, fidelity in love, and artistic ambition. From a lyrical standpoint, its purer intensities are established through its few passages of poetry: the songs of Decima, the "player queen" of the title.

In the play, Decima is a supremely talented, ruthlessly am-bitious actress married to the unfaithful but loving Septimus. It is she who sings the ballad (printed earlier in *Responsibilities* as "A Song from 'The Player Queen'") that defines the premise of her ambition and, finally, the major action of the play. She has inherited her mother's dream that Decima "was born to wear a crown"; and there are vague hints in the song that her father was some sort of mythic, brutally indifferent male force, like Leda's swan-lover. Their mating—of maternal dream and paternal power—underlies her des-tiny. Decima's last song in the play confirms her sense that such matings are natural to her. Thus, the opening stanza:

> Shall I fancy beast or fowl?
> Queen Pasiphae chose a bull,
> While a passion for a swan

Made Queen Leda stretch and yawn,
Wherefore spin ye, whirl ye, dance ye,
Till Queen Decima's found her fancy.

But the songs, definitive as they are in essential ways, make up only a tiny portion of this hyperactive and centrifugal play. What they reveal about its driving motives might perhaps be grasped by unusually sensitized members of a theater audience (assuming the actress's diction to be clear enough), but even that possibility is an unlikely one. Too much else is going on all around these rare poetic moments. And in any case audiences, even as solitary readers, are usually unprepared to recognize the dramatic weight of a song in the midst of a bustling, crowded plot.

How bustling and crowded it is defies rapid summation. The play is divided into two "scenes." The short first scene, a venture into seriocomic fantasy, opens like a puppet show or animated cartoon, with two "Old Men" in "grotesque masks" leaning from upper-story windows, "one on either side of the street," and exchanging banalities. What they say is a combination of elderly grousing and simple exposition: that the sun is now rising over the Queen's castle on its "great rocky hill"; that a crowd of fifty men passed by a short while ago; that "the young are at some mischief,—the young and the middle-aged"; and that "the world has grown very wicked." Indifferent to the human actions down on the street, they are mainly interested in an old dog that comes by daily. ("Yesterday he had a bone in his mouth.") Nevertheless, their clownish incomprehension provides an amusing prelude to the political and emotional turmoil in the rest of the play. They see everything and grasp nothing.

The rest of Scene I, all on the street, is extremely busy. First, Septimus the poet staggers onstage, drunk and exhausted after searching all night for Decima. He knocks on doors asking for a place to sleep, is refused everywhere, and explodes into his own brand of image-popping rodomontade: a form of absurdist prose-poetry.

Treat Septimus, who has played before Kubla Khan, like this!
Septimus, dramatist and poet! [*The Old Woman opens the window*

again and empties a jug of water over him.] Water! drenched to the skin—must sleep in the street. [*Lies down.*] Bad wife—others have had bad wives, but others were not left to lie down in the open street under the stars, drenched with cold water, a whole jug of cold water, shivering in the pale light of the dawn, to be run over, to be trampled upon, to be eaten by dogs, and all because their wives have hidden themselves.

As he lies there, various characters approach. The first ones are a pair of "bad, popular poets" he exchanges insults with. Next comes a mob of "Citizens and Countrymen." Most of them are bent on killing their Queen, whom they accuse of being a witch and of "coupling with a great white unicorn." Septimus, in eloquently absurd language, defends the honor of unicorns and derides a hostile "Big Countryman" who then fells him with an angry blow. An "Old Beggar" now appears who, "at the hour when there is to be a new King or a new Queen," will turn into "the donkey that carried Christ into Jerusalem" and will bray its annunciation of the great change. He seeks straw to roll about on when the moment comes and his donkey-back begins to itch. His prophetic blasphemy, raspingly gross and yet an offshoot of the New Testament, adds an odd sense of sacred meaning to the events of the play.

All these busy doings—something new for a Yeats play—occur in a scene just over eight pages long on the printed page. The surface is mostly farce and verbal horseplay, as in Septimus's grandly ridiculous speech just mentioned, or in the crowd's ignorant arguments about witches and about the devout, retiring, and dowdy Queen. Yeats's humor throughout the scene can become cloyingly whimsical. At the same time, it masks the play's satirical dimension, as in the scornful treatment of mob logic and the implied mockery of conventional morality and institutionalized religion. Thus, old taboos are violated by the frank sexual talk—however ridiculous—in the mob's speculative gossip about the Queen and the unicorn. (In Scene II, this talk is echoed in Decima's song "Shall I fancy beast or fowl?" and in her free behavior generally.) The Old Beggar-donkey-prophet, too, whose braying will usher in a new turn in history, signals the mysterious workings of fatality: a subject that absorbed Yeats's imagination and that he "systematized" in several poems in *The Wild Swans at Coole* (1919) and in his prose work *A Vision* (1925).

Also, Septimus's ranting about his "bad wife" and her disappearance has its comic edge but introduces a serious motif as well. His clownishness is that of a romantic Harlequin. He remains a wayward, vulnerable poet whose love has been rejected, as in many poems in *Responsibilities*. In fact, he has written just such a poem, which Decima sings in Scene II:

> O would that I were an old beggar
> Without a friend on this earth
> But a thieving rascally cur,
> A beggar blind from his birth;
> Or anything else but a man
> Lying alone on a bed
> Remembering a woman's beauty,
> Alone with a crazy head.

Scene II takes place in the Throne-Room of the Queen's Castle, with Decima the center of the eccentric action. She has been chosen to play the role of Noah's very old wife in a performance of *The Tragical History of Noah's Deluge* commanded by the Prime Minister, but she "would drown rather than play a woman older than thirty." Decima (who is hiding under the throne) is the last person except Septimus to accept arbitrary authority.

While the enraged Prime Minister indulges in a tantrum, the devout young Queen enters. She has planned to let herself be martyred by her angry subjects, who have never seen her. But she now realizes that she fears both the people and her own inclinations: "I have never known love. Of all things, that is what I have most fear of. . . . I am not naturally good, and they say people will do anything for love, there is so much sweetness in it." Hence, she gives her throne, her dress of gold brocade, and her golden slippers to Decima and retires to a convent. Decima, "born to wear a crown," plays the regal role eagerly and wins over the people at once by her authoritative manner and proud beauty.

That is the great turn of the mechanical plot, the kind of reversal that gives a comedy a happy ending. At the same time, there is a wholesale reversal of another kind, analogous to the cyclical disruptions in the history of cultures. In the world of the play, a new era begins with Decima's rise to power. Not only does she forget the jealousy she had felt because of Septimus's affair with another actress, but she also exiles him and chooses the elderly Prime Minister, the embodiment of repressive rule, to be her new husband. She also banishes the acting troupe, since they all know she is not the true Queen. And in the classic way of rulers with martyrs since Pontius Pilate, she allows the Bishop and the Prime Minister to condemn the Old Beggar to death as a "conspirator" and an "impostor" posing as "the Voice of God."

Given his association with the entrance of Jesus into Jerusalem, the Beggar's death-sentence is especially indicative. As Septimus has proclaimed with drunken clarity, "I announce the end of the Christian Era, the coming of a New Dispensation, that of the New Adam, that of the Unicorn; but alas, he is chaste, he hesitates, he hesitates." If the life of uninhibited pagan freedom is to come into its own once more, artists like Septimus must bid the Unicorn "trample mankind to death and beget a new race." But that time of regenerative energy must await its turn. Meanwhile, Decima and her world have entered the new phase now coming into its own. The old phase of romantic love, magical beasts, and passionate imagination has been exiled, or worse, along with Septimus, the players, and the Old Beggar.

How many of these thoughts and implications, all present in the printed text, would be evident to an audience that had not read the play is difficult to gauge. From a *presentative* standpoint—that is, the succession of visual and tonal impacts that make up the play in process—*The Player Queen* is a kaleidoscope of broad comedy, angry confrontation, mystical or poetically suggestive rhetoric and ballads, revelatory moments of personal feeling, and quick shifts of relationship. The fairy-tale fulfillment of Decima's dreams, and the wry outcome for Septimus, provide a simple basic curve of movement despite the welter of effects. Had the more philosophical and harshly cynical aspects of the play received more emphasis, they would doubtless have proved indigestible. Yet the curious, contradictory fact is that without them it would lack true seasoning of any kind.

The reason may well lie in a subconscious pressure, one that Yeats hinted at in a baffled way in his note to the 1922 printings of the play. In it he confesses to having "wasted the best working months of several years" trying to write a verse tragedy

> where every character became an example of the finding or not finding of what I have called the Antithetical Self; and because passion and not thought makes tragedy, what I made had neither simplicity nor life. I knew precisely what was wrong and yet could neither escape from thought nor give up my play. At last it came into my head all of a sudden that I could get rid of the play if I turned it into a farce; and never did I do anything so easily, for I think that I wrote the present play in about a month.

Making a farce of the play meant not pursuing the hares it had started to the kill. Thus, Septimus, who holds Yeats's own views on basic matters of poetic art and life attitudes, remains enough of an affectionate self-parody to avoid requiring deep self-scrutiny. Septimus's loss of Decima, his recognition of her ultimately impersonal self-sufficiency and attachment to power, and his recourse to another love would indeed be difficult to deal with in a seriously probing drama, since they mirror Yeats's own situation in life and also as presented in the confessional poems of *Responsibilities*. His obsession with the unicorn symbol (it is interesting that he placed the much earlier *The Unicorn from the Stars* next to *The Player Queen* in his *Collected Plays*) is a related psychological matter. In light of all the sexual issues of this play, Yeats's urge to convert that "chaste beast" of tradition into a supremely phallic power might well have proved a barrier in a more serious play. "The Unicorn," his alter ego Septimus proclaims, "will be terrible when it loves." But, as Yeats wrote, everything became simpler once he could see the piece as farce and let its possible implications fend for themselves.

The Cat and the Moon is a brief, delightful prose comedy of some six pages. It wears its symbolism lightly and is as simple in structure as *The Player Queen* is complicated. Its characters are two beggars wearing "grotesque masks" and three musicians in the background. The beggars, a blind man and a lame man he carries on his back, make their quarrelsome way to "the holy well of St. Colman," hoping to be cured. After reaching the well, they are about to come to blows over the question of whether saints prefer the company of sinners to that of their own kind. Suddenly the saint, invisible to them but played by the First Musician, answers them indirectly by presenting them with a choice:

> *First Musician* [*speaking*]. Will you be cured or will you be
>   blessed?
> *Lame Beggar.* Lord save us, that is the saint's voice and we
>   not on our knees. [*They kneel.*]
> *Blind Beggar.* Is he standing before us, Lame Man?
> *Lame Beggar.* I cannot see him at all. It is in the ash-tree
>   he is, or up in the air.
> *First Musician.* Will you be cured or will you be blessed?
> *Lame Beggar.* There he is again.
> *Blind Beggar.* I'll be cured of my blindness.
> *First Musician.* I am a saint and lonely. Will you become
>   blessed and stay blind and we will be together always?

The Blind Beggar, having regained his sight, sees that the Lame Beggar has stolen his black sheepskin coat, beats him for a while ("the beating takes the form of a dance and is accompanied on drum and flute"), and then goes off on his own. The Lame Beggar, who has chosen to be blessed and now wonders if it will do him any good, learns that he too is cured when the saint—so the First Musician says, speaking in that role—hops onto his back and then gets him to start dancing, again to music.

The rapid movement and dialogue of *The Cat and the Moon,* which depends so much in production on choreography, musical effects, and the witty device of having the First Musician speak for the invisible St. Colman, can only dimly be suggested by summary. The Punch-and-Judy exchanges of the two beggars in the presence of the lonely yet lighthearted miracle-making saint, the dance movements, and the whole sense of sunny magic make for a masterpiece of economy. Except for one beautiful song, the play is written in prose; but its rhythmic dialogue, often stichomythic, gives it qualities of lively free verse—as, for instance, in this passage between the First Musician (i.e., the saint) and the Lame Beggar near the end:

—Bend down your back.
—What for, Holy Man?
—That I may get up on it.
—But my lame legs would never bear the weight of you.
—I'm up now.
—I don't feel you at all.
—I don't weigh more than a grasshopper.
—You do not.
—Are you happy?
—I would be if I was right sure I was blessed.
—Haven't you got me for a friend?
—I have so.
—Then you're blessed.

The "beautiful song" mentioned earlier is sung by the same First Musician. It is part of the play's magic that this character has a double role as unseen saint and, in the song, as entranced questioner of unfathomable meanings. In *The Wild Swans at Coole,* Yeats's 1919 volume of poems, the song had appeared as "The Cat and the Moon." A continuous verse-unit there, it was broken up in the play so that the first eight lines are sung before the action begins, the next eight just before the beggars reach the well, and the final twelve at the end. Thus the play is enveloped in a music of wonder at the mystery of the relation between mortal life and cosmic forces, while the whimsy of having a cat embody the former state sustains the play's own light touch with similar mysteries. The song gives the play just the edge of

lyrical strangeness it needs. The opening lines epitomize its eerie
beauty:

> The cat went here and there
> And the moon spun round like a top,
> And the nearest kin of the moon,
> The creeping cat looked up.
> Black Minnaloushe stared at the moon,
> For, wander and wail as he would,
> The pure cold light in the sky
> Troubled his animal blood.

In his plays of 1917 to 1924, including the two Cuchulain plays
mentioned earlier, Yeats felt free to take experimental risks. His
earlier theatrical experience, and the poetic reorientation that re-
sulted in both *Responsibilities* and the poems that were to make up
The Wild Swans at Coole (1919) and *Michael Robartes and the Dancer*
(1921), had readied him for this change. So had his political brooding
in the years after World War I and the Easter Rising, mirrored in the
clash of feelings projected in *The Dreaming of the Bones* and in the
scorn for both mass ignorance and the authority of church and state
in *The Player Queen*. The latter play, too, broke from religious orthodoxy as much, in its fashion, as did the treatment of Christ in *Calvary*. Also, like the poems of the period—if one may say so without
translating his art into autobiography—it reflects the poet's maturing
attitudes toward love after the years of confusion and disappointment
during which the play was gestating. *The Cat and the Moon,* on the
other hand, embodies his new freedom to follow his fancy wherever it
leads, secure in the sense that lightness of spirit is not the same as
mere triviality.

2. The Cuchulain Plays and Poems

It seems useful to consider Yeats's plays and poems centered on the
Cuchulain legend as a group or "cycle." This is so despite their

appearance at infrequent intervals over many years and despite the very different character and usually superior quality of the plays after 1917. Nevertheless, the earlier pieces create a context of reference Yeats relied on heavily in his later ones.

The plays in the cycle are *On Baile's Strand* (1903), *The Green Helmet* (1910), *At the Hawk's Well* (1917), *The Only Jealousy of Emer* (1919), and *The Death of Cuchulain* (1939). These are enveloped by two poems: "Cuchulain's Fight with the Sea" (1892: called "The Death of Cuchulain" until 1925) and "Cuchulain Comforted" (1939). The poems illustrate not only the evolution of Yeats's artistry but also the profound change over the years in his image of Cuchulain.

In his twenties, as a young nationalist poet, he saw that figure as the equivalent in Irish tradition of the heroes of Arthurian and other European legendry. Works like Tennyson's *The Idylls of the King* and Arnold's "Sohrab and Rustum" are obvious models for "Cuchulain's Fight with the Sea." This is especially true of Arnold's poem, for it, like Yeats's, describes a combat in which a father unwittingly kills his own son. In phrasing and meter as well, Yeats is close to Tennyson and Arnold, although their poems are in blank verse while his poem uses the open rhyming couplets favored by Chaucer.

Stylistically, the 1892 "The Death of Cuchulain" was a mixture of actively direct and evocative writing with verbose effects. It was marred by artificially archaic touches of the sort that could infect even the best verse of the nineteenth century. After forty years of gradual tightening, the 1933 "Cuchulain's Fight with the Sea" still retains a few hapless phrasings. Thus, Cuchulain's wife, Emer, who is shown dyeing clothes as the poem begins, is described as "raddling raiment in her dun." And upon hearing the good news that her husband has returned from the wars, she "parted her lips with a sudden cry." In turn, the messenger, who had less welcome further news for her, "cried his word" that Cuchulain had brought home with him a lovely young mistress. A few lines farther on, we see the girl kneeling beside him as she "stared on the mournful wonder of his eyes." All of which does not contradict the lyrical purity of some of the rest of

"Cuchulain Mask," by Edmund Dulac

Yeats's poem. The hero's new love, for instance, is "sweet-throated like a bird." And at the end, after three stunned days of "dreadful quietude" upon learning that the youth he has fought and killed was his own son, he awakes to a fit of madness and, under a Druid spell, storms forth to do battle against the imagined armies of the sea:

> The Druids took them to their mystery,
> And chaunted for three days.
>
>   Cuchulain stirred,
> Stared on the horses of the sea, and heard
> The cars of battle and his own name cried,
> And fought with the invulnerable tide.

Prosodically, the poem deploys internal rhyme, breaks within and between verse-units, and enjambment to avoid overemphasizing its end rhymes. In many respects its technique is close to Tennyson's and Arnold's, whose scattered half-rhymes and many repetitions of key words at the ends of lines often suggest patterned rhyme. In his youth Yeats was a responsive if unsystematic student of these and other predecessors. His experiments with traditional prosody, plus his interest in Whitman and, later, in Pound and other younger contemporaries, helped him develop his remarkably "natural" rhythmic and syntactic control of conventional metrics.

"Cuchulain Comforted" is a perfect instance. Despite its surreal uncanniness, this very late poem is as straightforward in narrative style as "Cuchulain's Fight with the Sea," and even more straightforward in its diction. It is written in Dante's terza rima, an appropriate choice since its dialogue and action take place in the realm of the dead. The beginning will illustrate the poem's powerful immediacy:

> A man that had six mortal wounds, a man
> Violent and famous, strode among the dead;
> Eyes stared out of the branches and were gone.

> Then certain Shrouds that muttered head to head
> Came and were gone. He leant upon a tree
> As though to meditate on wounds and blood.

The renowned, mighty, uniquely individualistic Cuchulain has died and is about to be transformed into a totally opposite state of being. He will become a small, terrified, anonymous "bird-like thing" called a "Shroud" that does everything in common with its fellow Shrouds. What they do is thread needles, sew new linen shrouds, and sing without human words or human musical notes. ("They had changed their throats and had the throats of birds"—a long-range echo of "sweet-throated like a bird" in "Cuchulain's Fight with the Sea.") One of them explains to Cuchulain that they are "Convicted cowards all by kindred slain // Or driven from home and left to die in fear." Even here, Cuchulain is told, "The rattle of those arms makes us afraid." Yet Cuchulain must become one of them. "Your life," he is promised, "Can grow much sweeter if you will // Obey our ancient rule and make a shroud." And Cuchulain does so. He picks up a bundle of linen and begins.

If there is a certain ambiguity in "Cuchulain Comforted," it is not because of unclear language or symbolism but because of the poem's sheer strangeness. Yeats has invented a Dantean setting and situation within which the hero of the greatest Irish saga will enter a new phase of his existence, a phase in which he will become one with the despised and cowardly denizens of the earth: an anonymous laborer, but also a bird-throated singer. It is the last step in the poet's reshaping of the Cuchulain-figure into an image containing within itself both its original epic heroism (re-embodied, in various passages of poems and plays, as all who have given themselves to the struggle for Irish freedom) and its subjective anti-self: fearful, self-analytical, ridden with guilt. Yeats, nearing death, begins to assimilate his own character and experiences to those of the hero whose symbolic nature he has brooded over and remolded over so many years. He does not spell out this final link between Cuchulain and himself, although he perhaps hints as much in the image of the Shrouds patiently working to achieve whatever they are able to do: "Now we shall sing and sing the best we can."

The difference between the two poems represents, in the simplest way, the progression of Yeats's Cuchulain cycle. The plays, on the other hand, mark out the complex winding between these two points. Thus, the first play, *On Baile's Strand,* repeats the tragic-ironic action of the poem that preceded it. But also it spins a complex web of additional plot that connects with the later works in the cycle. For one thing, it adds the pre-Beckett, almost vaudevillian subplot of the Blind Man and the Fool, the former of whom will return more grimly in Yeats's final play, *The Death of Cuchulain.* For another, it superimposes a crucial moral and political conflict on the elemental struggle between father and son.

This superimposed conflict is similar in character to the struggle in *The King's Threshold.* It is between King Cuchulain of Muir-themne, the quintessential free spirit, and the older, more ambitious Conchubar, High King of Uladh, who wishes to establish a dynastic state to replace the old separate kingships. Conchubar—the calculating, treacherous figure Yeats was to portray again in *Deirdre* a few years later—desires Cuchulain to vow fealty to him, renounce his uncompromised independence, and marry and settle into a stable life under the new rulership. Unable to prevail by sheer argument, he cleverly persuades the gathered women and lesser kings who dread their invisible supernatural enemies the Sidhe (pronounced "Shee") —the "Shape-Changers that run upon the wind"—to beg Cuchulain to yield for security's sake.

Despite himself, out of sheer magnanimity, the hero agrees and thus traps himself. Almost at once, his son appears and announces he has come to "weigh this sword against Cuchulain's sword." And because of his vow, Cuchulain must accept the challenge despite his instinctive liking for the unknown youth. An important implication of the play, something absent from the poem, is the unpredictable, deadly self-betrayal involved in accepting external authority for even the most benign purposes.

A related aspect of the play is its distrustful view of love as another form of commitment that is best resisted. In this play as in the poem, Cuchulain's son is commanded by an embittered mother to kill his father but is himself slain by the more seasoned fighter. Because of chivalric rituals that the mother knows will be honored, neither man can discover the other's identity until too late. The play, however, makes two important linked changes in this familial circumstance. First, Cuchulain is not yet married; indeed, he rejects the very thought of marriage. And second, the mother is no longer Emer but Aoife, a Scottish warrior-queen Cuchulain had once made love with after overcoming her in battle. She is now aggressively allied with the Sidhe against Conchubar's forces. Although Aoife does not actually appear onstage in this play, she is such a passionate driving force behind it that we are well prepared for her powerful emergence, years later, in *The Death of Cuchulain*. It is she who especially comes to mind when, in a surprising passage in *On Baile's Strand* during his agon with Conchubar, Cuchulain sums up what "love" has meant to him:

> I never have known love, but as a kiss
> In the mid-battle, and a difficult truce
> Of oil and water, candles and dark night,
> Hillside and hollow, the hot-footed sun
> And the cold, sliding, slippery-footed moon—
> A brief forgiveness between opposites
> That have been hatreds for three times the age
> Of this long-'stablished ground.

Cuchulain's idea of love as "a brief forgiveness" between hostile opposites sounds more like the thought of a Schopenhauer or Strindberg, or even Ibsen in a certain mood, than of a legendary warrior-king. It in fact flirts with a modern anarcho-primitivist view, rejecting absolute bondage of any kind. In what he thus represents, Cuchulain—though he lives in a mythical, timeless past—is far ahead of his timelessness. What he says here matches other modulations by Yeats, which we have noted in some of his later work, toward a detached and even cynical psychological realism concerning love: in *Responsibilities,* for instance, and in *The Player Queen.* The increasingly sophisticated Cuchulain plays written after the poet turned fifty explore this attitude symbolically, through the hero's tangled and ambiguous relationships with various female figures.

As Yeats wrote in a note to his *Poems, 1899–1905* (1906), *On Baile's Strand* "is a kind of cross-road where too many interests meet and jostle for the hearer to take them in at a first hearing unless he listen carefully, or know something of the story of the other plays of the cycle." The 1906 volume contained a version of the play very close to the final one. It omitted a great deal of the background exposition, some of it having to do with Conchubar's treatment of Naoise and Deirdre, that had marred the first edition and performances. After sloughing off the clutter, Yeats still felt the remaining complexities were a bit of a burden; nevertheless, he had created a lively dramatic structure.

That structure seems clear enough. The play moves rapidly forward through its successive phases. It opens with the busily amusing scene, in prose except for brief patches of song, between the quarreling, gossiping Blind Man and the Fool. Then comes the angry argument, in blank verse (as in the play generally when major figures converse), between the two great kings. Next, we see Cuchulain's gracious yielding to the pleas of the women and the other kings, and the ritual chant afterwards.

His concession is the great turn in his destiny. Very swiftly thereafter the Young Man arrives with his bold challenge. Cuchulain, much taken with him, would rather not accept ("His head is like a woman's head / I had a fancy for") but finally must. The forebodings of the women after father and son go off to fight hold center stage briefly. Then follows the return of the Blind Man and the Fool, who reveal to Cuchulain the identity of the son he has killed and also give the play a secondary ironic turn at the very end. As they watch the maddened Cuchulain plunge into the sea to fight the waves that overmaster him, the Blind Man realizes what a great moment this is to rob the ovens of all the people who have rushed out of their houses to the shore. Despite what they know and have seen, he and the Fool are indifferent to any meaning beyond this opportunity—much as Judas, Lazarus, the Roman soldiers, and "the birds" in *Calvary* are indifferent to the meaning of the Crucifixion.

In addition, these two characters act out a parody of the main plot. The Blind Man manipulates the Fool as Conchubar manipulates Cuchulain. The manipulation is trivial—a matter of cheating the Fool out of his share of a stolen hen, rather than the High King's tricking the hero into killing his son—but still, the absurd parallel underlines Conchubar's coldly selfish exploitation of Cuchulain's noble nature.

This is particularly true because the Blind Man is not merely a clownish trickster but also has the Tiresian gift of foreseeing the future. One could hardly overlook the parallel here to Sophocles' *Oedipus Tyrannos*. Even less could one miss the unconscious pitting of father against son, though with opposite results, in the two plays. But these resemblances are not precise echoes. At most, they help darken the play's timbre, its sense of irreversible fatality pressing the dramatic action forward. Cuchulain's mad fury when he learns the truth is a very different emotional quantity, informed by a different mythical tradition, from Oedipus' overriding, self-punishing guilt.

As for the Fool, he is not only an innocent gull but a companion of witches and water deities. His incantatory songs, like the fire-ritual song of the women meant to ward off the seductive but murderous Shape-Changers, enhance the feeling of unseen presences forever plotting against human happiness. The songs are of a piece with Cuchulain's references to his own kinship with the world of witches and divinities—including his father, the sun-god who once

> came to try me, rising up at dawn
> Out of the cold dark of the rich sea.
> He challenged me to battle, but before
> My sword had touched his sword, told me his name,
> Gave me this cloak, and vanished. It was woven

By women of the Country-under-Wave
Out of the fleeces of the sea.

It is this very kinship that Conchubar seizes on to convince
Cuchulain that he is under a malign spell: "Witchcraft has maddened
you." The youth's apparent resemblance to Aoife must be an illusion,
Conchubar says, created by "some witch . . . floating in the air
above us" to make him forget his vow. In his confusion, the hero
agrees. The battle-rage comes upon him and the outcome is inevitable. Yeats was certainly right about the "many interests [that] meet
and jostle" in *On Baile's Strand*. But they come together, after all, in
the concentrated momentum of the play as it advances into Cuchulain's suicidal effort to punish an unjust universe.

The next Cuchulain play, *The Green Helmet,* originally a prose
work, was first printed and produced in 1908 as *The Golden Helmet.*
In a note that year, Yeats wrote that it "is founded on an old Irish
story, *The Feast of Bricriu,* given in [Lady Gregory's] *Cuchulain of
Muirthemne,* and is meant as an introduction to *On Baile's Strand.*"
The improved 1910 version, in verse, is the one he included in his
Collected Plays, placing it before the earlier *On Baile's Strand* as befits
an "introduction."

It cannot be said, though, to introduce the tragic strain of the
other plays in any manner. Nor does it share their partial reflection,
in the hero's inner feelings, of Yeats's self-image. In *The Green Helmet,* Cuchulain *has* no inner feelings. He is a hearty-spirited, extroverted figure who, as one of his companions says, "was born to luck
in the cradle." He is married to a happy Emer, is clearly the first
among would-be equals, and deals joyously with a test similar to the
one Gawain undergoes in *Sir Gawain and the Green Knight.*

Although the hero must cope with this apparently suicidal test,
and Emer shows fierce anxiety on his behalf, the whole ambience is
too lighthearted for our concern to go very deep even here. "Suspense" in *The Green Helmet* mainly creates an agreeable readiness to
be surprised. What delightful turn of pseudo-melodrama or eerie
mumbo-jumbo will the piece take next? And how will the ever-ready

Cuchulain deal with it? As for the other characters, mighty kings and queens in the original Red Branch cycle of legends, they are so laughably oafish or petty that the play could well be read as an affectionate satire on the Irish sagas. (Fortunately, Yeats abandoned the prose version's last-minute effort to wrench a rousing modern patriotic meaning from his mythical sources.) The verse form, too, contributes its own carefree jollity. Except for a little chant of self-praise by one of the two leading oafs and a love song by Emer exalting her man, it consists of rollicking six-stress couplets in Kiplingesque triple verse. The piece has scattered passages that achieve a pure lyric pitch even within this pattern, which lapses so readily into doggerel. But Yeats's subtitle, "An Heroic Farce," remains absolutely to the point.

At the start, the youthful Cuchulain has just returned from Scotland. (It was there he encountered Aoife—something he might be alluding to in his exchange later on with Emer, although it would be inconsistent with his supposed bachelor state then in *On Baile's Strand*.) He finds his fellow kings Laegaire and Conall in the loghouse near the sea where they have been keeping nervous watch. They are awaiting "The Red Man, a Spirit." Two years earlier he had appeared to them at midnight and accepted their convivial hospitality. And then:

Conall: He promised to show us a game, the best that
　　ever had been;
　　And when we had asked what game, he answered "Why,
　　whip off my head!
　　Then one of you two stoop down, and I'll whip off his,"
　　he said.
　　"A head for a head," he said, "that is the game that I play."
Cuchulain. How could he whip off a head when his own had
　　been whipped away?
Conall. We told him that over and over, and that ale had
　　fuddled his wit,
　　But he stood and laughed at us there, as though his sides
　　would split,

> Till I could stand it no longer, and whipped off his head at
> a blow,
> Being mad that he did not answer, and more at his laugh
> ing so,
> And there on the ground where it fell it went on laughing
> at me.
> *Laegaire.* Till he took it up in his hands—
> *Conall.*   And splashed himself into the sea.

The speakers' simplemindedness and the bouncy playfulness of
the verse lead us to laugh along with the severed head, rather than
shuddering at it. In contrast to his baffled mates, Cuchulain faces
down the Red Man when he arrives for his turn at whipping off
heads. Mocked and defied, the sea-spirit pretends he meant no harm:

> A drinking joke and a gibe and a juggler's feat, that is
> all,
> To make the time go quickly—for I am the drinker's
> friend,
> The kindest of all Shape-Changers from here to the
> world's end,
> The best of all tipsy companions.

"And now," he says, as if to compensate for having jested so
grimly, "I offer you a gift." The gift is another piece of mischief,
intended to set them all fighting. The Loki-like Red Man's successive efforts to incite confusion and conflict are the key to the play's
whole comic structure. A great deal of the fun lies in the fatuous
boasting, volleys of insults, and black-magic visual fireworks attending his tricks. In this instance, he lays his green helmet on the ground
"for the best of you all to lift / And wear upon his own head." Laegaire
and Conall naturally take the bait once again, quarreling childishly
over who is "best." But canny Cuchulain restores harmony for the
moment. He fills the helmet with ale and proclaims it a drinking cup
henceforth for all three alike.

So the pattern continues, like a comic boxing match in which
the Red Man keeps attacking and Cuchulain keeps knocking him

down. Foiled in his helmet maneuver, the Red Man stirs up fighting among the servants, which Cuchulain ends quickly, and then incites Emer and the wives of Conall and Laegaire to squabble over precedence in entering the house. Quick-witted Cuchulain solves this problem humorously. He bars the door with his spear and gets Conall and Laegaire to break down the wall next to it; all three ladies can now enter side by side. When the Red Man sets them quarreling again, over which husband has the best right to possess the green helmet, Cuchulain throws the divisive thing into the sea. And now, as a spectacular next-to-last resort, the Red Man uses his unearthly powers to try frightening the human characters out of their wits.

Suddenly, we are told, "black hands come through the windows and put out the torches," so that the stage grows pitch-black. As faint moonlight enters the room soon thereafter, "the Red Man is seen standing in the midst of the house" while "black cat-headed men crouch and stand about the door." He harshly demands that the debt owed him be honored. Cuchulain, true to his heroic nature, kneels down at once to be beheaded. But this is a comedy, and the Red Man, for all his joy in making trouble, has no finally wicked purpose after all. He spares Cuchulain because of his gay, uncalculating courage and because he has "the hand that loves to scatter; the life like a gambler's throw." In his weird way, he is a whimsically experimental administrator:

I have not come for your hurt. I'm the Rector of this land,
And with my spitting cat-heads, my frenzied moon-bred band,
Age after age I sift it, and choose for its championship
The man who hits my fancy.

Even the flightiest comedy has its serious side, and this play does certainly introduce the traditional Cuchulain, possessor of supremely noble qualities and superhuman powers. It also, immediately before the passage just quoted, suggests the passionate and difficult relationship he has with Emer and paves the way for the other Cuchulain plays (even, in retrospect, for the events in the earlier *On Baile's Strand* despite the possible inconsistency noted a few pages back). The exchange with Emer must be taken seriously in its characterization and also because it is the seed, though planted in comedy, that will flower in the tragic works to come:

Red Man. I demand the debt that's owing. Let some man
    kneel down there
  That I may cut his head off, or all shall go to wrack.
Cuchulain. He played and paid with his head, and it's
    right that we pay him back,
  And give him more than he gave, for he comes in here as a
    guest:
  So I will give him my head.   [*Emer begins to keen.*]
            Little wife, little wife, be at rest.
  Alive I have been far off in all lands under the sun,
  And been no faithful man, but when my story is done
  My fame shall spring up and laugh, and set you high above
    all.
Emer [*putting her arms about him*]. It is you, not your
    fame that I love.
Cuchulain [*tries to put her from him*]. You are young, you
    are wise, you can call
  Some kindlier and comelier man that will sit at home in
    the house.
Emer. Live and be faithless still.
Cuchulain [*throwing her from him*]. Would you stay the
    great barnacle-goose
  When its eyes are turned to the sea and its beak to the
    salt of the air?
Emer [*lifting her dagger to stab herself*]. I, too, on the
    grey wing's path!
Cuchulain [*seizing dagger*]. Do you dare, do you dare, do
    you dare?
  Bear children and sweep the house.
      [*Forcing his way through the servants who gather round.*]
            Wail, but keep from the road.

[*He kneels before Red Man. There is a pause.*]
Quick to your work, old Radish, you will fade when the
cocks have crowed.

Yeats made sure to place *The Green Helmet,* with its pre-tragic
Cuchulain, before *On Baile's Strand* in his *Collected Plays.* For a
similar reason he placed *At the Hawk's Well,* which he wrote much
later than either, ahead of both those plays because its plot antedates
theirs in mythical time. In that obvious sense, it is an "introduction."
And in another, more telling sense, it introduces a huge change in
the formal character of the cycle. As the first of the final three Cuchulain plays—highly compressed symbolic works that draw on elements of Japanese Noh drama, including its serious use of ghost-
characters as natural presences—it makes a new start. Yet at the same
time, it harks back to a romantic obsession driving Yeats's poems
and plays from the beginning. He was fascinated by the compelling
appeal, and also the pity, of self-sacrifice: of forgoing life's normal
joys for the sake of a dream of perfection or of some uncompromis-
ing ideal. Intertwined with this double fascination was the call
of the forbidden, usually expressed—or, psychologically speaking,
masked—as the dangerous seductiveness of unholy spirits or of
death.

This complex obsession revealed itself in varied, often elusive
ways over the years. The lovely early poem "The Stolen Child"
(1886), in which a little boy is lured from the security of his home by
the ambiguous promises of faeries, is one of the simpler instances.
The famous elegy "Easter, 1916" (1916), in which the political sin-
glemindedness of the martyred leaders of the Easter Rising is seen as
having led them into what was perhaps "needless death after all," is
stronger and more challenging fare. And *The Only Jealousy of Emer*
(1919) and *The Death of Cuchulain* (1939), the two plays of the cycle
after *At the Hawk's Well,* reflect the obsession most subtly of all. In
these plays, Emer and Cuchulain, respectively, retain a sense of their
ideal selves while they cope with the deceptions of hostile Shape-
Changers until, finally, they must accept defeat. *At the Hawk's Well* is

The "Guardian of the Well" for At the Hawk's Well, *by Edmund Dulac*

closer, at the beginning, to the clearly romantic European origins of this tragic motif. But once its action is galvanized by the cries and dancing of the mysteriously changing female spirit called "the Guardian of the Well," its Noh-like unfolding foreshadows that of the later plays.

Two characters, an "Old Man" and a "Young Man" who soon identifies himself as Cuchulain, pursue a will-o'-the-wisp ideal as the play opens near the "hawk's well" of the title. There, on a Scottish mountainside, they seek to drink of the water of immortality. Ordinarily nothing but a dry "hollow among stones half-full of leaves," the well is a barren-looking spot

> wherein
> Three hazels drop their nuts and withered leaves,
> And where a solitary girl keeps watch
> Among grey boulders. He who drinks, they say,
> Of that miraculous water lives forever.

For over fifty years, the Old Man complains, he has stayed close by, watching for the rare opportunity that may come at any time:

> A secret moment when the holy shades
> That dance upon the desolate mountain know,
> And not a living man, and when it comes
> The water has scarce plashed before it is gone.

During all those years of watching, the well has "plashed" up only three times, always while he slept under the malign spell of the dancers. Cuchulain, who naturally believes his luck will be different, promises to share the blessed water with the Old Man when it next appears. But he is distracted in another way by the hitherto virtually invisible Guardian of the Well, who for over half the play has seemed nothing but an odd heap on the ground under a black cloak—a vague, subliminal distraction at most. Now, suddenly, she utters loud hawk-cries and explodes into view. Costumed "like a hawk" and mimicking its flight, she rises and begins to dance. Her burst of sound and symbolic movement are the single most dynamic effect of the play. Cuchulain, mesmerized, pursues her when she disappears offstage.

Thus, like the sleeping Old Man, he misses the water of eternal life that has meanwhile risen and disappeared in a twinkling. The Guardian of the Well, a woman of the Sidhe, has deceived him doubly by her dancing. At the crucial moment, she has first led him to forget his original purpose and then eluded his desire for her. In another surprising turn here, as the play is about to end, the three musicians who have been present all along suddenly cry out "Aoife! Aoife!" and strike a gong. The Old Man, now awake, explains to Cuchulain that the fleeing dancer

> has roused up the fierce women of the hills,
> Aoife, and all her troop, to take your life,
> And never till you are lying in the earth
> Can you know rest.

Cuchulain rushes out to face them, and thus the action ends. We have received just enough information to connect this play with the others in the cycle; but that fact, at this particular dramatic moment, is only incidental to Cuchulain's unconsidered leap into the chaotic unknown. As a violent turn away from overwhelming competing pressures, it is a resolution psychically akin to the plunge into war by the protagonists of Tennyson's *Maud: A Monodrama* and Thomas Mann's *The Magic Mountain*.

The compressed interlocking of diverse elements in *At the Hawk's Well* is born of more than clever dramatic structure or exciting spectacle. The active role of the poetry is vital to the play's emotional movement. The highly charged blank verse of the main characters' dialogue is masterfully controlled in pitch and intensity. Even more effective, however, are the varied forms of the songs and the speeches of the Musicians. They start the play off and bring it to an end, they describe imagined scenes and events, and they philosophize lyrically like a chorus of Delphic oracles. And their language evokes feelings and perceptions far beyond the literal plot. Thus, their opening song presents Cuchulain surprisingly, almost shockingly:

> I call to the eye of the mind
> A well long choked up and dry
> And boughs long stripped by the wind,

> And I call to the mind's eye
> Pallor of an ivory face,
> Its lofty dissolute air,
> A man climbing up to a place
> The salt sea wind has swept bare.

"Pallor of an ivory face" and "lofty dissolute air" are not expressions normally used for warriors of epic stature. Rather, they create an aura of aristocratic and aesthetic decadence, as though great endeavor were a species of dissipation. Classical statuary might come to mind as well, but the image of an "ivory" (not "marble") face is exquisite rather than heroic: a tonal echo of Poe and the 'nineties. Associated with "pallor," the image also suggests a ghostly apparition. The suggestion is enhanced by the incantatory tone of the whole passage.

As they sing, the Musicians—masked and moving, like all the characters, with the staccato rhythm of marionettes—begin to ponder the meaning of the young hero's life even before he appears onstage. Their pondering anticipates a moving passage in Yeats's poem "Among School Children" (1927). The thought they introduce is essential to the meaning of Cuchulain's life, although he, immersed in the immediacies of the dramatic situation, will remain untrammeled by any such introspection:

> What were his life soon done?
> Would he lose by that or win?
> A mother that saw her son
> Doubled over a speckled shin,
> Cross-grained with ninety years,
> Would cry, "How little worth
> Were all my hopes and fears
> And the hard pain of his birth!"

The songs and exchanges of the Musicians are brooding and elegiac. They stress the pitiful waywardness of human desires, our inability to be content with any one choice:

> The heart would be always awake,
> The heart would turn to its rest.

And they see in Cuchulain's hunger for immortality—a mode of keeping "always awake"—a terror worse than the "rest" that is death. Three of their lines, almost a shriek of mystical dread, recall the morbid shudder of transformation that runs through the hero in Keats's "Hyperion":

> O God, protect me
> From a horrible deathless body
> Sliding through the veins of a sudden.

At the end of the play, as Cuchulain goes off to do battle with Aoife's deathless hosts, the Musicians' final song evokes, in purely lyrical fashion, the mixed central emotions of the play. As so often in Yeats, its dramatic import will be mostly lost on a theater audience, except as a lingering aftertaste of wry feeling. The fact that the words are sung—and sung to instrumental accompaniment—militates against the kind of focused attention such poetry demands. For the *reader,* however, the song precipitates out the essential life and movement of the play, as its first three stanzas will show. These stanzas, in their own right, make up a memorable poem that responds, not only to the fear-ridden vision of the play, but also to the psychological pressures creating such a vision:

> Come to me, human faces,
> Familiar memories;
> I have found hateful eyes
> Among the desolate places,
> Unfaltering, unmoistened eyes.
>
> Folly alone I cherish,
> I choose it for my share;
> Being but a mouthful of sweet air,

I am content to perish;
I am but a mouthful of sweet air.

O lamentable shadows,
Obscurity of strife!
I choose a pleasant life
Among indolent meadows;
Wisdom must live a bitter life.

The brief but crucial sequence of changing tones in the lines just quoted is centered around the appalled report in the powerful opening stanza. That stanza presents a hellish realm, tyrannized by the "unfaltering, unmoistened eyes" of raptor-like powers. Its imagery—after its appeal for the comforting support of "human faces" and "familiar memories"—is nightmarish, a language of sheer terror. It echoes, but far more intensely, the Old Man's prophetic warning to Cuchulain against the "Woman of the Sidhe." A curse, he has said, will fall "on all who have gazed in her unmoistened eyes." The warning foretells, indirectly, the hero's fight with his yet unconceived son and also the darker perplexities of sexual love that will emerge in the later Cuchulain plays—and that are of course important in so many of Yeats's poems:

That curse may be
Never to win woman's love and keep it;
Or always to mix hatred in the love;
Or it may be she will kill your children
  . . . .
Or you will be so maddened that you kill them
With your own hand.

In the context of the play, this warning provided an "explanation" of two events: Cuchulain's mad enchantment by the Guardian of the Well and his leap into war against the weird powers. It also provides dramatic substance for the imagery of dire terror in the first stanza of the Musicians' choral song. The song's next two stanzas

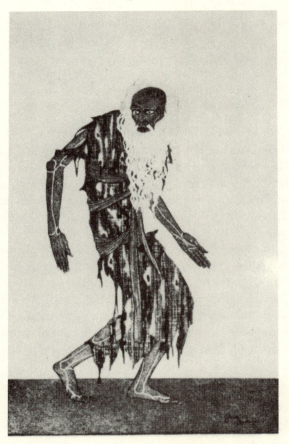

The "Old Man" for At the Hawk's Well, *by Edmund Dulac*

experiment with postures to cope with the terror. In the second stanza, the tone shifts to a wistful bravado, a flourish at once devil-may-care and self-depreciative. The third stanza then takes on the fatalistic edge of a Sophoclean chorus. It ends on a note of longing for simple contentment instead of the "bitter life" of "wisdom," which can see all too imaginatively into the more sinister realities of existence.

Thus, the successive tonalities within the play's unfolding action are absorbed and condensed into the Musicians' lyrical insights. And thus, too, Yeats, perhaps not altogether consciously at this stage, begins to connect his own deepest poetic preoccupations with Cuchulain's character and purposes. To accept the risks of passion, to fling into battle against forces of unpredictable power and terror not entirely alien to one's own nature, and to penetrate the realm beyond death—these aims connect the hero's nature and the poet's dreams.

At the Hawk's Well and *The Only Jealousy of Emer,* both first conceived in 1916, have obvious affinities in spite of the latter play's greater complexity. The most obvious formal affinity is the decisive role of the Musicians in the emotional dynamics of each of these pieces. Another kind of affinity lies in what might be called the plays' erotic turbulence. Without receiving central emphasis, this sexual aspect is graphically implied (for example, by the Guardian's dance and Cuchulain's response to it) in *At the Hawk's Well. The Only Jealousy of Emer,* though, fairly spills over with it. For one instance, the Guardian—or "Woman of the Sidhe"—reappears in the latter play and is openly seductive both in the way she dances and in her speech. One cannot help thinking of the love-entangled poems in *Responsibilities* and of the turmoil that Yeats confronted in the years immediately afterward.

It was, of course, the generally tragic period of the Easter Rising—to say nothing of the Great War. But also, in Yeats's personal life, it was a time when a long affair ended badly and he proposed unsuccessfully to two women—Maud Gonne and her daughter Iseult—and then, in October 1917, stabilized his life by marrying Georgie Hyde-Lees. The later Cuchulain plays, without anything like direct confession, seem occasionally to reflect the circumstances and problems of these involved relationships. Without undue speculation in a discussion devoted to Yeats's poetic art rather than his biography, one can nevertheless see the bite of his own deeply considered private experience in Cuchulain's exchanges with his wife and his other loves in the final two plays of the cycle.

Be all that as it may, *The Only Jealousy of Emer* begins with a song by the First Musician about the long, mysterious, and perilous evolution of "woman's beauty." Although "that loveliness" is described in delicate images—"a white / frail bird," "a fragile, exquisite, pale shell"—it nevertheless is seen as the result of terrifyingly painful labors through the centuries. (The implied analogy with the sufferings an artist must endure to bring a vision of beauty, epitomized as *female* beauty, to birth is clear.) The song ends in language, reminiscent of Blake's "The Tyger," that defines the creation of woman's beauty as a destructive, impersonal process:

> What death? what discipline?
> What bonds no man could unbind,
> Being imagined within
> The labyrinth of the mind,
> What pursuing or fleeing,
> What wounds, what bloody press,
> Dragged into being
> This loveliness?

Having begun at such a pitch of dread-filled, adoring wonder at womanly beauty, the same Musician now calls upon us to envision the scene of the play. What is happening is the aftermath of Cuchulain's mad fight with the sea once he realizes he has killed his own son—a piece of information easy to surmise but withheld for the moment. Those events are not the central ones of *The Only Jealousy of Emer*. As a result, the play's first emphatic impact is to give dramatic substance to the Musicians' association of erotic love and female beauty with suffering and death:

> I call up a poor fisherman's house;
> A man lies dead or swooning,
> That amorous man,
> That amorous, violent man, renowned Cuchulain,
> Queen Emer at his side.
> But now one comes on hesitating feet,
> Young Eithne Inguba, Cuchulain's mistress.

She stands a moment in the open door.
Beyond the open door the bitter sea,
The shining, bitter sea, is crying out. . . .

Thus, very early on, affinities are set up between suffering and "woman's beauty," and between Cuchulain's "amorous, violent" nature and his supposed death. In the series of agons that follows, these free-floating affinities linking the erotic and the tragic, or love and sacrifice, encompass the whole work and attach themselves to each specific situation.

The Musicians blend into the play at the start, but then they grow silent until the very end. The first exchange within the main action, between Emer and Eithne Inguba, provides some necessary exposition and the elements of an unusual love triangle, within which jealousy has become irrelevant. Emer is sure Cuchulain is not dead, and that "an image has been put into his place" by hostile spirits. She has invited the younger woman to help recall him from the spell he is under: "We two, / And we alone, may watch together here, / Because we loved him best." Eithne Inguba, she hopes, can win him back to life with her "sweet voice that is so dear to him."

The effort at salvation involves two suspense-fraught questions. The first question—which is the true Cuchulain?—is visually suggested in the stage directions for the scene in which we first see the two women. They describe a "curtained bed or litter on which lies a man in his grave-clothes" who "wears an heroic mask," while "another man with exactly similar clothes and mask crouches near the front."

The question is answered further along, when we learn that the man on the bed (called "The Figure of Cuchulain") is really the trickster Bricriu of the Sidhe, "maker of discord among gods and men." He has taken on the appearance of her husband's corpse to frighten Emer into bargaining with him. She cannot, at first, see the hero's true self, the crouching man ("The Ghost of Cuchulain") who is hovering on the edge of death. But Bricriu's whole aim is to thwart an enemy spirit—Fand, the "Woman of the Sidhe" who eluded Cuchulain in *At the Hawk's Well* but is now tempting him to cross the line of death and become her lover. Bricriu therefore "dissolves" the darkness that had kept Emer from seeing, and recognizing, the true Cuchulain.

Thus a new sexual dimension has entered the picture, adding further suspense while the first question is being answered. As the play unfolds, it centers more and more on the second question: whether or not Fand will win the day; and if not, how Emer and Eithne Inguba can draw their man back into the human world. Not to spell out all the intricacies of the plot, the upshot is that Emer must renounce her dearest hope—that one day Cuchulain will again love her as in their youth—in order to save him. As soon as she does so, he is allowed to replace the false image on the bed and to embrace Eithne Inguba, who is convinced that "it is I that won him from the sea." In this fashion, the tragic burden has shifted, without an ounce of bathos, from Cuchulain to Emer; and the arena of mortal conflict has been moved from pride of tribal authority and the clash of swords to the intricacies of passionate desire and marital loyalty.

Once again, it seems necessary to stress the importance, in a play like this, of its poetic aspect. Yeats has provided genuine suspense and interesting spectacle; yet both his plot and staging may confuse watchers unaccustomed to spoken verse—especially verse at a somewhat demanding level of evocativeness. He hardly possessed the theatrical genius of Shakespeare, who could graft wonderfully suggestive, sometimes difficult lines and passages into his five-act poetic plays and still keep the action galloping ahead for all viewers. But Yeats's short, concentrated pieces are serious experiments—essentially for modern audiences with little experience of any verse drama apart from revivals of Shakepeare and certain classics—in mating lyrical craftsmanship with stagecraft. We have seen how, from his earliest verse onward, he built poems in dialogue form. Conversely, his plays, at chosen points, extend the limits of dialogue to imaginative reaches beyond a given dramatic situation but not irrelevant to it.

The colloquy between the Ghost of Cuchulain and the Woman of the Sidhe after her seductive dance provides an instance. To isolate its eerie enchantment, Yeats shifted from the play's basic blank verse to rhyming four-stress couplets. The passage begins:

> *Ghost of Cuchulain.* Who is it stands before me there
>   Shedding such light from limb and hair
>   As when the moon, complete at last
>   With every labouring crescent past,
>   And lonely with extreme delight,
>   Flings out upon the fifteenth night?
> *Woman of the Sidhe.* Because I long I am not complete.
>   What pulled your hands about your feet,
>   Pulled your head down upon your knees,
>   And hid your face?
> *Ghost of Cuchulain.*   Old memories:
>   A woman in her happy youth
>   Before her man had broken troth,
>   Dead men and women. Memories
>   Have pulled my head upon my knees.

Cuchulain's Ghost, with his moon-imagery derived from the system of fatality Yeats and his wife were working out (published in 1925 as *A Vision*), seems at first to be speaking a symbolic language far removed from the play's action. And yet the passage becomes so humanized in his second speech that the moon-imagery comes to sound perfectly natural: the dreaming wisdom of a man whose life has gone through many phases, who is weighed down by the memories he speaks of, and who feels remorse for having "broken troth" with Emer, the woman he has most loved. Thus, the abstract imagery of the moon "with every labouring crescent past" enters the drama of Emer's intimate suffering.

The same sort of modulation occurs at the beginning of the play. There the Musician's song, like the Ghost of Cuchulain's first speech, has the initial effect of a pure and moving but quite detached success. But soon we see that the whole play, with its female personae striving painfully to win Cuchulain—whether from death or into the world of wild chthonian spirits—is prepared for by the opening lines of that song. The versification, too, is very much a part of the song's emotional movement. The continuous enjambment until the fourth line, the delayed and identical rhymes, and the abrupt, condensed reprise in the fifth and sixth lines contribute to the effect of straining against imminent disaster. At the same time, the repeated images of a frail, storm-driven sea-bird and of "dark furrows upon the ploughed land" are finely suggestive of the play's precarious balances and romantic sensuality:

> A woman's beauty is like a white
> Frail bird, like a white sea-bird alone
> At daybreak after stormy night
> Between two furrows upon the ploughed land:
> A sudden storm, and it was thrown
> Between dark furrows upon the ploughed land.

The Musicians' final song, at the close of the play, at first seems even more independent of the main action than the opening song and the Ghost's first speech did. But again, it proves to have picked up, by way of associative reverie, a decisive image of the tragic solitude of each human life as it passes through its phases. The clearest, most poignant instance in the play is the dénouement itself: the sacrificial, self-isolating triumph of Emer on Cuchulain's behalf. The Musicians do not speak directly to this point. Their language is somewhat tangential, even abstract, but it carries the feeling of the play to something like a universally inclusive level. The song begins:

> Why does your heart beat thus?
> Plain to be understood,
> I have met in a man's house
> A statue of solitude. . . .

And later:

> Although the door be shut
> And all seem well enough,
> Although wide world hold not

A man but will give you his love
The moment he has looked at you,
He that has loved the best
May turn from a statue
His too human breast.

O bitter reward
Of many a tragic tomb!
And we though astonished are dumb
Or give but a sigh and a word,
A passing word.

What makes your heart so beat?
What man is at your side?
When beauty is complete
Your own thought will have died
And danger not be diminished;
Dimmed at three-quarter light,
When moon's round is finished
The stars are out of sight.

Without being tendentious, these passages in the concluding song again bring the play into the orbit of the human insights underlying *A Vision*. They implicitly link Emer's change of fortune with cycles of destiny the song calls the "moon's round." There is no effort to force the play itself into an illustration or proof of the system. But the suggestion of its "bitter" relevance and of "our" inability to do more than give "a sigh and a word" makes the ending a beautiful, dirge-like choral interpretation of the action.

Yeats completed *The Only Jealousy of Emer* in January 1918. It was almost twenty-one years later that its main human characters—together with the Blind Man of *On Baile's Strand,* the crow-headed war-goddess called the Morrigu, and the elusive Aoife (hitherto an important offstage figure only) made their next and final appearance. Yeats finished work on *The Death of Cuchulain* in December 1938, about a month before he died on 28 January 1939 in Cap Martin,

France. A December letter to a friend, Edith Shackleton Heald, says: "I have tired myself finishing the play and writing a lyric that has risen out of it, and also talking." The "lyric" was most likely "Cuchulain Comforted." He seems to be referring to both works again in an interesting New Year's Day letter to Miss Heald, in which he writes: "I think my play is strange and the most moving I have written for some years. I am making a prose sketch for a poem—a kind of sequel—strange, too, something new."

These details are relevant not only to the circumstances of Yeats's final creative period but also to the affective character of what he was writing. Despite the tragic bent of both plays, the elegiac, submissive spirit of the energy-spent hero in *The Death of Cuchulain* (and of "Cuchulain Comforted") is very different from his sexual entrancements and perplexities in *The Only Jealousy of Emer*. They are indeed psychological decades apart: the distance between the author's passionate, introspective middle age and his imaginative coping, in old age, with the crisis of approaching death.

In the play, of course, it is the imminence of *Cuchulain's* death that saturates the emotional atmosphere with a mixture of bitterness, resignation, and suicidal heroism. The presiding deity, the Morrigu, is a death-force. Cuchulain learns that his beloved Eithne Inguba either wishes his death or is being manipulated in a plot against him. He nevertheless chooses to act on her professed message from Emer, advising him to "ride out and fight" his enemies (Queen Maeve's armies) at once—against, as he knows, "odds no man can face and live"—instead of awaiting the "great host" that will arrive to support him in the morning. His reason is his customary defiant courage, adapted to Yeats's equally defiant but desperate solipsistic stance as expressed in a poem like "The Tower." Cuchulain says, with superb unreason: "I make the truth! / I say she brings a message from my wife." And in "The Tower" (1927) Yeats had written:

> Death and life were not
> Till man made up the whole,
> Made lock, stock and barrel

> Out of his bitter soul,
> Aye, sun and moon and star, all . . .

But the most compelling "reason" for Cuchulain's decision is simply that his time to die has arrived. This is the essential condition of the play, underscored by the constant repetition of the words "die" and "death" and "kill," always in relation to Cuchulain no matter who is speaking. In addition, it is symbolized by the Morrigu's sudden apparition early in the play and her return—even more overwhelming in its stark impact than the Guardian's dance in *At the Hawk's Well*—after Cuchulain's death. Earlier in the play, after Cuchulain has been given "six mortal wounds," Aoife appears to take her long-delayed revenge by killing him. But the *coup de grâce* comes, not from any glamorous or supernatural character or rival hero, but from the calculating Blind Man. He is no longer the amusingly greedy figure of *On Baile's Strand,* except in the much altered sense of black comedy. But he does retain that character's uncanny knowledge and remains the most squalid minor prophet in literature. Maeve, he explains, had promised him twelve pennies "if I brought Cuchulain's head in a bag." And so it is that the old beggar, in every way Cuchulain's total opposite, becomes the bound and helpless hero's executioner. Although the pennies are reminiscent of Judas' pieces of silver, the Blind Man is not a traitor but a dread embodiment of death itself: the most common, and utterly impersonal, scourge of humanity.

The Death of Cuchulain moves rapidly through what amounts to barely nine pages of text. It begins with a prose monologue by "a very old man looking like something out of mythology" but sounding very much like W.B.Y. in full manic splendor. He combines an attack on popular and realistic art ("I spit upon the dancers painted by Degas") and its audience with a witty, scornful apologia for the play's character and its appeal to people who "know the old epics and Mr. Yeats' plays about them." The action then shifts to the three increasingly grim agons that make up the main body of the work. Three afterbeats follow: the Morrigu's brief, chillingly distanced address "to the dead," a symbolic dance by Emer around Cuchulain's severed head, and a song by the hitherto silent "Street-Singer." The song connects some of Yeats's most haunting preoccupations with the Cuchulain legend. Its sensual lyricism, its stirring questions, and its deep thrust into how mythic memory enters the modern mind carry the play to a new, passionately elegiac awareness at the very end.

Cuchulain's first agon, with Eithne Inguba, is charged both with his doubts concerning her truthfulness and with his own frank ambivalence—a kind of ambivalence we normally find in the subjective reverie of poets rather than in the confident thought of archetypal heroes. Cuchulain, knowing he is about to die, obliges destiny with a wry grace, plunging into battle prematurely instead of awaiting reinforcements. He knows Eithne Inguba has been treacherous, yet arranges for her future welfare before he sets out. And he remembers, ruefully, the steadfast love of the forsaken Emer, whose sacrifice had once saved him from the powers of the sea. When the sudden appearance of the Morrigu confirms the imminence of his death, the importance of romantic love in itself recedes from him and he reminds Eithne Inguba—and himself—that "everything sublunary must change." It would be hard to distinguish the dying hero's feelings from the poet's at this point.

The second agon, after the battle in which Cuchulain has received his six mortal wounds, is with Aoife. She has come to kill him at last, in revenge for their son's death. He cooperates by letting her bind him tightly to a stone pillar so that he is totally helpless. But then she hears someone coming and goes off to hide until whoever it is passes. Since it is the Blind Man, who seizes his opportunity with little delay, this is the last we see of Aoife. Her exchange with Cuchulain now that both are old, however, has been extremely touching in its intimacy despite her purpose. In part it is a sharing of reminiscences, slightly at cross-purposes, between former lovers after long estrangement. Once Cuchulain realizes who she is, he has complete sympathy with her intention:

> I have put my belt
> About this stone and want to fasten it
> And die upon my feet, but am too weak.
> Fasten this belt.

> [*She helps him do so.*]

> And now I know your name,
> Aoife, the mother of my son. We met
> At the Hawk's Well under the withered trees.
> I killed him upon Baile's Strand, that is why
> Maeve parted ranks that she might let you through.
> You have a right to kill me.

His whole nature is changing. When she begins to bind him more securely with her delicate veil, he is solicitous: "But do not spoil your veil. / Your veils are beautiful, some with threads of gold." The shimmering veil softens and feminizes his appearance. And for a moment, also, the two converse as proud parents. "Our son," she asks, "—how did he fight?" And Cuchulain replies, reassuringly: "Age makes more skilful but not better men."

The third and briefest agon, with the Blind Man, is mostly a swift movement of savage irony. The Blind Man gloats over the reward of twelve pennies he is to receive for handing over Cuchulain's head to Maeve. "But this has been my lucky day," he tells his victim. The ensuing dialogue brings out both his inhuman relentlessness and Cuchulain's reversal of personality:

Cuchulain.   Twelve pennies!
Blind Man. I would not promise anything until the woman,
    The great Queen Maeve herself, repeated the words.
Cuchulain. Twelve pennies! What better reason for killing
    a man?
    You have a knife, but have you sharpened it?
Blind Man. I keep it sharp because it cuts my food.
[*He lays bag on ground and begins feeling Cuchulain's body, his hands mounting upward.*]
Cuchulain. I think you know everything, Blind Man.

My mother or my nurse said that the blind
Know everything.
Blind Man.   No, but they have good sense.
How could I have got twelve pennies for your head
If I had not good sense?
Cuchulain.   There floats out there
The shape that I shall take when I am dead,
My soul's first shape, a soft feathery shape,
And is not that a strange shape for a soul
Of a great fighting man?
Blind Man.   Your shoulder is there,
This is your neck. Ah! Ah! Are you ready, Cuchulain?
Cuchulain. I say it is about to sing.

                                   [*The stage darkens.*]
Blind Man.   Ah! Ah!
          [*Music of pipe and drum, the curtain falls . . . .*]

Cuchulain's final words connect directly with the situation and feeling of the poem "Cuchulain Comforted," which could well be taken as a narrated epilogue to the play.

Within *The Death of Cuchulain* itself, though, the image of the soul's future shape as a "soft feathery" bird is only a momentary, if enormously suggestive, effect. The play shifts abruptly, when the curtain next rises, to "a woman with a crow's head," the Morrigu, standing on a bare stage and giving her account of how Cuchulain received his battle wounds. She "holds a black parallelogram, the size of a man's head," and "there are six other parallelograms near the backcloth." Her account begins with the solemnity of a Doomsday report in Hades:

          The dead can hear me, and to the dead I speak.
          This head is great Cuchulain's, those other six
          Gave him six mortal wounds. . . .

Unless beautifully choreographed and performed, *and* not prolonged in this otherwise short piece, Emer's subsequent dance around the parallelogram representing her husband's head is a truly awkward interlude. One wonders if Yeats could ever have found the dancer the Old Man calls for in the prologue: "the tragi-comedian dancer, the tragic dancer, upon the same neck love and loathing, life and death"—in other words, a dancer whose nature would be the very essence of the play itself. Her dance, symbolizing rage, adoration, and mourning (as described in the stage directions) would still confuse an audience unless a printed program informed it that Emer is the character being represented. For until this point, Emer has taken no part in the action; nor has her entrance been expected.

The dance also makes the Street-Singer's song a bit anticlimactic. Nevertheless the song, arising from amidst "the music of some Irish Fair of our day," ends the play superbly. Its three verse-units of uneven length—in ballad meter not divided into quatrains and sometimes slightly irregular—are purportedly what "the harlot sang to the beggar man" out of the depths of the folk-mind. No living men, she says in the first and longest unit, can match the sexual perfection (no longer available) of Cuchulain and his legendary comrades. The best that modern women can know in the flesh are bodies "I both loathe and adore." Is that condition, then, our "sole reality"?

The second verse-unit imagines an answer. It is made up of further questions, premised on the resurrection of those heroes and their supernatural passion through visionary struggle for national freedom. There is an implied analogy—not put propagandistically, as this description may have suggested—between the martyrs of the Easter Rebellion, who made a stand at the Dublin Post Office, and the bringing down of Cuchulain in the play:

> What stood in the Post Office
> With Pearse and Connolly?
> What comes out of the mountain
> Where men first shed their blood?
> Who thought Cuchulain till it seemed
> He stood where they had stood?

The final unit is softly retrospective. It repeats, but in a restrained tone, the first unit's lament for the deterioration of ancient ideals; then refers, as if in a guidebook, to Oliver Sheppard's statue of Cuchulain, commemorating the Rebellion, outside the Post Office; and recalls, with only slightly greater emphasis, the rage of frustration vented in the prologue: "But an old man looking back on life / Imagines it in scorn." The play's dream of violent greatness humanized into gentle acceptance but no less great as a result now recedes— but will be pursued further in "Cuchulain Comforted."

In the interest of viewing the whole Cuchulain cycle as a sequence, we have leapt ahead—though not for the first time—of our basically chronological review of Yeats's achievement. But the leap has enabled us to see, not only the gathering richness of these poems and plays, but the increasing fusion of the mythical material with the poet's private realm of self-exploration. And in contemplating *The Death of Cuchulain* we have also looked ahead to the remarkable advance in dramatic power and economy that marked the very last plays, and sometimes the last poems, that Yeats wrote.

V

Poetry of Transition II
(1914-1919)

Yeats's next books of new poetry after *Responsibilities* were *The Wild Swans at Coole* (1917; enlarged edition, 1919) and *Michael Robartes and the Dancer* (1921). All the poems in these books had been written by early 1919, for the most part during the preceding three or four years. The two collections reveal interesting reciprocities and, since the later book is very short, might well have been combined. This chapter will therefore consider them together, or at least as companion volumes.

Yeats had good enough reasons, no doubt, to print them separately. *Michael Robartes and the Dancer* does have important new emphases, in some degree connected with his work on *The Only Jealousy of Emer* and other plays during the same general period. Seven of its fifteen poems are related to war and vital Irish political experience, the Easter Rising in particular. The others, written in the wake of Yeats's late marriage at fifty-two, reflect deepened human perspectives generally. All in all, brief as the book is, it anticipates the long gestation of *The Tower* as the poet entered his late fifties and early sixties. And besides, as a practical matter, he had already significantly expanded *The Wild Swans at Coole,* first issued by the Cuala Press in 1917, for its 1919 publication by Macmillan.

171

Given the reciprocities that have been mentioned, however, the shorter work serves in effect as a powerful coda to the longer one.

To turn now to *The Wild Swans at Coole*: it is, on the whole, marked by its elegies and its rueful meditations, though leavened by some exuberant counter-notes. At the same time, the volume is subtly controlled by a buried sequence at its center that both sustains and goes beyond its pervasive sense of loss. (It is "buried" in that it is not separated by an overall title or other external indication from the rest of the book.) This sequence, which makes a striking turn from the passionate reconsiderations of failed love in *Responsibilities,* consists of eight intensely personal poems: "Memory," "Her Praise" (called "Her Phoenix" in the 1917 edition), "The People," "His Phoenix," "A Thought from Propertius," "Broken Dreams," "A Deep-sworn Vow," and "Presences."

The psychological moment of the sequence is the period preceding Yeats's marriage in October 1917: something not mentioned in the poems. Nor do they say "Maud Gonne"—even if the name springs to mind for obvious reasons, especially when one reads "The People." No matter. The poems, like those of Catullus or Propertius or Wordsworth (in his Lucy poems), hold up in their own right. One can hardly doubt their confessional immediacy, but it serves as an affective energy within the sequence rather than as autobiographical documentation.

The most obvious unifying element in what we may call the "Memory" sequence is that it consists of an unusual group of love poems. They are not the familiar expressions of present rapture or anticipation or painful uncertainty or desire. Rather, their character is best indicated by the titles "Memory," "Broken Dreams," and "His Phoenix"—the last because the sequence fixes on the persistent domination of the poet's sensibility and imagination by his lost beloved's ineradicable impress. She is "his phoenix" in that their once-close relationship—whatever its literal nature—has been destroyed and yet she constantly rises from its ashes as a commanding presence in the poet's emotional life. Her power is seen first in the simple and unforgettable physical image, in "Memory," of the hollow the moun-

Maud Gonne (photograph c. 1900)

tain hare has left in the mountain grass. This image—although we meet it only once, and it is replaced in later "Memory" poems by the "phoenix" metaphor—remains the key symbol of reference of the entire sequence. It is mirrored in the more explicitly personal language of the penultimate poem, "A Deep-sworn Vow," and of the closing "Presences," which adds dimensions of supernatural awe and terror. But, meanwhile, the reach of the beloved's remembered force has, in successive poems, directed the poet toward unexpected moral and political insights. And simultaneously, the sequence has also been playing with varied thoughts about her—a lover's thoughts, sometimes worshipful, sometimes lighthearted, sometimes critical— as if indeed the relationship were an actual ongoing reality. The pathos implicit in such dreaming gives these poems an elegiac cast, while the larger effect is of a self-created world of quickened arousal rooted in a past that refuses to disappear.

For the duration of these eight poems, we are totally within that world. It is interesting that they are preceded by "The Hawk," a poem of self-reproach in which the poet reminds himself how easily the "hawk of [his] mind" loses its self-possession. This sharp stab of humility clears the way for the poems of submission to a nobler, tutelary spirit. Similarly, the sequence is followed by "The Balloon of the Mind," which pulls the volume back into its previous orbit after immersion in a haunted realm of unrequited love and its unexpected permutations. The "Memory" sequence is, vividly, an anticipatory reply to the question Yeats was later to raise in "The Tower": "Does the imagination dwell the most / Upon a woman won or woman lost?"

"Memory," a six-line masterpiece of imagist resonance, sets the emotional pitch at the start. It begins in cavalier fashion, its tone that of a man totally free of romantic enslavement:

> One had a lovely face,
> And two or three had charm,
> But charm and face were in vain . . .

And then it swerves wrenchingly into an image, at once delicate and earthy, of irrevocable possession by one being of another:

> Because the mountain grass
> Cannot but keep the form
> Where the mountain hare has lain.

Because it is called "Memory," and because the mountain hare is no longer lying in the mountain grass, the poem expresses loss as well as undying subjection to a stronger personality and its sexual force. The initial language of shallow, indifferent gallantry is thrust away by the ungenteel image of animal physicality. The sensual turn at the end seems all the more graphic because of the reversed sexual roles that the image implies. The unrelenting enjambment, too, presses the excitement of that turn urgently.

This tiny poem of direct yet complex impact is quickly followed by "Her Praise," whose opening line—"She is foremost of those that I would hear praised"—becomes its refrain although it is repeated only once. (In retrospect it seems tinged with plaintive obsessiveness.) The word "praise" recurs three more times, the last time at the very end. The human situation is both homely and touching: a lover's desire to speak his beloved's name and introduce it into all conversation. Whereas "Memory" has the form of pure song and the impact of an arrow shot from a crossbow, "Her Praise" is more openly confessional, a confiding, unfolding, musing incantation. Its language is restless, impatient:

> I have gone about the house, gone up and down,
> As a man does who has published a new book,
> Or a young girl dressed out in her new gown . . .

This tone is not *passionate*—not exactly. What it conveys, in context, is a confusion of excited feeling rather than helpless enthrallment. At the end, the poem takes on an aura of almost commemorative adoration, preparing us for the brilliant turn in the next poem,

"The People." The "mountain hare" of "Memory" has left its imper-
ishable emotional imprint, but now we see how much more was
involved than the comparative tameness of other loves:

> I will talk no more of books or the long war
> But walk by the dry thorn until I have found
> Some beggar sheltering from the wind, and there
> Manage the talk until her name comes round.
> If there be rags enough he will know her name
> And be well pleased remembering it, for in the old days,
> Though she had young men's praise and old men's blame,
> Among the poor both old and young gave her praise.

Once again, energetically sustained enjambment helps press
home a striking emotional recognition: in this instance, of a woman's
engulfing compassion. The insight carries the poem's celebratory
momentum into something like attribution of divine grace. An irresistible surge of illumination, transcending private concerns, has reoriented the poem. The lover's restless excitement at the beginning,
and his need to praise his beloved everywhere, are still present, but a
whole new world of social bearing now encompasses them. The
long, loosely four- or five-stress lines and the intricately reflexive
rhyme scheme allow room for the somewhat complex development of
this poem. Yet ultimately it depends on the same kind of torque in its
second half that we find in the much shorter "Memory"; and by the
end almost inevitably, its focus is on "remembering."

The third poem, "The People," is just over twice the length of
the eighteen-line "Her Praise." My first chapter has already com-
mented on this poem in some detail, though not on its place in the
"Memory" sequence. There it was compared with the earlier poems
"Ephemera" and "Adam's Curse" because all three pieces give dialogue a major role in their lyrical structure. In addition, "Adam's
Curse" and "The People" share other vital characteristics. Each begins with the poet's vehement protest against public ingratitude,
involves a beautiful woman's rejoinder, and ends with a startlingly
intimate shift of feeling.

But here we must stress an important difference, related to the special turn "The People" gives to the "Memory" sequence. In writing it, Yeats avoided anything like the lovely, fragile, 'ninetyish desolation of "Adam's Curse." Instead, he chose a language of serious argument, in which the woman called "my phoenix" speaks with stern though unpretentious authority. The poet has started the dialogue by voicing his not altogether-noble resentment against the people:

> "What have I earned for all that work," I said,
> "For all that I have done at my own charge?
> The daily spite of this unmannerly town . . ."

Instead of showing sympathy, "my phoenix" speaks of her own bitter experience but refuses to blame the whole "unmannerly town." She has suffered more aggressive persecution than the poet from "the drunkards, pilferers of public funds, / All the dishonest crowd" of officials and exploiters; but her revolutionary faith in the people—despite their having been manipulated into thinking her an enemy—is unshakable:

> Yet never have I, now or any time
> Complained of the people.

Her staunchness leads the poet to defend himself. "You," he tells her, "have not lived in thought but deed" and therefore "have the purity of a natural force." He, on the other hand, *does* live in thought, and must put what "the eye" of his "analytic mind" sees into words. But this reply is to no avail; she has compelled him to face his own self-indulgence and unconscious pettiness, reflected in the cash metaphors of the poem's opening question: "What have I earned" and "at my own charge." In the poem's closing lines, he confesses that, even before he attempted his self-justifying explanation, he had yielded inwardly to the preternatural moral authority of "his phoenix": a "natural force" like that of the mountain hare in "Memory."

Its position in the buried sequence helps "The People" build on the preceding poems. "Memory" gave an ardent, warmblooded anchorage to the idealizing of the beloved. "Her Praise," in turn, revealed the particular luster of her bountiful spirit. Thus, we were prepared for her steadfast refusal, in "The People," to demean her faith in the poor and oppressed by "complaining" of their ingratitude. Her power to dominate is by now a moral force even more, perhaps, than an erotic one. Suddenly we have the extraordinary experience of seeing the poet forced, by a pang of simple shame, off his high horse of intellectual and aristocratic distance:

> And yet, because my heart leaped at her words,
> I was abashed, and now they come to mind
> After nine years, I sink my head abashed.

Without pressing any theoretical assumption, one can see that this poem presents a magnificent instance of artistic self-transcendence. That is, the associative process has brought the poet to a point beyond his ordinary expressed attitudes: a point of humble recognition of psychological self-deception and irrefutable human realities. The sequence has reached a climax of introspective discovery. It has moved quickly from its original metaphor of passionate obsession, centered on an enduring private emotional state, through a shift of attention to the goddess-like beloved and her rebuke of his attitude toward the people, and then back to the private self, now vulnerable and "abashed" at the core of its pride.

The ending of "The People" reminds us, too, of the double time-stream of the poems. The climactic moment described took place in the past, and the sequence derives much power from its refusal to relinquish the immediacy of what once happened. Therefore the affective coloration of the sequence depends on its vibrant sense of repossessing the past, with its lost possibilities, in the *present* volatile circumstance. Memory here is the return of experience as it was, though necessarily with an added, elegiac dimension. To repeat the preceding quotation:

And yet, because my heart leaped at her words,
I was abashed, and now they come to mind
After nine years, I sink my head abashed.

But this is a true poetic sequence, with the organic structure
of a lyric poem writ large. It must needs break away from this moment of transfixed, remorseful acknowledgment and go on to other
modes of celebrating "her" authority. The next poem, "His Phoenix," does so with a vengeance. A piece of deliberate buffoonery
verging on doggerel, it dances to a rollicking ballad rhythm and a
cleverly overlapping rhyme scheme capped by the refrain: "I knew a
phoenix in my youth, so let them have their day." Yet within this
happy, vaudevillian, drinking-song frame it rings many emotional
changes—something the refrain itself, with its mixed nostalgia and
jollity, would suggest. The range of reference, too, is sophisticated
from the start despite the colloquial air, so that the effect (though
certainly not the meter) somewhat resembles that of Byron's *Don
Juan:*

There is a queen in China, or maybe it's in Spain,
And birthdays and holidays such praises can be heard
Of her unblemished lineaments, a whiteness with no stain,
That she might be that sprightly girl trodden by a bird;
And there's a score of duchesses, surpassing womankind,
Or who have found a painter to make them so for pay
And smooth out stain and blemish with the elegance of his mind:
I knew a phoenix in my youth, so let them have their day.

"His Phoenix" is, after its fashion, a ballad of fair women of every
sort: grand ladies, dancers, actresses, and beauties "who live in pri-
vacy." The "phoenix" of the refrain might seem to have been but one
love among the many—apart, of course, from the word's not incon-
siderable mythical resonance—until the final stanza. There, however, the poem turns from its free and easy gaiety and exalts one
woman's unique glory when she was young. An added sharp turn

comes in the stanza's closing lines, which swing the mood back into
the nostalgic exaltation of the previous poems:

> There'll be that crowd, that barbarous crowd, through all
>   the centuries,
> And who can say but some young belle may walk and talk
>   men wild
> Who is my beauty's equal, though that my heart denies,
> But not the exact likeness, the simplicity of a child,
> And that proud look as though she had gazed into the
>   burning sun,
> And all the shapely body no tittle gone astray.
> I mourn for that most lonely thing, and yet God's will be
>   done:
> I knew a phoenix in my youth, so let them have their day.

These final lines recall both a real person and a vision. The next
poem, "A Thought from Propertius," intensifies both aspects. "That
most lonely thing" has become a goddess, the worthy companion of
wise Athena; at the same time, her sensual magnetism surrounds her
like an aureole. In this one poem, she alone holds the stage:

> She might, so noble from head
> To great shapely knees
> The long flowing line,
> Have walked to the altar
> Through the holy images
> At Pallas Athena's side,
> Or been fit spoil for a centaur
> Drunk with the unmixed wine.

In this single, lapidary poetic sentence, with its careful rhythmic
balances and almost secret off-rhyming ($abcdb'a'd'c$), the tangible
sexuality of "Memory" and the supernatural aura evoked in "Her
Praise" and "The People" come together as they might in some
marvelous piece of Grecian sculpture. The whole poem exists as an
image of pure pagan divinity, whose true life would have come into

its own in some ancient world of mythical earthiness. Its shining isolation is enhanced by its placement between the largely boisterous "His Phoenix" and the touching, normally human "Broken Dreams." In the latter poem, the lover addresses his lost beloved directly for the first time, as older man to older woman:

> There is grey in your hair.
> Young men no longer suddenly catch their breath
> When you are passing . . .

He even makes free to favor her with a denial of her perfection:

> You are more beautiful than anyone,
> And yet your body had a flaw:
> Your small hands were not beautiful . . .

In lines like these, she is for the first time brought into the ranks of ordinary mortal women and made more believable thereby. In this poem, too, memory itself is for one poetic instant reduced to average proportions:

> Your beauty can but leave among us
> Vague memories, nothing but memories.

All this plain realism humanizes and makes familiar the image of the beloved. Yet its function in "Broken Dreams" is to prepare us for a counter-assertion of hair-raising poignancy, one that brings into the foreground of the sequence the anguish that has been lurking offstage all the while. The deeper music of this exquisitely articulated poem is that of the grieving mind's passion to defeat fatality itself by the sheer strength of its desire. Hence its insistence on renewing the past from the altered standpoint of the dream-driven present. The counter-assertion:

> Vague memories, nothing but memories,
> But in the grave all, all, shall be renewed.

The certainty that I shall see that lady
Leaning or standing or walking
In the first loveliness of womanhood,
And with the fervour of my youthful eyes,
Has set me muttering like a fool.

The chilling force of this verse-unit, and the pathos of the lines
in the next unit that imagine her changing to a magically perfect
swan and losing her beloved "flaw," are correctives to any impression
of reconciliation to loss. The poet sizes himself up accurately. He is
not a lover who has triumphed through indomitable imagination, nor
is he one who has gone beyond the follies of romantic desire. Rather,
he is merely "the poet stubborn with his passion." At the end, as "the
last stroke of midnight dies," the mood dwindles into pathetic self-
dismissiveness: "From dream to dream and rhyme to rhyme I have
ranged / In rambling talk with an image of air."

Yet the sequence ends with two poems that reaffirm the inescapable power of that "image of air." The first, "A Deep-sworn Vow,"
begins in resentment: "Others because you did not keep / That deep-
sworn vow have been friends of mine." The lines are a quickening of
the gently critical, but not unfriendly, tone that sometimes enters the
preceding poem; and they echo, though in a drastically different
context, the angry opening of "The People." They are an accusation
and an apology, and they continue the humanizing direction of "Broken Dreams." Nevertheless, we are told, the image of the beloved
once more takes over as powerfully as ever when the conscious mind
lets down its guard. Whenever "I look death in the face" or "clamber
to the heights of sleep" or "grow excited with wine"—the poem
confesses—"suddenly I see your face."

The closing poem, "Presences," intensifies this new emphasis
on states of fierce psychic arousal, ending the sequence on a note of
awestruck bafflement and perturbation but still entranced by the
sexually charged mystery it has been coping with. The woman-
figure who has been in control all along has split, as in a dream, into

her three major aspects: sexual, innocently childlike, and regal or divine. She has taken many symbolic forms, all studying *him* (as the iconic faces study "the bestial floor" in "The Magi"—but for a different purpose) to find the ultimate meaning of his theme: "that monstrous thing / Returned and yet unrequited love."

The buried "Memory" sequence has its unique character, yet is very much a part of *The Wild Swans at Coole*. It has obvious affinities with poems like "On Woman" and "The Double Vision of Michael Robartes"; and "Solomon to Sheba" might well be called a happier alternative vision. Also, it provides an elegiac dimension different from the important literal elegies it accompanies. And there are other shared concerns elsewhere: weariness with oneself, changes of perspective in old age, the desire to recapture the feelings of "burning youth." Most of all, these poems at the heart of the book reveal the deeply subjective current of introspection underlying—and implicit in—the supposedly schematic "The Phases of the Moon" and related pieces.

It is interesting, in the context of this sequence, that the Cuala Press edition of *The Wild Swans at Coole* (1917) ended with *At the Hawk's Well*—a play, as we have seen, without dramatic resolution in the usual sense. Its competing emotional pressures interact very much as do those in the "Memory" group, though much less complexly and subjectively. In the play, the pressures are of two kinds. The first comes from the Old Man's helpless persistence in the face of total frustration, like that of "the poet stubborn with his passion" in "Broken Dreams." The second comes from the erotic turbulence suggested by the Guardian's dance and Cuchulain's irresistible attraction to Aoife (with no suggestion of its outcome, however). It was, in fact, in *At the Hawk's Well* that Yeats first projected aspects of his own struggles and relationships onto the Cuchulain figure he was creating. That projection, discussed in the preceding chapter, was even more in evidence in *The Only Jealousy of Emer* (completed in January 1918), which comes closer than any other play in the Cuchulain cycle to the emotional positioning of the "Memory" poems.

And in the very late and doom-obsessed *The Death of Cuchulain,* it recurs at least as poignantly.

At the Hawk's Well makes an appropriate close for the 1917 edition of *The Wild Swans at Coole,* not only because of its affinity with the "Memory" poems but also because it provides a strategic final fillip. The volume begins with a title poem that opens on a deceptively quiet note. Following the model of any number of meditative romantic poems, it starts by describing an enchanting natural scene with calm appreciation. For a moment the language is actually trite ("The trees are in their autumn beauty") and flat ("The woodland paths are dry"). Then the enchantment sets in, although the tone remains matter-of-fact:

> Under the October twilight the water
> Mirrors a still sky;
> Upon the brimming water among the stones
> Are nine-and-fifty swans.

Gradually, the pitch becomes more exciting and the emotion more personal. The second stanza culminates in the memory of the first time—nineteen years earlier—that the poet saw the swans "suddenly mount / And scatter wheeling in great broken rings / Upon their clamorous wings." The third, turning mournfully nostalgic, tells us his "heart is sore" and that "all's changed" for him sincethat first occasion. Then comes his envious description of the swans, giving them human and even divine attributes, in the climactic fourth stanza. By implied contrast, the description conveys his own bitter aftertaste of grief and disappointed love:

> Unwearied still, lover by lover,
> They paddle in the cold
> Companionable streams or climb the air;
> Their hearts have not grown old;
> Passion or conquest, wander where they will,
> Attend upon them still.

Yeats's full prosodic virtuosity is seen in this penultimate stanza. With no loss of rhythmic continuity, each line but the last manages to stress a separate aspect of the idealized swans' blissfully mated life. The poem's stanza-form (ballad-like in the first four lines, and then a rhymed pair of lines of uneven length: the first a sweeping five-stress movement, the second a tightened three-stress one) allows readily for sudden shifts in tempo and tone. Thereafter, the final stanza releases the poem, if a bit too patly, from its tangle of powerful feeling.

Thus, "The Wild Swans at Coole" serves as an overture to the elegiac music of high dreams and their inevitable frustration that dominates both the original edition and the expanded and reorganized one of 1919. The Cuala edition, though, has a far less complex overall structure. It moves from its emotionally contained yet almost explosive opening poem though three pieces of increasing melancholy that are later placed elsewhere. These are the ironically titled "Men Improve with the Years," the delicately rueful "The Collar-Bone of a Hare," and the poet's lament, called "Lines Written in Dejection," for his lost past of dangerous passions and visions. The next poem, "The Dawn," might be added to this group, because of its yearning to escape the burden of awareness through total impersonality:

> I would be ignorant as the dawn
> That merely stood, rocking the glittering coach
> Above the cloudy shoulders of the horses;
> I would be—for no knowledge is worth a straw—
> Ignorant and wanton as the dawn.

But desiring the freedom to be "ignorant and wanton" can obviously mean more than just wishing to shake off one's cares once and for all. It also implies cultivating whatever awakens our keenest sense of life, regardless of its moral bearing or whether or not it brings happiness. Exquisitely designed in its varied placement of rhyme and in its balanced weighting of line-lengths (the key to masterful "free verse"), "The Dawn" is from this standpoint a brilliant segue to the next two poems, "On Woman" and "The Fisherman," both of which explore its implications in unexpected ways.

The former of these pieces, the exuberant "On Woman," locates a crucial awakening in an unforgettable, tormented past love, anticipating the "Memory" sequence. It daringly converts that still unresolved anguish into a state of carefree liberation that actually relishes the painful memory. Indeed, the dearest hope the poem expresses at the end is to recover, in some later incarnation,

> what once I had
> And know what once I have known,
> Until I am driven mad,
> Sleep driven from my bed,
> By tenderness and care,
> Pity, an aching head,
> Gnashing of teeth, despair;
> And all because of one
> Perverse creature of chance,
> And live like Solomon
> That Sheba led a dance.

The poem's jaunty pattern of alternately rhyming trimeter in joined quatrains is broken only once, by the omission of a single expected line after "Until I am driven mad." This slight jolt catapults us into the piled-up catalogue of the specifics of being "driven mad" in the next four lines, while the poem delays completing the rhyme with "known" until its closing quatrain. All this prosodic play has a joyous bounce despite the language of love-suffering: a mixture whose sardonic overtones of romantic self-parody derive from a long tradition. (One should normally say the tradition goes back at least to the Roman lyric poets of the first century B.C., but Yeats ends his poem by gleefully pushing it back to the days of Solomon and Sheba. Do not consult the Bible to confirm his happy fantasy!)

Its mixture of strong, direct feeling and humorous self-irony is essential to the whole character of "On Woman." Neither aspect is excluded by the other, something essential to remember in reading the eight-line opening verse-unit. This passage is a mischievous, yet serious and compelling overture to the much longer unit that makes up the rest of the poem. It is an outburst of genuine enthusiasm whose central image is engagingly persuasive, suggesting as it does that harmonious physical love between the sexes has its counterpart in their psychological reciprocity:

> May God be praised for woman
> That gives up all her mind,
> A man may find in no man
> A friendship of her kind
> That covers all he has brought
> As with her flesh and bone,
> Nor quarrels with a thought
> Because it is not her own.

"Giving up all her mind" does not imply, as a too-hasty interpretation might claim, any denial of the value of independent intelligence in women. Rather, it is an erotic image of mutuality in all aspects of a relationship, comparable to lovers' "giving up" their bodies to one another. The mischievousness of Yeats's phrasing here lies in its momentary teasing of a banal conventional viewpoint. He creates the deliberately false impression, at first, that his poem "praises God" for making women naturally—or, at any rate, ideally—mindless and yielding. The impression is set up only to be corrected almost at once: first by the powerful simile of a friendship that actively "covers all he has brought / As with her flesh and bone"; and second, more explicitly, by the witty lines that start the second verse-unit:

> Though pedantry denies,
> It's plain the Bible means
> That Solomon grew wise
> While talking with his queens,
> Yet never could, although
> They say he counted grass,

> Count all the praises due
> When Sheba was his lass,
> When she the iron wrought, or
> When from the smithy fire
> It shuddered in the water . . .

So neither Solomon's many wives nor Sheba (when she taught him the art of forging iron—a double-entendre, to be sure) merely listened to him in passive adoration. Hardly! Nor, of course, did "my phoenix," who not only reigns over the poet's imagination in the "Memory" sequence and elsewhere, but also unhesitatingly "quarrels with a thought" of his in "The People." Yet all are singled out for praise in the course of this poem—at least if we assume that "my phoenix" must be the desired but maddening woman referred to in the closing lines, who has caused the poet so much "gnashing of teeth" and "despair" along with his "tenderness and care."

After the lines just mentioned come two passages of high intensity. The first, just four lines long, imagines the orgasmic "shudder" of Solomon and Sheba in language echoing the earlier image of the forged iron that "shuddered in the water." The second is the prayer the poem ends with—that "God grant me" once more, if only in some other existence, a passionate involvement with however "perverse" a "creature of chance." In this context, to be "ignorant and wanton as the dawn" is to yield oneself up—whether man or woman—to the impersonal working of a sexual principle that animates every aspect of our lives. The "Memory" sequence, shortly to follow, gains its freedom to acknowledge the power of Yeats's "phoenix" and yet distance it much in the same way.

The next piece, "The Fisherman," is a curious variant on the motif of "The Dawn." For a long time, the poet says, he has "looked in the face" the kind of poetry he had once planned to write "for my own race" and the kind of audience it must needs be written for. The poetry should be "cold and passionate as the dawn." In "The Dawn," Yeats expressed the desire to become "ignorant and wanton as the dawn." Here he is thinking of the altered quality of his art, at once astringently impersonal and highly charged, that would result if he could cast off intellectual and moral constraint and turn his thoughts away from the social forces that torment them. The fit audience for such a poetry would be "wise and simple," not hyper-sophisticated or corruptly self-seeking like "the living men that I hate": the "craven," "insolent," and cynically "witty" persons in power under whose reign the country has seen "the beating down of the wise / And great Art beaten down."

The ideal representative audience the poem summons up is a figure so self-contained and unpretentious, so much perhaps the author's anti-self, that he is "a man who does not exist, / A man who is but a dream." The poet imagines him in his

> grey Connemara cloth,
> Climbing up to a place
> Where stone is dark under froth,
> And the down-turn of his wrist
> When the flies drop in the stream.

Apart from its dream of a genuine poetry written for such a man (whether or not he ever would read it), "The Fisherman" echoes earlier complaints against the philistine enemies of free art and thought and anticipates the beautiful exchange in "The People." It thus, in its own fashion—though without any allusions to love's entanglements—also helps ready the way for the "Memory" sequence.

That sequence, enclosed between the self-depreciating transitional poems "The Hawk" and "The Balloon of the Mind," now follows. As has already been suggested, it forms the rich center of both editions of *The Wild Swans at Coole*. But it does so more clearly in the shorter 1917 edition whose structure we have so far been following. The poems succeeding it in that edition turn away from its specific preoccupations, which re-enter the book only obliquely— but to great effect nevertheless—in *At the Hawk's Well*.

The main poems in that final group are "Upon a Dying Lady" (a seven-part sequence written during a friend's unsuccessful struggle against cancer) and "Ego Dominus Tuus." The volume has another elegy, "In Memory"—called in later editions "In Memory of Alfred Pollexfen"—written dutifully to honor Yeats's maternal grandfather but surprisingly flat and undistinguished. So much of the book, however, has been *self*-elegiac in its drift of feeling that even this piece helps bring other human worlds into view. But it is "Upon a Dying Lady," with its attention to the physical suffering and imminent death of another person, the actress Mabel Wright (sister of Aubrey Beardsley), that adds the specific dimension of compassion to the volume.

The short pieces that make it up, written at various intervals during her illness, are uneven in quality. One of them, "Her Race," shows Yeats's social attitudes close to their worst and his art not far behind in a passage intended to show her natural superiority:

> She knows herself a woman,
> No red and white of a face,
> Or rank, raised from a common
> Unreckonable race . . .

Another, "Her Courage," places her with Nietzschean grandiosity among figures of heroic legend (Grania and Achilles among them) "who have lived in joy and laughed into the face of Death." The five remaining pieces, though, are moving in their gentle, grieving concern and in a certain appealing quietness of tone.

On the whole, individual lines in "Upon a Dying Lady" tend to stand out more memorably than whole poems. The restrained yet graphic first lines of "Her Courtesy" start off the sequence at just the appropriate pitch: "With the old kindness, the old distinguished grace, / She lies, her lovely piteous face amid dull red hair." Sometimes the feeling is paternal, as in "The End of Day": "She is playing like a child / And penance is the play." Only once does a harsh ferocity come through—in the poem "She Turns the Dolls' Faces to the Wall," which expresses anger on her behalf. Her friends, knowing how much she loves beautiful and exotic dolls, have brought her some as gifts—but the hospital authorities keep her from enjoying them at once:

> Because to-day is some religious festival
> They had a priest say Mass, and even the Japanese,
> Heel up and weight on toe, must face the wall . . .

and later, at the end of the same poem:

> Because the priest must have like every dog his day
> Or keep us all awake with baying at the moon,
> We and our dolls being but the world were best away.

But the final piece, "Her Friends Bring Her a Christmas Tree," puts aside any anger. It brings the sequence to a close on a touchingly buoyant note of gallantry, both humane and curiously detached: an appeal to Death to forgive her friends' frivolity at such a time. "Pardon, great enemy," it splendidly begins, explaining that they have decorated the tree with "pretty things" to please her "fantastic head" when she sees them from her bed. Therefore, it pleads,

> Give her a little grace,
> What if a laughing eye
> Have looked into your face?
> It is about to die.

It is probably too obvious a comment to observe that the compassionate solicitude of "Upon a Dying Lady" deepens the mournful shading of much of the Cuala edition by coming so close to literal elegy. The "lady" is "about to die"; and Death, personified, is a tangible presence who perhaps frowns on her playfulness under his awesome gaze. One might almost insert Poe's powerful line, "Death looks gigantically down," into this poem, which in fact has its faint links with an obsession of Poe's: namely, that the death of a beautiful woman is the most moving of poetic themes. But of course Yeats's dying lady, like his phoenix, is neither a poor, lorn, lovely Lenore nor a demonically possessive Ligeia whose fierce will outlives her body. She is a gifted person who counts in the real world of artists and spirited companions who are her peers.

In any case, the modulation from the dominant tone of the "Memory" sequence and surrounding poems to that of "Upon a Dying Lady" is subtle and most interesting: from one kind of admiring tribute to such a person, shot through with a profound romantic sadness at having lost her love irrevocably, to another in the more immediately wrenching circumstance of a friend's onrushing death.

Most of "Ego Dominus Tuus," the next poem in the 1917 volume, stands in sharp contrast to the intensely emotional lyrical writing it follows. Its analytical character anticipates that of two more brilliant poems added in the 1919 edition: "The Phases of the Moon," inserted directly after it, and "The Double Vision of Michael Robartes," now the closing poem. Taken together, the three poems create a strong counterpoise to the intimate subjectivity of the sequences. (*At the Hawk's Well,* as a play centered on its own characters and action rather than on its author's private feelings, had a similar distancing function in the earlier edition. But once he had bolstered "Ego Dominus Tuus" with the two added poems, Yeats dropped the play from *The Wild Swans at Coole.*)

In essence, the relatively low-key "Ego Dominus Tuus" is what we may call a "program poem." Its discursive blank verse has its weaknesses, but Yeats used it almost as a prose exploration of the competing yet interlocked aspirations driving his art. Seeking to objectify what he was doing, he couched the poem as a friendly argument between two alternative poetic selves called, somewhat absurdly, "*Hic*" and "*Ille*" (Latin for "This One" and "That One"). *Hic* aims only to ferret out secrets of his own inner being. *Ille,* on the other hand, yearns to connect with the supernatural and everything we feel must be unknowable:

> By the help of an image
> I call to my own opposite, summon all
> That I have handled least, least looked upon.

Hic's models of poetry of the self are the works of Dante and Keats. Dante "made that hollow face of his / More plain to the mind's eye than any face / But that of Christ." And "No one denies to Keats love of the world; / Remember his deliberate happiness." But *Ille,* who is given the better of the argument, sees these supposed self-revelations by Dante and Keats as images of what they longed to be, not what they were. When *Hic* declares that "I would find myself and not an image," *Ille* responds with an intellectually telling—if stylistically clumsy—critique of the current state of art in general:

> That is our modern hope, and by its light
> We have lit upon the gentle, sensitive mind
> And lost the old nonchalance of the hand;
> Whether we have chosen chisel, pen, or brush,
> We are but critics, or but half create,
> Timid, entangled, empty and abashed,
> Lacking the countenance of our friends . . .

Since *Ille* says "our" and "we" in this passage, Yeats clearly includes some tendencies of his own in the indictment. *Ille,* who has the last word, speaks for him in pointing the way toward an art neither indifferent to the inner realities of "myself" nor confined to the limits of any one sensibility. This concept, at once linking and transcending the supposedly opposed positions, fascinated Yeats and animates a number of his most vital poems. Even more important, *Ille*'s closing speech has the authority of a high lyric charge beyond anything else in the poem. Mainly by being full-bodied poetry rather than prosaic verse, its tremulous evocation of a desired state of transport and awe overwhelms the mere good sense of what *Hic* has to say:

> I call to the mysterious one who yet
> Shall walk the wet sands by the edge of the stream
> And look most like me, being indeed my double,
> And prove of all imaginable things
> The most unlike, being my anti-self,
> And, standing by these characters, disclose

All that I seek; and whisper it as though
He were afraid the birds, who cry aloud
Their momentary cries before it is dawn,
Would carry it away to blasphemous men.

The "characters" *Ille* speaks of here are cabalistic "magical shapes" he has traced in the sand. He is "enthralled," as *Hic* has put it, by "the unconquerable delusion" that there are mystical secrets they may help him discover—in this instance by magnetically attracting a visionary "anti-self" who will convey the secrets to him. *Hic*'s use of the word "delusion" reflects the sceptical side of Yeats. But *Ille*'s dream of self-transcendence (at least through *imagining* such revelation) nevertheless dominates the poem and carries the greater weight. It has the "mastery," in the sense of the poem's title, which of course means "I, Thy Master."

Yeats added one final poem after "Ego Dominus Tuus" in the 1917 volume. The short, sardonic "The Scholars" mocks the "old, learned, respectable, bald" pedants, "forgetful of their sins," who "edit and annotate" the passionate, unruly poets they would be shocked ever to meet in the flesh: "Lord, what would they say / Did their Catullus walk that way?" The little squib, a reminder that its author was a volatile poet and not primarily a theorist, served as a buffer between his poems and *At The Hawk's Well*. Yeats moved it elsewhere in later editions.

The 1919 *The Wild Swans at Coole* buttresses and also complicates the book's original structure in two ways especially. First, it adds three poems—"In Memory of Major Robert Gregory," "An Irish Airman Foresees His Death," and "Shepherd and Goatherd"—all of which center on the death of Lady Gregory's son in the Great War. The first two of these now directly follow the title poem, and the third is saved for another added group a bit further along. One result is to underscore the volume's elegiac burden and therefore, also, to prepare the way for "Upon a Dying Lady." Another is to give particular emphasis to the image of Gregory as an ideal, almost deified figure rooted in Coole, where he was born. The title poem has already established the profound importance of Coole in the poet's emotional life—so that Gregory, like the fantasy-born hero of "The Fisherman," may serve as one model of an "anti-self": an image of the kind of man Yeats might have become, had his karma not confined him to what he called his "sedentary trade." But the Gregory poems' reinforcement of the elegiac element in *The Wild Swans at Coole* is their most important contribution to the volume.

Similarly, the new edition adds a number of poems at the end that strengthen the turn introduced by "Ego Dominus Tuus." Chief among these are two already mentioned: "The Phases of the Moon" and "The Double Vision of Michael Robartes."

Yeats invented the characters Michael Robartes and Owen Aherne in three stories he published in 1897: "Rosa Alchemica," "The Tables of the Law," and "The Adoration of the Magi"—all included in the posthumous prose collection *Mythologies* (1959). He conceived of the two men as carriers of mystical and revealed knowledge, and their names, that of Robartes especially, recur in his work in a context of such lore. In "Ego Dominus Tuus," for instance, *Hic* observes that *Ille* has been studying a book "that Michael Robartes left." And in "The Phases of the Moon," they turn up again near Yeats's tower one dark night and see from the light in his window that he—like *Ille*—must be toiling to find "in book or manuscript / What he shall never find."

Thereupon they conduct a wondrous dialogue, gleefully gloating over the "truths" they know but will not pass on to him. The reason they will not do so, says Robartes, is because, in those early stories,

> He wrote of me in that extravagant style
> He had learnt from Pater, and to round his tale
> Said I was dead; and dead I choose to be.

Yeats had found a way to unfold, in a poem that mixed witty, chillingly strange, and surreal effects, the basic scheme he would publish in 1925 as *A Vision*. That book—fundamentally serious but occasionally whimsical—uses the twenty-eight phases of the moon to symbolize the stages of cosmic, human, and individual history. The poem offers a highly condensed version, focusing on the stages of a single human life, but avoids bogging down in prosaic dullness.

For one thing, there are the poem's eerie setting and the absurd yet poignant dramatic situation already described: that of the poet in his lonely tower striving to discover what Robartes and Aherne, his own creations, know but will not disclose to him. The ironies here are delightfully many, given that the information they mockingly rehearse beyond his hearing is after all of his own making—although we have to step out of the poem to offer this obvious comment—just as these characters themselves are.

Everything in "The Phases of the Moon," including its handling of blank verse, is more alive and compelling than the writing in "Ego Dominus Tuus." One reason is the folk-story atmosphere, epitomized at the start by the way the two old, travel-worn phantasmal mockers are introduced and at the end by the shivery image of a bat that circled around Aherne "with its squeaky cry" as "the light in the tower window was put out." Another is the humorously conceived malice of the pair toward their creator. But most important are the lyrical purity and volatility of Robartes' exposition of the mysteries imaged in the moon's successive changes, while Aherne contributes to the dynamic shifts by urging him on, asking transitional questions, and adding his own vivid responses.

The exposition itself, then, while lyrical moment by moment, is also a dialogue and a story: an account of the progress of the human psyche from birth to death. Aherne calls it a "song" and gets Robartes going by appealing to him to

> Sing me the changes of the moon once more;
> True song, though speech: "mine author sung it me."

And Robartes begins, in the grave beat of a sacred text:

Twenty-and-eight the phases of the moon,
The full and the moon's dark and all the crescents,
Twenty-and-eight, and yet but six-and-twenty
The cradles that a man must needs be rocked in:
For there's no human life at the full or the dark.

His "song" reaches its mystical height in its imagery of life "at the full." In this phase, Robartes says, one's will and imagination are so powerfully ascendant they transform external reality into a reflection of themselves. "All thought becomes an image and the soul / Becomes a body," and the self becomes an entranced, specter-like being isolated from the changes of ordinary life:

When the moon's full those creatures of the full
Are met on the waste hills by countrymen
Who shudder and hurry by: body and soul
Estranged amid the strangeness of themselves,
Caught up in contemplation, the mind's eye
Fixed on images that once were thought;
For separate, perfect, and immovable
Images can break the solitude
Of lovely, satisfied, indifferent eyes.

And thereupon with aged, high-pitched voice
Aherne laughed, thinking of the man within,
His sleepless candle and laborious pen.

The moments of Aherne's happy laughter at the thought of the poet's ignorance are among the various leavening effects in the poem. So are the two revenants' serious yet exuberant exchanges concerning love, beauty, and the physically self-transforming effects of suffering and desire. "The Phases of the Moon" reaches a special kind of exaltation, similar to that of *Ille*'s final speech in "Ego Dominus Tuus" but more fully realized. Although so different in character from the earlier poems in the book, these pieces and the others at the end of the 1919 volume share with them an elusive turn of perspective. The sequences, and poems like "On Woman," win through to a certain freedom—and sometimes, even, a touch of joy—by recalling emotional pain and turmoil and, in retrospect, finding a way toward acceptance of the irrevocable. "The Phases of the Moon" and the pieces around it continue the liberating process by seeing the heights and depths of our individual experience as merely incidental to an impersonal, unending cycle of universal change. Thus, in the whimsically charming yet touching "The Cat and the Moon," the nocturnal "dance" of the "troubled" animal and the "spinning" heavenly body ("the pure cold light in the sky") symbolizes humanity's subjection to cosmic forces beyond our ken.

The relation of all this to the book's structure is simple enough. Throughout the earlier part, the poet had dealt with the nearly unbearable realities of tragic death and drastic disappointment in love, and at a certain point he needed to detach himself without denying those realities. The gently comic irony of "Two Songs of a Fool," for instance, shows one way Yeats found to do so. The simple Fool frets over his "great responsibilities," described in his first song as "a speckled cat and a tame hare," both of whom "look up to me alone / For learning and defence / As I look up to Providence." His constant fear has been that the hare would escape and be "found / By the horn's sweet note and the tooth of the hound." Alas, in the second song the worst has happened; he has forgotten to shut the door and the hare is gone. Our pathetic inability to know or control reality could not be conveyed more lightly yet genuinely. The hare is not "tame" and the fool has no mastery. Inevitably, they evoke the mountain hare and the lover in "Memory."

The closing poem of *The Wild Swans at Coole* is a far grimmer affair. "The Double Vision of Michael Robartes" says nothing about Yeats's personal relationships, or about particular, cherished people of the kind his elegies mourn and celebrate. Nevertheless, in the guise of an allegorical monologue by Michael Robartes, it is one of the poems ("The Phases of the Moon" is another) that Yeats said presented "my philosophy of life and death." This three-sectioned poem begins in dark despair at the mechanical forces, "cold spirits" with "blank eyes" and "wire-jointed jaws and limbs of wood," which determine our destinies without reference to what we ourselves might choose to be. Robartes associates his nightmare image with the dark of the moon: the phase that symbolizes the obliteration by death of human will and personality and the total triumph of those "abstract" powers. This is the first part of Robartes' "double vision."

The next section adds a second vision in the same place—"the grey rock of Cashel," that evocative site of an ancient Irish kingdom. This time what Robartes sees happens at the full of the moon, when human will and personality are in the ascendancy, as in the passage just quoted from "The Phases of the Moon." It is a vision of a girl dancing between a "Sphinx" and a "Buddha." At first the phrasing suggests statuary, but soon these two figures seem alive despite their entranced stillness. The poem describes their reciprocal symbolism, the one embodying pure contemplation and knowledge, the other the troubled realm of love and feeling reflected in so many of the preceding poems:

> One lashed her tail; her eyes lit by the moon
> Gazed upon all things known, all things unknown,
> In triumph of intellect
> With motionless head erect.

> That other's moonlit eyeballs never moved,
> Being fixed on all things loved, all things unloved,
> Yet little peace he had,
> For those that love are sad.

The dancer between them, meanwhile, is an image of art in action, in one sense a fusion of thought and feeling, in another beyond both by virtue of that very fusion. Together, the three embody human triumph over death and time, despite the way the poem emphasizes—partly in acknowledgment of the horror engraved by the first vision—the fact that all three are "dead." As the section's closing stanza puts it:

> In contemplation had those three so wrought
> Upon a moment, and so stretched it out
> That they, time overthrown,
> Were dead, yet flesh and bone.

The poem's first two sections, balancing these opposed visions without indulging in easy sentimentality, have the stateliness of revelatory awe and of the restraint of powerful emotions. The third section, by contrast, releases its feeling in an outburst of recognition. The dancer, Robartes realizes, is not only an image of self-absorbed art but also a girl he has known in dreams but never before remembered. She is an elusive, havoc-causing figure of reverie and desire, like Helen of Troy, "who never gave the burning town a thought." Here of course we are very close to Yeats's "phoenix" and the intensities of the "Memory" poems, and the carefully constructed, relatively impersonal final section of the volume is suddenly in danger of being drawn back into the maelstrom of personal passion:

> To such a pitch of folly I am brought,
> Being caught between the pull
> Of the dark moon and the full . . .

The poem catches itself in time, however, and pursues its confessional impulse no farther. Yeats's preparation for the next great turn in his work was now almost complete. The brief *Michael Robartes and the Dancer* (1921)—fifteen poems in all—was, as its title might suggest, his vehicle of transition.

A rather arch but sexually charged dialogue in the title poem of the new book introduces the transition. It connects especially with Part III of "The Double Vision of Michael Robartes." Even the earlier parts of that poem have their obvious physical and sensual side: the dark sense of mechanical forces our wills cannot control, the awesome but humanly conceived Sphinx with her "woman breast and lion paw," and the Buddha totally immersed in love and its absence. But Robartes' passionate frenzy when he remembers his erotic dream-life centered on the dancing girl is the strongest link to "Michael Robartes and the Dancer."

In this new poem, an older man and a young woman still at school—*He* and *She*—have been discussing an altar piece in which a knight is shown slaying a dragon to save a lady. The man seizes the opportunity to arouse the girl's awareness of her own desires by interpreting the painting allegorically. The dragon the knight attacks, he says, is the lady's "thought"—that is, her idea of virtue, which prevents her yielding to the knight. Lovely women, the girl must learn, should find in what their mirrors show them the key to the sexual joy that makes everything worthwhile. He presses the argument by praising her bodily beauty—"that beating breast,/ That vigorous thigh, that dreaming eye"—and then citing the paintings of Michelangelo and Veronese as "proof / That all must come to sight and touch." He even makes subtle theological points to support his seductive aim. But *She* pretends not to understand. "My wretched dragon is perplexed," she replies at one point. And at the end she dismisses the whole subject: "They say such different things at school." The dialogue, with its comedy-of-manners ring, is partly a self-parodying echo of the speaker's vain dream-pursuit of the dancer in "The Double Vision of Michael Robartes."

The title poem, although its bearing is significant enough, is only an overture to the poems on love that are to come: the boisterous "Solomon and the Witch" and the painful "An Image from a Past Life" and "Towards Break of Day." The first of these completes the series of three poems that began in *The Wild Swans at Coole* with "Solomon to Sheba" and "On Woman." In the new piece Sheba is still instructing Solomon in the glorious reciprocities of passion, and these two—the wisest of mortals—still find a perfect fusion of knowledge and ecstasy at the height of their orgiastic union. But the pitch of their shared feeling and wild release in this poem surpasses even its very taking predecessors.

"Solomon and the Witch" is yet another dialogue, written in the same alternately rhyming four-stress pattern as "Michael Robartes and the Dancer." But it is far more free-wheeling than that intriguing

but intellectually overloaded poem. Every turn in the biblical lovers'
exchange sparkles and crackles. Sheba speaks first. She has a mystery to report, and at the same time her language is simple and
ardent:

> And thus declared that Arab lady:
> "Last night, where under the wild moon
> On grassy mattress I had laid me,
> Within my arms great Solomon,
> I suddenly cried out in a strange tongue
> Not his, not mine."

Solomon's response is introduced with a joyous spontaneity:

> Who understood,
> Whatever has been said, sighed, sung,
> Howled, miau-d, barked, brayed, belled, yelled, cried, crowed,
> Thereon replied . . .

What the great polylinguist of animal as well as human utterance "thereon replied" must pale beside this alliterative and inter-
nally rhyming catalogue of his range of knowledge. Still, his fanciful
answer, with its happy, punning play of wit, its improvised fable, and
its unexpectedly dark thoughts on love, justifies his reputation for
wisdom. So does his gratefulness, at the end of this speech, that "a
blessed moon last night / Gave Sheba to her Solomon." He begins
with the fable, concocted to explain her sudden outcry "in a strange
tongue" while he held her in his arms:

> "A cockerel
> Crew from a blossoming apple bough
> Three hundred years before the Fall,
> And never crew again till now,
> And would not now but that he thought,
> Chance being at one with Choice at last,
> All that the brigand apple brought

And this foul world were dead at last.
He that crowed out eternity
Thought to have crowed it in again."

One of Yeats's favorite jokes, often in work of serious bearing, was to parody theological authority and invent his own Apocrypha. A simple instance is the passage, in "On Woman," that tells us: "It's plain the Bible means / That Solomon grew wise / While talking with his queens." The tale of the cockerel and, in fact, the whole of "Solomon and the Witch" are pure Yeatsian Apocrypha of this sort. While he plays whimsically on the word "crowed" (the last in the catalogue of animal sounds we were told he understood), Solomon also identifies it with Sheba's outcry. He interprets the outcry as a new annunciation, in the form of a cockerel's crowing, arising from the pure sexual ecstasy of the night before. That ecstasy has meant humanity's repossession of Paradise, undoing the Fall foretold in the imaginary cockerel's first annunciation.

This fabling is only the first part of Solomon's speech. The concluding part, a single long sentence, drops whimsy entirely and picks up the thread of thought, introduced earlier on, concerning "Chance" and "Choice." But it does not lapse into philosophical abstractions. In this sentence, Solomon, like Michael Robartes and Cuchulain in other work, almost becomes an alternative persona for the poet. He speaks of the kind of emotional wretchedness reflected in Yeats's confessional love poetry and even of "despair" that the "bride-bed" can bring—a confessional hint foreshadowing two poems of marital unhappiness in this volume: "An Image from a Past Life" and "Towards Break of Day." The Yeats of the "Memory" sequence might well be speaking for a few bitter lines here, before turning his attention away from all that, when Solomon says of the cockerel's triumphant crowing that

> "though love has a spider's eye
> To find out some appropriate pain—
> Aye, though all passion's in the glance—
> For every nerve, and tests a lover

With cruelties of Choice and Chance;
And when at last that murder's over
Maybe the bride-bed brings despair,
For each an imagined image brings
And finds a real image there;
Yet the world ends when these two things,
Though several, are a single light,
When oil and wick are burned in one;
Therefore a blessed moon last night
Gave Sheba to her Solomon."

It is these lines that give the poem its depth. They dramatically set their ruthless "spider's eye" image of destructive love and ruinous marriage against the blazing counter-image of the "single light, / When oil and wick are burned in one," of blissful union. Some welcome comic relief follows—a bit of lovers' badinage whose easy facetiousness makes a gentle frame for the extraordinary passage just quoted. And then we have a final, dynamic leap into an atmosphere of pure enchantment and passion in Sheba's closing speech:

"The night has fallen; not a sound
In the forbidden sacred grove
Unless a petal hit the ground,
Nor any human sight within it
But the crushed grass where we have lain;
And the moon is wilder every minute.
O! Solomon! let us try again."

We need to thank the Solomon-and-Sheba poems, and this one in particular, for giving us the sweetest imaginative triumphs of love-fulfillment in all of Yeats's work. The two other poems of love and marriage in *Michael Robartes and the Dancer* are another matter entirely.

The first, "An Image from a Past Life," immediately follows "Solomon and the Witch." Once again, it is a dialogue, but this time between a modern man and wife and rooted in a difficult, ultimately impassable psychological barrier between them. And again we have the riddle of a strange cry that sets the dialogue going. This time it is a "scream" from outdoors that awakens the couple, who go to the window and look out. The husband, called *He,* sees only the starlit stream below and—because he has been "stirred" as never before—thinks the sound has come from some "terrified, invisible beast or bird: / Image of poignant recollection." The terrified wife, called *She,* says that she can see the image of another woman, a sweetheart of his "from another life," hovering out there above the water. *He* claims she only imagines the apparition, which she tries to hide from him by laying her hands over his eyes, and sets about comforting her and setting things right.

All this, of course, makes the "scream" very different from Sheba's primal cry of annunciation induced by the orgiastic delight of the two heroic, world-transforming figures Yeats kidnapped from a sacred text. A biographical reading might well take into account his wife's knowledge, from his writings and from common talk and from his own lips, of the poet's obsession with Maud Gonne—certainly an "image of poignant recollection" for him. Small wonder if anyone of either sex, under such circumstances, should sometimes feel "afraid / Of the hovering thing night brought me." The relevance to this poem of Solomon's comment that "maybe the bride-bed brings despair" seems clear enough.

But in the end the quality, and even the simple meaning, of the poem are nevertheless independent of these considerations. The poem's human interplay—tenderness, guilt, jealousy, fear, reassurance—is, despite individual differences, natural to love-experience. And the masterly lyrical movement, with its Poe-like evocation of a lost attachment that will not let go, has a haunting uneasiness. This effect is especially helped by the drawn-out opening lines, followed by the clustered rhyming in the short middle lines, of each stanza:

> *She.* A sweetheart from another life floats there
>   As though she had been forced to linger

From vague distress
Or arrogant loveliness,
Merely to loosen out a tress
Among the starry eddies of her hair
Upon the paleness of a finger.

"Towards Break of Day," though placed farther along in the volume, seems a sister piece to "An Image from a Past Life." Written in the first person, it is more immediately confessional in its impact although the poems reflect comparable marital sorrows. In "Towards Break of Day," husband and wife wake from dreams of frustration so reciprocal that the poet wonders whether they have not been sharing the same dream. In his, he has returned to a waterfall that, in his boyhood, gave him a "childish delight" much intensified since then in his memory:

I would have touched it like a child
But knew my finger could but have touched
Cold stone and water. I grew wild,
Even accusing Heaven because
It had set down among its laws:
Nothing that we love over-much
Is ponderable to our touch.

And as for his wife:

she that beside me lay
Had watched in bitterer sleep
The marvelous stag of Arthur,
That lofty white stag, leap
From mountain steep to steep,

These dreams, each imaging a fulfillment that is just out of reach, also deflate any ideal of perfect fulfillment. And in the intimate specific context of the poem, they clearly symbolize sexual disappointment. Rather than the joy of gratification, "cold stone and wa-

Georgiana Hyde-Leeds (Mrs. Yeats, c. 1917), photo by Brian Seed

ter" are all the husband can expect; and "the marvelous stag of Arthur" is even less attainable in the wife's "bitterer sleep."

Together with the "bridal-bed" lines in "Solomon and the
Witch," these two marriage poems record major shifts of sensibility
in the maturing Yeats. The poems still cope, as before, with the
defeat of marvelous hopes, and "An Image from a Past Life" has real
affinities with the "Memory" sequence. But Yeats had now fully
entered a world of middle-aged rather than youthful perplexities and
discoveries. The complex perspectives he felt pressed to deal with in
his poetry had increased in number over the years, especially after his
marriage to Georgie Hyde-Lees in 1917. Also, their collaborative
work leading to *A Vision* had made him acutely alert to the interaction of opposite personalities and states of feeling.

The passages of sheer rapture and lovers' teasing in "Solomon
and the Witch," alongside the darker thoughts in that poem, are an
instance. So, despite the sting of "poignant recollection" in one poem
and of unfulfillment in the other, are the sympathetic insights into the
wife's feelings in the marriage poems. And a simpler piece, "Under
Saturn," begins with the poet's apology to his wife, on one occasion,
for his "saturnine" demeanor that day. It is not, he explains a little
disingenuously, the result of "lost love, inseparable from my thought
/ Because I have no other youth." Rather, he has been ruefully recalling a childhood vow, "sworn in vain," that he would never leave
Sligo. (It is interesting thatYeats placed "Under Saturn," in which
he is at pains to praise his wife for "the wisdom that you brought" and
"the comfort that you made," immediately after "An Image from a
Past Life.")

The remarkable poem "Demon and Beast" marks the poet's
deepened maturity in another fashion. Its tone of confidingly personal conversation—somewhat unusual for Yeats when not writing
about love—is much like that in "Towards Break of Day," which it
follows. It has to do with a sudden state of pure "aimless joy" that left
him briefly free, one day, from "that crafty demon and that loud
beast": the rival forces of "hatred and desire," he says, that "plague
me day and night." The temporary release was the result, not of

mystical revelation such as Solomon and Sheba discovered together, but of physical weakness and vulnerability that had come with age. "I am certain," the poet claims,

> that mere growing old, that brings
> Chilled blood, this sweetness brought;
> Yet have no dearer thought
> Than that I may find out a way
> To make it linger half a day.

He has experienced this ecstasy while walking through the National Gallery in Dublin, near the park called St. Stephen's Green. Under its influence, various grim-faced portraits of historical figures seemed to smile and "beckon to sweet company." Even "the glittering eyes in a death's head" in a seventeenth-century painting "said welcome." Outdoors later, he wept with joy to see theantics of a gull and "an absurd / Portly green-pated" duck in the park's small lake.

The final verse-unit of "Demon and Beast" makes a remarkable leap of association, between the experience the poem has been describing and the "exultant" suicide of a fourth-century ascetic sect founded by St. Anthony in Thebaid, the area ruled by Egyptian Thebes. The shift of attention from a private state of feeling to a widened circle of historical and philosophical awareness is one of this volume's significant turns.

The turn emphasizes the self-sacrificial impulse riding the earlier sense of joy. The bliss of being loosed from the double pull "between my hatred and desire" came by accident, as it were, rather than from spiritual self-discipline. But the result was the same. The pressures of ambitious labor and of every kind of passionate intensity (a phrase used pejoratively in the next poem, "The Second Coming") have their obvious rewards, which people do not surrender easily. Yet the dream persists of surrendering them to gain a "sweetness" of existence beyond power and self-gratification. Hence the endearing attractiveness of the anecdote that sets off the poem, and hence also the climactic force of its ending:

O what a sweetness strayed
Through barren Thebaid
Or by the Mareotic Sea
When that exultant Anthony
And twice a thousand more
Starved upon the shore
And withered to a bag of bones!
What had the Caesars but their thrones?

The link between "Demon and Beast" and the next two pieces is a subtle one. "The Second Coming," a poem of ominous historical bearing, is in most ways poetry of a totally different order. Its powerfully prophetic blank verse (rich, though, in off-rhymes, internal rhymes, alliteration, and piled-up parallel constructions) builds from portent to portent. They are signs of cataclysmic change, like those described in the Gospels as accompanying the Crucifixion, but here they betoken a civilization gone murderously out of control. Yeats's lines interpreting them draw the biblical comparison and then add one final symbol of utter brute terror:

Surely some revelation is at hand;
Surely the Second Coming is at hand.
The Second Coming! Hardly are those words out
When a vast image out of *Spiritus Mundi*
Troubles my sight: somewhere in sands of the desert
A shape with lion body and the head of a man,
A gaze blank and pitiless as the sun,
Is moving its slow thighs, while all about it
Reel shadows of the indignant desert birds.

This is not the Sphinx of pure intellect that Michael Robartes saw. Rather, the poem's final lines suggest, it embodies the raw animal power that will reign in the coming age of barbarism:

And what rough beast, its hour come round at last,
Slouches toward Bethlehem to be born?

These lines are put as a question because the "vast" shape just described is a private vision of the poet's—only one possible form among the innumerable hideous ones in the ranks of what he calls "*Spiritus Mundi*": "the Spirits (or Phantoms) of the World." Which of these evil forms will replace the infant Jesus as the decisive symbol of the coming era? As yet the poet cannot tell.

One passage especially links this poem and "Demon and Beast." It comes at the end of the first verse-unit and is the key to the emotional pressure driving the whole movement:

> The blood-dimmed tide is loosed, and everywhere
> The ceremony of innocence is drowned;
> The best lack all conviction, while the worst
> Are full of passionate intensity.

"Passionate intensity" is precisely what Yeats has been turning away from in so many poems of this period. We should, naturally, make an exception of a poem like "Solomon and the Witch," since there the passion is certainly intense but also happy and carefree. But relief from the *driven* variety is what causes the "sweetness" and the sheer gratitude in "Demon and Beast," and it is what is ardently longed for in the lines just quoted. The world of the "blood-dimmed tide" is our world between the two great wars and within the period of civil war and revolutionary struggles in Ireland and elsewhere in Europe. Violent partisans, absolutely sure of themselves, are the people "full of passionate intensity" the poem refers to. And "the best," who "lack all conviction" because free of dogmatic ideology and unsure of what to do in the face of it, are at a loss when the simple courtesies of "the ceremony of innocence" are swamped. The pressures of this situation are intermixed in this volume with the personal pressures reflected in "Demon and Beast" and the marriage poems.

"A Prayer for My Daughter," which follows "The Second Coming," is a perfect instance. The prayer of the title is a plea, "because of the great gloom that is in my mind," that the newborn child will be spared those pressures. "I have walked and prayed," the poem goes—

> Imagining in excited reverie
> That the future years had come,
> Dancing to a frenzied drum,
> Out of the murderous innocence of the sea.

Everything the poet desires for the daughter seems in harmony with the spirit of "Demon and Beast." He prays that she "be granted beauty," but not so much as "to make a stranger's eye distraught" or lead her to rely on her beauty alone. He would have her life be blessed with tranquillity and "glad kindness." And, most of all, he prays that she will never be "choked with hate," especially with an "intellectual hatred." Free of that particular curse, her soul can constantly maintain the joyous "radical innocence" that her father once found away from his "demon and beast" for a few minutes in Dublin.

"An intellectual hatred is the worst, / So let her think opinions are accursed," says Yeats in this poem. The two lines together show the wider meaning he often gives to "hatred": namely, intolerant "opinion." (We may remember that the opening line of "Michael Robartes and the Dancer" is: "Opinion is not worth a rush." There *He* is trying to open the girl to the whole of life, as opposed to devotion to ideas only.) In the stanza that expands on "intellectual hatred," Yeats goes on to tell his daughter how "the loveliest woman born"—doubtless Maud Gonne, since this was the constant irritant in their disagreements—has "bartered" away all her best possibilities "because of her opinionated mind."

One "opinionated mind" Yeats was breaking away from was the lingering aftermath of his own youthful Fenianism as represented in a work like *Cathleen ni Houlihan* and in various early prose pieces. He had hardly surrendered his nationalism, but as he matured he reshaped it into something far beyond narrow militancy. The ambivalence we have seen in his play *The Dreaming of the Bones,* first published in 1919 (the same year he was to write "A Prayer for My

Yeats family photograph, c. 1927

Daughter"), came close to being a repudiation of absolute political intransigence. Its treatment of half-legendary lovers driven to betray their country is neatly balanced in sympathy with its presentation of the stalwart young patriot they encounter.

There are five specifically Irish political poems in this volume. They show a certain ambivalence in that two of them, "Sixteen Dead Men" and "The Rose Tree," are rousing ballads that celebrate the leaders of the failed Easter Rising, all but one of whom (a woman) were executed by the British. These poems, however, are printed immediately after "Easter, 1916," which, while also celebrating the "sixteen dead men," mourns them as possibly mistaken heroes who are to be cherished by the nation nevertheless. "Our part," the poem says, is

> To murmur name upon name
> As a mother names her child

When sleep at last has come
On limbs that had run wild.

This remarkable poem, which Yeats dared publish in 1916 only in a privately printed edition of twenty-five copies, presents two parallel tonal streams that coalesce in the overall elegiac feeling and in the famous tragic refrain (slightly varied throughout):

All changed, changed utterly:
A terrible beauty is born.

One of these tonal streams, dominating the two opening verse-units, is purely eulogistic. In the first unit, the poet speaks of how, before the Rising, the revolutionists had seemed mere clowns to him and his friends. In the second, he lingers over the characters of four of them, unnamed but identifiable: a beautiful, overly militant woman (Constance Gore-Booth Markievicz); two poets, one of them a teacher (Padraic Pearse and Thomas MacDonagh); and a man whom "I had dreamed / A drunken, vainglorious lout" (John Mac-Bride, Maud Gonne's husband for a brief, unhappy time). Whatever one might have known about them, it was all "changed utterly" by their great sacrifice.

The other tonal stream takes precedence in the final two units, which react against inflexible political postures that can lead to unnecessary sacrifice of human understanding as well as of lives. The third unit begins with an engaging image of the idealism attached to great causes:

Hearts with one purpose alone
Through summer and winter seem
Enchanted to a stone
To trouble the living stream.

And there lies the rub—in that image of being "enchanted to a stone / To trouble the living stream." For these lines are followed by a catalogue of endlessly changing, lovely elements of human experience and of nature that do the "troubling"—while, on the other hand, "Too long a sacrifice / Can make a stone of the heart." The hardness of stone suggests an inhuman intransigence, and so the question arises, and with it the challenge to nationalist ideology that made Yeats wary of publishing the poem too soon:

> Was it needless death after all?
> For England may keep faith
> For all that is done and said.
> We know their dream; enough
> To know they dreamed and are dead;
> And what if excess of love
> Bewildered them till they died?

After these lines, the poem returns, finally, to the spirit of eulogy it began with—but a spirit now more compassionate than hero-worshipping. "Intellectual hatred" has been rejected in the political as in the private realm, despite the risk of offending patriotic sensibilities. Yeats has catapulted his thinking into the realm of one of our most painful modern pressures: the constant need to take a stand on military actions—by governments or by guerrillas—that we may find hateful without condemning the innocent or misled individuals who do the fighting.

The two remaining poems of Irish political bearing sustain the standpoint of "Easter, 1916." One is the angry little poem called "The Leaders of the Crowd," which begins: "They must to keep their certainty accuse / All that are different of a base intent." The other, "On a Political Prisoner," has to do with Constance Gore-Booth Markievicz, the militant beauty of "Easter, 1916" who, because of her sex, was jailed rather than shot by the British. The poem contrasts her present condition with her happier youth in the countryside when, an accomplished horsewoman, "She seemed to have grown clean and sweet / Like any rock-bred, sea-borne bird." The first stanza describes her quiet presence in her prison cell, where she has become so patient that a gull flies through the window-bars and lets her feed it. And then the poem asks:

> Did she, in touching that lone wing
> Recall the years before her mind
> Became a bitter, an abstract thing,
> Her thought some popular enmity:
> Blind and leader of the blind
> Drinking the foul ditch where they lie?

Thereafter, the closing stanzas do the "recalling" of those years for her, so that the poem moves with delight into picturing her beautiful former existence. We see her, at the end, as if she had indeed been the "rock-bred, sea-borne bird," staring out over the sea from "some lofty rock," that the poet remembers. The contrast here between a condition of wild, unpredictable freedom and ideological self-entrapment is but one instance of Yeats's great effort, in this volume, to get out from under the constraints of destructive "passionate intensity" of every kind.

VI

The Tower

As with other poets' successive volumes, Yeats's sometimes overlap in the sense that they contain work begun and even completed before previous volumes had been printed. *The Tower* (1928) is the prize example. Some of its poems were in the making a decade or more before it appeared. One, "The New Faces," goes back to 1912 and is of a piece with poems of deep friendship like "These Are the Clouds" and "A Friend's Illness" in *The Green Helmet and Other Poems* and "To a Friend Whose Work Has Come to Nothing" and "Friends" in *Responsibilities*. Another, "Owen Aherne and His Dancers," goes back to 1917 and—despite its bitter theme (an older man whose love has been rejected by a young woman)—is stylistically close to Yeats's writing of two decades earlier. The great double sequence, "Meditations in Time of Civil War" and "Nineteen Hundred and Nineteen," is the work of 1921 to 1922 and might conceivably have been added to *Michael Robartes and the Dancer*. And "All Souls' Night," written in 1920, brings the book to an end.

These facts are worth mentioning as a reminder that the dates of successive volumes are useful but hardly absolute markers of a poet's development. We have occasionally seen Yeats leapfrogging himself by foreshadowing later methods and perspectives while still coping with earlier ones. But since he achieved the height of his powers in certain poems of *The Tower,* it is interesting to note—without laboring the point—how free he felt to marshal his resources and preoccupations from the whole of his artistic memory.

The Tower, Yeats's finest single volume, ushered in the triumphant last decade of his career. Its overall structure is simple in principle if complex in detail. Yeats started it off from sheer strength, in the dazzling series of poems "Sailing to Byzantium," "The Tower," and the double sequence already mentioned. Farther along, with careful strategy, he positioned the book's other outstanding pieces: "Two Songs from a Play," "Leda and the Swan," "Among School Children," parts of the sequence "A Man Young and Old," and the much neglected "All Soul's Night." Taken as a whole, the volume copes in widening circles with its initial recognition that the passion-driven physical world, with its "sensual music," is "no country for old men." The widening circles involve the resources of art, myth, and imagination, the defeat of cherished illusions in the course of civil war in Ireland, and the dream of communion with realms beyond death that we have seen acted out in the Cuchulain cycle of poems and plays.

The two opening poems face the shock of reaching old age head-on, as earlier poems had faced the bafflements of difficult love. But Yeats—as we have seen—had been learning how to express powerful feelings and yet keep his art from becoming mired in self-absorption. All his poems of old age (a deplorable way to describe them, but useful nonetheless if not sentimentalized or translated into biographical data) merge private feelings, often desperate, with larger, engulfing contexts. Thereafter, other poems, notably those in the double civil-war sequence but also "Two Songs from a Play," "Leda and the Swan," and "All Souls' Night," pick up and add to those larger contexts overwhelmingly. The result is that the book as a whole projects the long, introspective memory of a man acutely conscious not only of his own aging and mortality but also of the universe, human and cosmic, that has both shaped and balked him.

"Sailing to Byzantium" is a self-contained poem, but it can also be considered a compact prelude to the far-reaching title poem following it. Its four stanzas in ottava rima resemble an audio-visual mural in four panels. The first "panel" depicts a teeming "country" of endlessly ardent sexuality, enmeshing "the young / In one another's arms" and, indeed, everything else in nature that "is begotten, born, and dies." It is not, we have been told, "a country for old men," and so the speaker watches and listens from somewhere outside that pulsating domain of eternal summer. In the closing couplet he comforts himself with what seems, in the face of so much luxuriant excitement, a sadly pedantic consolation: "Caught in that sensual music all neglect / Monuments of unageing intellect."

The second stanza puts him at the center of its panel, in the image of a scarecrow. This stanza, however, moves rapidly through several phases. The image, at first static and pathetic, suddenly becomes animated and ecstatic. The metaphor of the scarecrow come to life, and then a further metaphor of "sailing" away on a holy pilgrimage to "Byzantium," lift the poem from its heavy mood. In fact, they catapult it into a realm of exalted desire—one created by will and aesthetic imagination to replace that of the flesh. In the process, the originally dull-seeming image of "monuments of unageing intellect" has been charged with associations of transcendent joy and beauty and with an atmosphere of passionate questing:

> An aged man is but a paltry thing,
> A tattered coat upon a stick, unless
> Soul clap its hands and sing, and louder sing
> For every tatter in its mortal dress,
> Nor is there singing school but studying
> Monuments of its own magnificence;
> And therefore I have sailed the seas and come
> To the holy city of Byzantium.

In the final couplet here, Yeats uses "I" for the first time in the poem. A romantic vision of the poet *in extremis,* a dreaming suppliant for entrance into "the holy city of Byzantium," now replaces the shabby scarecrow of the first lines. Ancient Byzantium has exotic artistic and religious associations, notably—in this poem—with the cathedral of Santa Sophia and its stylized mosaics, but is far short of Heaven. The whole mood is piercingly yearning. And so, in the third stanza, the poem bursts into prayer, addressed to the "sages standing in God's holy fire / As in the gold mosaic of a wall," begging them to swoop down and become "the singing-masters of my soul," and

> Consume my heart away; sick with desire
> And fastened to a dying animal
> It knows not what it is; and gather me
> Into the artifice of eternity.

The third panel, then, pictures the aged speaker facing the even more aged "sages": his opposite counterparts dwelling with God eternally. He is "sick with desire" in two ways: one as a living man who still feels, though to no avail, the pang of physical passion; the other as a suppliant for death and transfiguration. The climactic confessional intensity of this stanza is reflected in both its pictorial aspect (it is like a Blake engraving) and its incantatory use of urgent imperatives in imploring the sages' help.

The final stanza imagines how it will be when his prayer is granted. He will be reborn as pure artifact: a golden bird singing in a timeless world, with "such a form as Grecian goldsmiths make / Of hammered gold and gold enamelling." His song will no longer be addressed to the indifferent inhabitants of nature's summer world. Rather, he will sing for an ideal audience, free of sensual turmoil, about "what is past, or passing, or to come"—as do the creative mind's "monuments of unageing intellect." His ordeal in actual life has not disappeared; the stanza is in the future tense but the optative mood. Yet a consoling vision has emerged for his art.

The next poem, "The Tower," is so encompassing and so powerfully revealing of the level Yeats had reached by the time he wrote it (1926) that it calls for extended discussion. It begins with the same complaint that started off "Sailing to Byzantium," except that the *cri de coeur* here is even fiercer:

What shall I do with this absurdity—
O heart, O troubled heart—this caricature,
Decrepit age that has been tied to me
As to a dog's tail?

Thus begins the second, and far more expansive, of Yeats's great poems of the psychological crisis attending old age. He does not put the matter in that coolly clinical way, though. Rather, he opens his poem dramatically, with a desperate question that is at once romantic in its outcry ("O heart, O troubled heart") and edged with hysterical buffoonery in its image of "decrepit age that has been tied to me/As to a dog's tail."

"The Tower" is not limited in its scope by these highly compressed and excited opening lines, but—like "Sailing to Byzantium"—it takes its impetus from its beginning. The tangle of feeling presented in these lines is at the heart of its long and subtle dynamic unfolding. Thus, the next passage of special emphasis in this process occurs in the three stanzas that close the poem's second section. Driven by the same desperation that exploded in the outcry at the start, these stanzas develop it in a far different key. They, too, are couched in question form, but are dramatic without being frenzied. The two questions they raise are gravely intense ones. The first addresses the shades of fabled local personages the poem has been recalling; the second addresses Hanrahan, the poet's wildly free, imaginary alter ego:

Did all old men and women, rich and poor,
Who trod upon these rocks or passed this door,
Whether in public or in secret rage
As I do now against old age?
But I have found an answer in those eyes
That are impatient to be gone;
Go therefore; but leave Hanrahan,
For I need all his mighty memories.

Old lecher with a love on every wind,
Bring up out of that deep considering mind

> All that you have discovered in the grave,
> For it is certain that you have
> Reckoned up every unforeknown, unseeing
> Plunge, lured by a softening eye,
> Or by a touch or a sigh,
> Into the labyrinth of another's being;
>
> Does the imagination dwell the most
> Upon a woman won or woman lost?
> If on the lost, admit you turned aside
> From a great labyrinth out of pride,
> Cowardice, some silly over-subtle thought
> Or anything called conscience once;
> And that if memory recur, the sun's
> Under eclipse and the day blotted out.

All the questioning passages I have so far quoted are immediate in their human bearing: something one can always count on
in Yeats, even when being forced to confront disagreeable realities.
As we have seen, the poem's opening passage presented the humiliating predicament of a spirited, passionate person (identified as
the poet himself) in enfeebled old age. The second, longer passage,
with its pair of questions, picks up and deepens that current of
feeling. It returns to the predicament itself, but adds intensely conflicting associations of remembered love-experience and its after-
effects.

The first question is rhetorical. It expresses a nagging introspective concern: namely, whether or not the poet's "rage" at growing old
has been shared by "all old men and women" who have ever lived. In
a sense, he is merely wondering (though with unusual frankness)
whether or not his "rage" is normal. The implied answer of the
imagined, indifferent shades is "Yes," despite the tantalizing, ambiguous image that presents it: "But I have found an answer in those
eyes / That are impatient to be gone." Rationally speaking, the implied answer might provide reassuring solace. But ordinary rationality is not the point. The vision of the impatient shades is an

Thoor Ballylee ("The Tower"), photographed by Brian Seed

imperious one that changes the poem's emotional balance. It presents a sudden prospect of a realm beyond life: a mode of existence in which the shades of the dead are immersed. They have no wish to be distracted from its preoccupations even for an instant. The concerns of the living are no longer their own in the least.

The second question, charged with a dark, rueful introspection, returns to those concerns: "Does the imagination dwell the most / Upon a woman won or woman lost?" Again the unstated answer—"a woman lost"—seems obvious enough from the succeeding lines. We know this because (as if we didn't know anyway!) the poem shifts its full attention now to the complexities of unfulfilled love. The thought in itself here is remarkable. It was not "fate," or the beloved's free choice, that led to the loss. Rather, it was one's own decision, rooted in one's inner self. The loss need not have been. It was engendered by unconscious pride or fear or squeamishness—or, in a brutal, amoral phrase that is nevertheless beautifully to the point, by "anything called conscience once."

These questions and implied answers are not abstractions. They are sensual and emotional storm-centers. The poem began in an ecstasy of impotent embarrassment, a "rage" at growing physically old despite increased imaginative powers. This is the "rage" of frustration alluded to in the first of the later questions, directed to the unanswering dead who will not, or cannot, speak to us. Perhaps, though, some imagined alternative self—here the Hanrahan that "I myself created"—might bridge the realms of the living and the dead and clarify, at last, the enduring mystery of love's travails? For Hanrahan, affectionately called an "old lecher with a love on every wind" (yet also gifted with a "deep considering mind"), embodies the full rich memory of lovers' experience. He has

> Reckoned up every unforeknown, unseeing
> Plunge, lured by a softening eye,
> Or by a touch or a sigh,
> Into the labyrinth of another's being.

These lines present a dream of gratified desire, but the metaphor of love as a labyrinth is at the same time a forbidding one. It recurs, more grimly, near the close of the passage:

> admit you turned aside
> From a great labyrinth out of pride,
> Cowardice, some silly over-subtle thought
> Or anything called conscience once;
> And that, if memory recur, the sun's
> Under eclipse and the day blotted out.

The labyrinth metaphor is indeed forbidding. It drastically qualifies the notion of love's pure, uncomplicated delights. Yet the seductiveness of the companion images ("softening eye," "a touch or a sigh") remains overpowering. Truly, one would have to join the inhuman world of the shades to escape the conflicts of desire, confusion, and remorse in love.

And in fact, the poem finally opts for joining that world. In its next and final section it provides one of the most touching emotional "solutions" in our poetry, comparable to Milton's lines in *Paradise Lost* beginning "Some natural tears they dropped." This section of "The Tower" proposes the impossible: to nullify the competing forces of passionate experience by teaching the soul detachment from them, as though one were already one of the indifferent shades. We may note, not so incidentally, that this tropism toward death is the inevitable result of the struggle, begun as we have seen in *The Wild Swans at Coole* and *Michael Robartes and the Dancer,* to get out from under the existential pressure of one's particular past life. It throws its shadow over much of Yeats's later work.

The tonal shift here is the final turn on the poem's original cry for liberation from the bodily burden of old age. The detachment sought is not that of religious asceticism. It is characterized by a Berkeleyan assertion—with neither theological nor philosophical overlay, however—that human imagination alone is the sole begetter of everything we think of as reality. This part of "The Tower" is in no sense an argument; it is a beautiful and pathetic verbal act of need-driven will:

> And I declare my faith:
> I mock Plotinus' thought
> And cry in Plato's teeth,
> Death and life were not
> Till man made up the whole,
> Made lock, stock and barrel
> Out of his bitter soul,
> Aye, sun and moon and star, all,
> And further add to that
> That, being dead, we rise,
> Dream and so create
> Translunar Paradise.
> I have prepared my peace
> With learned Italian things
> And the proud stones of Greece,
> Poet's imaginings
> And memories of love,
> Memories of the words of women,
> All those things whereof
> Man makes a superhuman
> Mirror-resembling dream.

Let me repeat: this near-solipsistic proclamation is in no sense discursive argument. It is entirely metaphorical, a symbolic gathering of cherished ideals and memories for building a warmly protective mental nest against the despair revealed at the end of Part II. The poem itself closes in on the figure of a "nest" in the succeeding verse-unit. The poet has "prepared my peace," he says, just

> As at the loophole there
> The daws chatter and scream,
> And drop twigs layer upon layer.
> When they have mounted up,
> The mother bird will rest

On their hollow top,
And so warm her wild nest.

Thus, gently and graciously, the previous vigorous lines of will-ful assertion are shown to be only a defensive structure against the inevitable, a way-stop on the road to complete, shade-like detach-ment. The closing verse-unit then becomes a song of letting go disguised as transcendence, elegiac rather than triumphant:

> Now shall I make my soul,
> Compelling it to study
> In a learned school
> Till the wreck of body,
> Slow decay of blood,
> Testy delirium
> Or dull decrepitude,
> Or what worse evil come—
> The death of friends, or death
> Of every brilliant eye
> That made a catch in the breath—
> Seem but the clouds of the sky
> When the horizon fades;
> Or a bird's sleepy cry
> Among the deepening shades.

There is a *kind* of transcendence, after all, in the letting go and in the elegiac coloration. Neither of these is genuine detachment; but together, in lines just before the end, they help complete the libera-tion from self-absorption and self-pity the poem has been pressing toward. Brooding over his own bodily and mental deterioration to come, the poet suddenly introduces an even more painful subject. Though just quoted, the lines bear repeating:

> Or what worse evil come—
> The death of friends, or death
> Of every brilliant eye
> That made a catch in the breath.

The thought is normal, generous, and unforced, and yet not exactly an ordinary one. It breaks the heart without half trying. In its pure, lyrical way, it is a distillation of the central elegiac strain of "The Tower" and also of two other important, although subordinate, affective streams.

These affective streams, which make themselves felt in Sections II and III respectively, are somewhat complex. They include, first, a robust feeling for common humanity in the anecdotes, jests, and musings that precede the questioning stanzas I have quoted from Section II. Second, there is a tone of reverence for the magical power of memory—both personal and historical—in the same group of stanzas. And third, there is the high-pitched political and visionary exaltation in the opening lines of Section III.

To recapitulate for awhile: the poem's first section begins, we remember, with an outcry of personal distress and humiliation. It then broods over the "absurdity" of being in such a state and of being expected to forgo, because one has grown old, all further attempts at a passionately creative life. This sad predicament having been estab-lished, the second section opens with the poet pacing the battlements of his tower (a natural enough symbol here of his life-situation). In his existential agony, he seeks help from "images and memo-ries" called up in his imagination: "For I would ask a question of them all."

The figures of local tradition that he then conjures up are nearly as varied as Chaucer's pilgrims. They add boisterous life and color, lyrical celebration of a young girl's beauty, and historical depth to the body of this fundamentally elegiac poem. First the poet recalls the rich, notorious Mrs. French, who once had an "insolent farmer's" ears clipped off by a servant. Then a lovely peasant girl immortalized in song by the poet Blind Raftery comes to mind. In turn, this romantic memory and its joyous associations set off a comic tale about some men who, "maddened by those rhymes, / Or else by toasting her a score of times," went forth to gaze upon her with their own eyes—

But they mistook the brightness of the moon
For the prosaic light of day—
Music had driven their wits astray—
And one was drowned in the great bog of Cloone.

And then, in the midst of these anecdotes of bitter feeling, life's cruelties, delightful womanly beauty, poetic inspiration, and drunken fantasy, there is a crucial segue to the poem's major tragic burden. The passage both anticipates the book's final poem, "All Souls' Night," and—with an irony similar to that in Plato's myth of the cave—stresses the "madness" of poetic vision:

Strange, but the man who made the song was blind;
Yet, now I have considered it, I find
That nothing strange; the tragedy began
With Homer that was a blind man,
And Helen has all living hearts betrayed.
O may the moon and sunlight seem
One inextricable beam,
For if I triumph I must make men mad.

Yes, if he "triumphs," the poet—like Raftery—will "make men mad" with dreams of pure yet palpable beauty and of the triumph of human will over life's otherwise inexorable destructiveness. These lines linking "The Tower" with Raftery's song and the spirit of the *Iliad,* which make the illusion of triumph seem tragically misdirected, anticipate the poem's poignant ending. At this strategic point the figure of Red Hanrahan enters the poem. Created by Yeats as his own half-comic, half-tragic mirror image, he always aspires, never succeeds, but never abandons the hopeless struggle:

He stumbled, tumbled, fumbled to and fro
And had but broken knees for hire
And horrible splendour of desire;
I thought it all out twenty years ago.

In the section's final stanzas, this engaging but very imperfect oracle will be asked to impart to the poet, in words the poet himself instructs him to use, the truth about love, that "great labyrinth." Thus their two reciprocal voices will unite to stress the futility of the dreaming will.

After Hanrahan, certain figures out of the dim, all-but-eroded past are recalled. One is the "ancient bankrupt master" who last possessed the tower; he serves as a reminder of the inevitable fading away of identity itself. And similarly, the forgotten "rough men-at-arms," with heroes among them, who once manned the tower on military assignment are imagined present as they once were—but only, of course, as phantasmal figures

> Whose images, in the Great Memory stored,
> Come with loud cry and panting breast
> To break upon a sleeper's rest
> While their great wooden dice beat on the board.

These figures add to the poem's depressive saturation, against which the defiant assertions in Part III—including the poem's only political assertions—take their bravely fatalistic stance. The assertions sing the uncalculating "pride" that Yeats feels as a mysterious, impersonal force working both in nature and in uncorrupted humanity. The passage is a proclamation of triumphant defeat:

> The pride of people that were
> Bound neither to Cause nor to State,
> Neither to slaves that were spat on,
> Nor to the tyrants that spat,
> The people of Burke and of Grattan
> That gave, though free to refuse—
> Pride, like that of the morn,
> When the headlong light is loose,
> Or that of the fabulous horn,
> Or that of the sudden shower
> When all streams are dry,

Or that of the hour
When the swan must fix his eye
Upon a fading gleam,
Float out upon a long
Last reach of glittering stream
And there sing his last song.

Before we turn more centrally to the civil-war sequences following this poem, it seems useful to compare them in two respects with
"The Tower." First, obviously, the political element in the lines just
quoted foreshadows the major preoccupation of the sequences. But I
want to call special attention to the nobly compassionate and distressed poems "The Road at My Door," "The Stare's Nest by My
Window" (in "Meditations in Time of Civil War"), and Poem I of
"Nineteen Hundred and Nineteen." These are pieces reciprocal with
"The Tower" in their candor and tragic gravamen, and in addition
they are political in that term's most human meaning. What they
have to say about war is as much to the point today as when they
were written. Like the ending of "The People," they reveal a side of
the poet's political sensibility very unlike the aristocratic, eugenistic,
and even fascist attitudes he could adopt.

The second point of comparison that seems relevant here has to
do with structure. "The Tower," with its brave self-scrutiny and
varied formal handling of a very complex affective movement, may
well be Yeats's outstanding single poem. But the interlocking civil-
war sequences are a triumph on a different scale. From that point of
view, we can say that the form of the three-part, multifaceted "The
Tower" is a splendid modulation toward a true sequence. At this
point, in fact, it seems useful to emphasize that the whole volume can
be viewed as an extended sequence, as evidenced by its careful non-
chronological ordering. (For example, "Sailing to Byzantium" was
completed in 1926, "The Tower" in 1925, "Meditations in Time of
Civil War" in 1922, and "Nineteen Hundred and Nineteen" in 1921
or 1922.) The two opening poems have revealed both the mind-set
and the kind of intricate associative reverie to be developed in the rest

of the book. And now the civil-war sequences show the violent, uncontrollable post-1914 tidal waves crashing upon that mind-set and leaving it wounded and grieving: a predicament that the succeeding poems cope with in various ways.

The interaction between the seven-poem first sequence and the six-poem second one is clear from their basic emotional centers, whose titles I have already mentioned. These are "The Road at My Door" and "The Stare's Nest by My Window" (climactically positioned just before the final poem in the "Meditations" group), and the untitled opening poem of "Nineteen Hundred and Nineteen." What they share is their dismay at all the bloodshed and atrocities during the "Troubles" of 1919 to 1921. All camps were implicated: the Irish Republican Army's "Irregulars," the brown-uniformed troops of the provisional "Free State" government (which had accepted Dominion status), and the British troops ("Black and Tans") and their unofficial, undisciplined cohorts called "Police Auxiliaries."

The first two of the poems just named are in form the simplest in the first sequence. They are made up of four-stress cinquains rhyming *abaab,* but with a great many off-rhymes, so that their effect is like that of folk ballads despite their elegantly precise phrasing. Two stanzas of "The Stare's Nest by My Window," with its ballad refrain, will illustrate both the artistry of these poems and their horror at what is going on close to the poet's home:

> We are closed in, and the key is turned
> On our uncertainty; somewhere
> A man is killed, or a house burned,
> Yet no clear fact to be discerned:
> Come build in the empty house of the stare.

> A barricade of stone or of wood;
> Some fourteen days of civil war;
> Last night they trundled down the road
> That dead young soldier in his blood:
> Come build in the empty house of the stare.

The horror is picked up again in the climactic fourth stanza of the poem that starts off "Nineteen Hundred and Nineteen":

> Now days are dragon-ridden, the nightmare
> Rides upon sleep: a drunken soldiery
> Can leave the mother, murdered at her door,
> To crawl in her own blood, and go scot-free;
> The night can sweat with terror as before
> We pieced our thoughts into philosophy,
> And planned to bring the world under a rule,
> Who are but weasels fighting in a hole.

The traumatic images at the heart of these passages—"that dead young soldier in his blood"; "the mother, murdered at her door" and left "to crawl in her own blood"—do not of course represent the whole body of the double sequence. But they reflect the essential psychological shock that generates its particular formation. In reaction to that shock, the poet sees that he and his ideals for Irish life and culture have no part in the world of killers let loose in the land. In "The Road at My Door," fighters from various warring groups pass by, one of them "an affable Irregular" who "comes cracking jokes of civil war / As though to die by gunshot were / The finest play under the sun." A strain of personal depression, brought out bitterly in the self-dismissive stanza at the end of the poem, runs through the sequences:

> I count those feathered balls of soot
> The moor-hen guides upon the stream,
> To silence the envy in my thought;
> And turn towards my chamber, caught
> In the cold snows of a dream.

In "Meditations in Time of Civil War" these decisive emotional motifs are given a surround of psychopolitical philosophizing and of thoughts about Castle Ballylee, where Yeats lived. The second poem, "My House," begins by describing it:

> An ancient bridge, and a more ancient tower,
> A farmhouse that is sheltered by its wall,
> An acre of stony ground . . .

Michael Robartes and Owen Aherne would have recognized the place, and even its interior as presented a bit further on:

> A winding stair, a chamber arched with stone,
> A grey stone fireplace with an open hearth,
> A candle and written page.
> *Il Penseroso*'s Platonist toiled on
> In some like chamber, shadowing forth
> How the daemonic rage
> Imagined everything.
> Benighted travellers
> From markets and from fairs
> Have seen his midnight candle glimmering.

The "Meditations" sequence builds a dramatic tale around this scene and the poet's life within it. He has been "toiling on" late at night like John Milton, who had dreamed, in his "Il Penseroso," of calling up Plato's spirit to reveal to him "what worlds or what vast regions hold / The immortal mind" after death. We have seen how broodingly seductive his thoughts of reaching out to the realm of the dead were becoming to Yeats. They provide a dark shadow-stream of feeling alongside his distress at the wanton slaughter, and will be brought to a head in the climactic third poem of "Nineteen Hundred and Nineteen." This aspect of the sequences helps define the intricately dreaming yet vulnerable mind, which also had been creating a vision of a nobly civil Ireland of the future, that was so cruelly disabused by the course of the "Troubles."

A simple narrative line runs through the "Meditations," carrying the sequence through its lyrical changes. "Ancestral Houses," the opening poem, provides a point of departure in strong contrast to what follows. The one piece not rooted in Yeats's Norman tower and unpretentious farmhouse, it centers its attention on the forgotten responsibilities of the great houses of Ireland. Its leisurely ottava rima allows room for a stirring rhetorical development, starting with two stanzas of ironic disillusionment at the death of cherished aristocratic virtues. He mingles a glamorous sense of "the inherited glory of the rich" with contempt for the "mice" who have succeeded the "bitter and violent men" who laid the family foundations: men who called upon equally driven architects and artists to "rear in stone/ The sweetness that all longed for night and day." The closing stanzas modulate into a nostalgic lament for the unconscious betrayal of all that passionate creative energy and love of the idea of perfection.

The rest of the sequence then turns its back on any hope that the great magnanimous spirit of an idealized aristocracy can be revived by the "mice." Instead, the poet will try to sustain it in his own home so that, he says at the end of "My House," one day "my bodily heirs may find, / To exalt a lonely mind, / Befitting emblems of adversity." Those emblems are represented in the third poem, "My Table," by an ancient Japanese sword once given him. Its "moon-luminous" beauty reminds him that his labors and his ideals are justified despite all discouragement. "Only an aching heart"—like the hearts of the artists described in the first poem—"conceives a changeless work of art"; and our only salvation lies in refusing to betray the soul's love of beauty whatever the circumstances.

"My Table" reveals a great deal about the ideal of true aristocracy imbedded in the sequences. It assumes a standard of responsible privilege no actual ruling class has ever approached: a sort of tragically informed samurai-aestheticism, tempered at its best by genuine regard for the people's interests and by a desire to see a whole nation inspired to live by the same standard. Disillusionment with the weak descendants of presumably Cuchulain-like ancestors merges with revulsion at the current blood-drenched, "dragon-ridden" state of the country.

The serious yet make-believe game of establishing a model if humble fiefdom without serfs (a Jeffersonian feudalism, as it were) at Ballylee continues in the fourth poem, "My Descendants." Yeats

plays the game to the hilt in this poem, even unto fearing a deterioration of his family line like that of the great houses he has been
deploring. What if that should happen, he asks arrogantly, with no
apparent notion of the effect such a question—or his answer—might
have on his children:

> And what if my descendants lose the flower
> Through natural declension of the soul,
> Through too much business with the passing hour,
> Through too much play, or marriage with a fool?
> May this laborious stair and this stark tower
> Become a roofless ruin that the owl
> May build in the cracked masonry and cry
> Her desolation in the desolate sky.

Even the closing lines, meant to be a gracious turn expressing
affection for those closest to him, refer directly to his wife and to his
neighbor and close friend Lady Gregory, but not to his children—
who do, however, enter the picture in the dismissively impersonal
penultimate line:

> And I, that count myself most prosperous,
> Seeing that love and friendship are enough,
> For an old neighbour's friendship chose the house
> And decked and altered it for a girl's love,
> And know whatever flourish and decline
> These stones remain their monument and mine.

If the charm of this ending is unfortunately marred, we may find
some excuse at least in Yeats's larger purpose of contrasting the
diminished character of the great houses with his vision of the spiritual integrity needed to face the disasters of our age. The next two
poems, "The Road at My Door" and "The Stare's Nest by My
Window," shove the disasters, Goya-like, directly into the foreground of the sequence. The former of these closes with its despair-

ing self-portrait of the poet "caught / In the cold snows of a dream." The second points up the psychological trap that has him in its jaws together with his countrymen:

> We had fed the heart on fantasies,
> The heart's grown brutal from the fare;
> More substance in our enmities
> Than in our love . . .

The last poem of the "Meditations" sequence finds him in full retreat from everything he has been asserting. Its title is indicative: "I See Phantoms of Hatred and of the Heart's Fullness and of the Coming Emptiness." The chivalric vision of the middle poems has not been repudiated, but now the poet is a dreamer in retreat from intractable reality. "I climb to the tower-top and lean upon broken stone."

What he sees in the first stanza mirrors his own state of mind. A windblown misty landscape makes all outlines vague and confusing, while the moonlight seems "a glittering sword out of the east" and frenzied reveries take over: "Monstrous familiar images swim in the mind's eye." Even the stanza form, hexameter octaves rhyming *ababcdcd,* contributes through its long lines to the drawn-out visualization of those dream-images.

The three succeeding stanzas each develop one such image: first a senselessly "rage-driven, rage-tormented, and rage-hungry troop" crying for vengeance and tearing at one another like demons in Hell; then "magical unicorns" with ecstatic, lovely ladies on their backs; and finally, "brazen hawks" bereft of all emotion: "Nothing but grip of claw, and the eye's complacency, / The innumerable clanging wings that have put out the moon." This last image is even more nightmarish than the Sphinx of "The Second Coming" because purely mechanical, like the instruments of modern warfare. It drives the poet back into himself, makes him doubt his vocation and all his assumptions, and leads his imagination to retreat from torment to the safety of boyhood fancies and illusions:

I turn away and shut the door, and on the stair
Wonder how many times I could have proved my worth
In something others understand or share;
But O! ambitious heart, had such a proof drawn forth
A company of friends, a conscience set at ease,
It had but made us pine the more. The abstract joy,
The half-read wisdom of daemonic images,
Suffice the ageing man as once the growing boy.

"Nineteen Hundred and Nineteen" is in some important ways a compressed reprise of "Meditations in Time of Civil War." Its first poem, we have seen, reaches its climax in the lines on "the mother, murdered at her door" by "a drunken soldiery." Using the same ottava rima as the opening piece in the preceding sequence, it is an even stronger poem of shocked disillusionment—this time, though, with the idea, prevalent before the Great War, that society had been progressing toward a just and peaceful world. The contrary conception, that history is cyclical, not progressive, is only hinted at in the "Meditations"; but "Nineteen Hundred and Nineteen" asserts it boldly, sorrowfully, and fatalistically at the very start:

Many ingenious lovely things are gone
That seemed sheer miracle to the multitude,
Protected from the circle of the moon
That pitches common things about . . .

"Man is in love and loves what vanishes," another line tells us, suggesting an associative link between Yeats's earlier poems of thwarted passion and these of defeated historical ideals. And the next-to-last stanza presses the tragic purview to the point where it becomes our ultimate challenge to integrity. Each individual soul is doomed to solitude and extinction; this desolate truth must become the bedrock of our understanding:

He who can read the signs nor sink unmanned
Into the half-deceit of some intoxicant

From shallow wits; who knows no work can stand,
Whether health, wealth or peace of mind were spent
On master-work of intellect or hand,
No honour leave its mighty monument,
Has but one comfort left: all triumph would
But break upon his ghostly solitude.

The progress of this dire train of thought, so much grimmer than its parallel at the end of "The Tower," is momentarily halted by the brief second poem of "Nineteen Hundred and Nineteen." Like a choral song in a Greek tragedy, this poem recasts what has gone before it in more universal terms—in this instance singing of the "Platonic Year," the supposed two-thousand-year cycle in which cultures are born, rise to a height, and disappear. Unlike a Greek chorus, however, it adds a new symbol to give the conception color and vibrancy. A performance of a troupe of Chinese exotic dancers, who "enwound / A shining web, a floating ribbon of cloth" so that it seemed as if "a dragon of air" was whirling the dancers about, has provided the symbol—which in this case is far more buoyant in its feeling than the poem's dreary conclusion:

> So the Platonic Year
> Whirls out new right and wrong,
> Whirls in the old instead;
> All men are dancers and their tread
> Goes to the barbarous clangour of a gong.

The heavy feeling here is an apt follow-through from the dejected opening poem. It clears emotional space for Poem III, perhaps the most remarkable piece in the double sequence, by placing the previous poem's lament over the cruel failure of political hopes in a "whirling" context of universal process. The process itself may have a beautiful, free-patterned energy like that of the exotic dancers' "shining web" that seemed "a dragon of air" (an image at once delightful and ominous), yet it wreaks destruction upon societies nourished on the illusion of permanence.

Poem III swings into another orbit, related to what has gone before and at the same time independent of it. We are back in the realm of "pride" in the face of despair described so idiosyncratically in the final section of "The Tower." Now, though, the bearing of the poem is extremely personal in a new way. Having accepted the "ghostly solitude" that is the common fate, the poet almost joyously makes a virtue of it. His "pride" lies in his readiness to cope with the overwhelming cyclical forces that mock all human hopes. The first of the three intricately patterned ten-line stanzas begins by presenting the situation amiably, as though the poet were chatting with a friend. Then its near-whimsy explodes into one of the truly powerful moments in English poetry:

> Some moralist or mythological poet
> Compares the solitary soul to a swan;
> I am satisfied with that,
> Satisfied if a troubled mirror show it,
> Before that brief gleam of its life be gone,
> An image of its state;
> The wings half spread for flight,
> The breast thrust out in pride
> Whether to play, or to ride
> Those winds that clamour of approaching night.

Thrilling as this image is, the stanza could not quite stand by itself without seeming too much akin to the easy inspirationalism of much Victorian and post-Victorian poetry, from Tennyson's "Ulysses" to Henley's "Invictus." Perhaps the closest approximation, and the fairest to both sides of the comparison, would be with Browning's "'Childe Roland to the Dark Tower Came.'" But the poem does go further. The heroic stance, though genuinely assumed, is not finally sustained. The swan image itself takes on a reverse implication, after all, in the concluding stanza:

> The swan has leaped into the desolate heaven:
> That image can bring wildness, bring a rage

To end all things, to end
What my laborious life imagined, even
The half-imagined, half-written page;
O but we dreamed to mend
Whatever mischief seemed
To afflict mankind, but now
That winds of winter blow
Learn that we were crack-pated when we dreamed.

The poem has reached this point partly by following through on its image of the swan's readiness for flight. The implied question arises: *Flight whither?* And the answer given is: "Into the desolate heaven"—the dead end beyond which no vision is granted, and the thought of which induces suicidal "rage."

The startling quantum jump here from pride to self-abasement seems very sudden. But it was prepared for in the deceptively un-dramatic middle stanza, which begins with a quiet, introspective confession that also deflates all who would speak grandly for human-ity: "A man in his own secret meditation / Is lost amid the labyrinth that he has made / In art or politics." Next, the stanza thinks with longing of how desirable it would be to shed one's whole past self— "body and trade"—in death, and thus free the soul to exist in pure solitude. But on the authority of "some Platonist" (doubtless Yeats himself, who is also the "moralist or mythological poet" of the poem's first line), it warns us that the shedding would not be easy. The mystical metaphysics involved may be a bit elusive, but the language here has a curious confidentiality, as though the "Platonist" had passed on a chancy practical tip to a friend who was passing it on to us:

if our works could
But vanish with our breath
That were a lucky death,
For triumph would but mar our solitude.

Thus the middle stanza turns the poem, and the sequence, around. The slightly riddling words of extreme despair in Poem I—

"all triumph would / But mar our solitude"—are echoed here, but as an expression of probably impossible hope. We are prepared for the solitary soul's leap into nothingness, and for its inability to penetrate the unknown and isolate its own pure essence, and for the "desolation" of "heaven" itself. And we are prepared, too, despite the sophisticated metaphysical paradoxes along the way, for the homely colloquial ending of the poem: "we were crack-pated when we dreamed." The self-castigating ironies of the fourth and fifth poems, directed against "our" weasel-like behavior and shallow mockery of our betters in time of crisis, come naturally in the wake of Poem III. They humanize the sensibility at work. We hear the voice of a fellow citizen sick of the world in which he too has played a demeaning part.

And then, in Poem VI of "Nineteen Hundred and Nineteen," a final prophetic vision takes over. The first five lines summon up the essential feeling of the whole double sequence in a new image of fearful, yet partly seductive, chaos:

> Violence upon the roads: violence of horses;
> Some few have handsome riders, are garlanded
> On delicate sensitive ear or tossing mane,
> But wearied running round and round in their courses
> All break and vanish, and evil gathers head.

This poem moves cinematically, with its opening lines providing an overview (and, if this were an actual film, with appropriate music). Then the camera closes in on the riders, the legendary Sidhe of ominous beauty and power who had long intrigued Yeats's imagination:

> Herodias' daughters have returned again,
> A sudden blast of dusty wind and after
> Thunder of feet, tumult of images,
> Their purpose in the labyrinth of the wind;
> And should some crazy hand dare touch a daughter
> All turn with amorous cries, or angry cries,
> According to the wind, for all are blind.

In a note on the Sidhe in *The Wind Among the Reeds,* Yeats had described them as

> the gods of ancient Ireland . . . or the people of the Faery Hills [who] still ride the country as of old. Sidhe is also Gaelic for wind. They journey in whirling wind, the winds that were called the dance of the daughters of Herodias in the Middle Ages, Herodias doubtless taking the place of some old goddess.

We may readily add the obvious folk-association with Herodias and her dancing daughter Salome—scheming women responsible for the beheading of John the Baptist. In any case, the poem's closeup of the blind, tumultuous "daughters of Herodias," now "amorous," now "angry," shows them as the very embodiment of sinister confusion amid the age's "blast of dusty wind."

And then the camera moves to an entirely different symbol, a lurching apparition—like the Sphinx in "The Second Coming," withits "gaze blank and pitiless as the sun." The new apparition, although also devoid of mercy and intellect, has a human form and is therefore an even more terrifying portent. The Sphinx that appeared to the poet's imagination was a warning of a monstrous world waiting to be born. The new figure is simply gross power in action:

> But now wind drops, dust settles; thereupon
> There lurches past, his great eyes without thought
> Under the shadow of stupid straw-pale locks,
> That insolent fiend Robert Artisson
> To whom the love-lorn Lady Kyteler brought
> Bronzed peacock feathers, red combs of her cocks.

The opening line of Poem VI—"Violence upon the roads: violence of horses"—connects directly with the central preoccupation of the double sequence: the Civil War. Apart from that line and a more abstract half-line ("and evil gathers head"), the rest of the poem retreats to "the half-read wisdom of daemonic images" the despairing poet turned to at the end of the "Meditations." Here they are the images of the Sidhe and of Robert Artisson, the supposed incubus whose sexual attentions Alice Kyteler, condemned as a witch in 1324, was accused of buying with her gifts. The poem has raced, without stanza breaks, from the violence of current guerrilla warfare, to the realm of stormy, dangerous female desire and anger, and then to its counterpart, male ruthlessness in its stupidest, most insolent form.

Attraction to the "rough beast" of power as well as fear of it, whether it be military and political power or sexual power, has revealed itself in the unfolding of the double sequence. One remembers the poet's secret "envy" of the fighting men who come by his tower and go off again to play their part in the country's destiny. Perhaps, too, an altered light has been thrown on his earlier poems of willing yet unhappy subjection to the power of his "phoenix." All this is not to deny that the expressed revulsion against the bloodshed, let alone the atrocities, of the civil war is the dominant feeling and motivation of the sequences. But they also carry the admission of the psychological complexities accompanying that revulsion. The swift movement of Poem VI is remarkable. It is made up of two long sentences and, prosodically, of three six-line stanzas, each rhyming *abcabc,* that are jammed together in a single verse-unit. In the final six lines it hardly stops for breath: one end-stop and one caesura altogether. And it is packed with images and verbs of whirling action that give it the cinematic character mentioned earlier. The psychological associations involved, essential to the discoveries the sequences have been making, could not be "explained" poetically without this sort of presentative rush of successive visions.

After "Nineteen Hundred and Nineteen," *The Tower* slackens its pace for a few quieter pieces. First come two bits of very incidental verse: the lugubrious "The Wheel," fortunately only eight lines long, and the flip four-line squib "Youth and Age." At this point Yeats inserted "The New Faces," an intense, moving little poem he had written in 1912 but delayed publishing anywhere for almost a decade. It was apparently addressed to Lady Gregory, who would then have been sixty years old. While her name is not mentioned, details in the poem emphatically suggest her Coole Park estate. These facts, significant only biographically, seem worth mentioning because the poem reflects just the kind of close, collaborative relationship, rooted in deep friendship, that Yeats had with Lady Gregory. But read simply in its own right, it is an adult love poem, partly in the elegiac mode, and is near-Catullan verse of a rare variety:

> If you, that have grown old, were the first dead,
> Neither catalpa-tree nor scented lime
> Should hear my living feet, nor would I tread
> Where we wrought that shall break the teeth of Time.
> Let the new faces play what tricks they will
> In the old rooms; night can outbalance day,
> Our shadows rove the garden gravel still,
> The living seem more shadowy than they.

"The New Faces" stands out brilliantly amidst the somewhat desultory little group of four poems following "Nineteen Hundred and Nineteen." That group concludes with "A Prayer for My Son," written after the birth of the Yeatses' son Michael in 1921. Its feeling seems strained, especially in its comparison of the dangers the poet says the child will confront (such as enemies jealous of his achievements) with those faced by the Holy Family. It has none of the rich force of "A Prayer for My Daughter," yet is to a tiny extent redeemed by its initial whimsical tenderness:

> Bid a strong ghost stand at the head
> That my Michael may sleep sound,
> Nor cry, nor turn in the bed
> Till his morning meal come round;
> And may departing twilight keep
> All dread afar till morning's back,
> That his mother may not lack
> Her fill of sleep.

The volume recovers full strength, however, in certain poems whose strategic placement has already been mentioned: namely, "Two Songs from a Play," "Leda and the Swan," "Among School

Children," sections of "A Man Young and Old" (especially I, IV, VIII, and IX), and "All Souls' Night." In their several ways, these are all universalizing works. That is, their major emphasis is given more to all-encompassing—even apocalyptic—perspectives than to personal or political tensions and crises. To some extent they seem reactions against the vastly depressive insights reached in the civil war sequences (and underpinned by the death in 1922 of Yeats's father, which also aroused long-dormant feelings about the loss of his mother years earlier). The reactions were by no means sunnily optimistic. They took the form of seeing human tragedy in a cosmic or at least impersonal context, and sometimes of grasping for communion with realms beyond death.

This reactive direction is clearest for "Two Songs from a Play" and for "Leda and the Swan," whose starting points are, respectively, "God's death" (especially the Crucifixion) and the myth of Leda's ravishment by Zeus. It is least obvious for "Among School Children." That poem begins as another personal account, leavened by humor and romantic memory, of the discomforts of old age. It then becomes, first, a lament for life's inevitable disillusionments and, finally, a mystical affirmation of the way that nature and art hold time at bay. "A Man Young and Old" subordinates its private, confessional basis to the moon imagery the "system" of *A Vision* is based on. And, despite important differences, "All Souls' Night" oddly parallels the structure of "Among School Children." It is in part whimsy, in part a one-man séance, in part multiple elegy, and in part a madly fierce act of will "in the world's despite"—yet it moves, similarly, from personal memories to asserting a way to transcend the limits of mortality.

The play the title of "Two Songs from a Play" refers to is *The Resurrection,* first published in 1927 but reprinted in its much improved present form in 1932 and presented at the Abbey Theatre in 1934. In a prefatory note (1931), Yeats wrote: "Before I had finished this play I saw that its subject-matter made it unsuited for the public stage in England or in Ireland." He therefore "wrote songs for the unfolding and folding of the curtain that it might be played in a studio or a drawing-room like my dance plays or at the Peacock Theatre [Dublin] and before a specially chosen audience." The "songs" were the "Two Songs" included in *The Tower*. (The final stanza, however, had not yet been written in 1928. It was added three years later.)

Fears remaining from early attacks by clerics and religiously conservative audiences were clearly still with Yeats in 1931. When production by the Abbey (Ireland's outstanding "public stage") was planned after all just a couple of years later, he changed the prefatory note to read "might make it unsuitable" instead of "made it unsuitable." We shall look at the play more fully in the next chapter; but I should note here that, despite the fact that the Resurrection of Christ is its main focus of attention, it is by no means a Christian play. The "two songs"—really two halves of a single song, the first half sung by "Musicians" at the beginning, the second half at the end—are even more pointed than the play in subordinating both the Crucifixion and the Resurrection to the cyclical scheme of *A Vision*. That is, the language of non-faith is "pointed" if read carefully enough to penetrate its thinly protective Delphic surface.

Both play and poem convey what Yeats, in a 1934 note to *The Resurrection,* called "the terror of the supernatural described by Job"—although, he wrote, "my intellect rejected" it. His phrasing succinctly conveys his deep emotional engagement, quite lacking in rational conviction or even rational comprehension, with mystical traditions nurtured in the human psyche over the centuries.

Precisely this contradictory subjective mixture, of terrified awe at the "supernatural" and cool intellectual distancing, defines "Two Songs from a Play." It makes the paired songs a perfect expression of the depressive-apocalyptic turn of Yeats's work noted earlier. The opening song, with its references to Greek mythology and its echoes of Vergil's Eclogue IV and of Shelley's chorus in *Hellas* beginning "The world's great age begins anew," is densely allusive. It begins as inspired prophecy but ends in despair. Like so much literature of this century, it is indebted to Sir James Frazer's *The Golden Bough* and to the work in comparative myth and ritual of the Cambridge

anthropologists—work that of course called into question the unique
authority of any given religion.

Luckily, the *poem* is not crushed under the weight of all its
influences. It is helpful to be aware of them, but only if we can keep
them in their place somewhere offstage. For onstage the poem presents a sequence of effects, each of them simple and immediate in
itself. Thus the first stanza opens the curtain upon a vibrant initial
tableau followed by a shockingly violent action. Although it describes mutilation of a god's body, the phrasing recalls the lines in
"Nineteen Hundred and Nineteen" about the "mother, murdered at
her door" and left "to crawl in her own blood." And after that the
stanza focuses on a new scene: the Muses, somewhere in the em-
pyrean of art, singing to celebrate the birth of a new era "as though
God's death were but a play." Again, despite the supernatural scene,
we have an echo of the civil-war sequences: specifically, of the passage in "The Road at My Door" in which a jolly Irregular "comes
cracking jokes of civil war / As though to die by gunshot were / The
finest play under the sun." Like the sequences, the stanza is at once
visionary, elegiac, and charged with exultant horror:

> I saw a staring virgin stand
> Where holy Dionysus died,
> And tear the heart out of his side,
> And lay the heart upon her hand
> And bear the beating heart away;
> And then did all the Muses sing
> Of Magnus Annus in the spring,
> As though God's death were but a play.

As the poem progresses, it becomes clear that Yeats is conflating
the story of Christ with pagan myths of the death and resurrection of
gods, in particular the virgin goddess Athena's salvaging of Dionysus' heart after he had been rent apart by the Titans. Mythical
history has it that she carried the heart to Zeus, who swallowed it and
then impregnated Semele, a mortal, to give Dionysus a second birth.
These are among the details that a host of scholars have been glad to

elucidate, but that the poem omits in favor of dramatic immediacy and mystery and even a certain exciting ambiguity.

Within the poem, what emerges beyond this context is a lament, not for the deaths of specific sacrificed divinities but for the necessary displacement of all that we live by and love as new historical phases take over. Cyclical change is endless and demoralizing. Christianity itself, for instance, ushered in the death of Grecian values of intellectual openness of spirit and rigor of method:

> Odour of blood when Christ was slain
> Made all Platonic tolerance vain
> And vain all Doric discipline.

So the first stanza of the second "song" closes. Originally, it ended the poem on a note of sharp dismissal of Christian doctrine. But the final stanza added later begins with a lament for mutability—

> Everything that man esteems
> Endures a moment or a day—

and it ends with a sad turn of thought that accords with Poem III of "Nineteen Hundred and Nineteen" and with the basic premise of modern secular humanism. Granted our tragic predicament of having to leap into a "desolate heaven," our only resource is the values we ourselves create:

> Whatever flames upon the night
> Man's own resinous heart has fed.

This burning image, with its melancholy echo of Shakespeare's metaphor (Sonnet LXXIII) of a dying fire "consumed with that which it was nourished by," is nevertheless a kind of affirmation. In its fashion it prepares us for the spirit of "Among School Children," which ends by presenting the creative process as our one hope in the face of the disillusion that comes with time. In the context of the tragic human predicament, "whatever flames upon the night" is a miracle, even though it consumes its source: "man's own resinous heart." The miracle occurs when the artist, unselfconsciously absorbed in the act of making, becomes inseparable from the organic growth of the work—just as the different parts of a tree are intrinsic to its whole living identity:

> Labour is blossoming or dancing where
> The body is not bruised to pleasure soul,
> Nor beauty born out of its own despair,
> Nor blear-eyed wisdom out of midnight oil.
> O chestnut-tree, great-rooted blossomer,
> Are you the leaf, the blossom, or the bole?
> O body swayed to music, O brightening glance,
> How can we know the dancer from the dance?

The stanza is a last-ditch defense of art, but also of every kind of creative endeavor that the individual ego can lose itself in. It stands as a willful affirmation, a hold (as in "The Tower") against the preceding stanzas' accumulated sense of life's futility. At the same time, it is a reflex of those stanzas in what it implies: namely, that even a poem of increasing ruefulness and despair can be an example of "labour . . . blossoming or dancing." "Among School Children" is a perfect model of such a poem.

The poem is in the ottava rima that Yeats often found a congenial form. With it he could shift tones gracefully within or between large six-line units that might be primarily description or narration or lyrical contemplation. The seven earlier stanzas, with their leisurely five-stress lines rhyming *abababcc,* provide many instances. Yeats sometimes uses the fifth line as though it were a turning point in a sonnet; and his closing couplets, as in a Shakespearian sonnet, offer a natural opportunity for a significant heightening of some sort. The movement of "Among School Children" is a superb instance of his mastery of this form.

Thus, the first stanza begins with quiet simplicity. The poet is making an official visit to a girls' school: "I walk through the long schoolroom questioning; / A kind old nun in a white hood replies." A mild irony enters the summary of what she tells him: "The children learn to cipher and to sing," etc., "in the best modern way." At the stanza's close the irony grows sharp and self-directed as he realizes with a pang how he must look to the little students:

> the children's eyes
> In momentary wonder stare upon
> A sixty-year-old smiling public man.

The second stanza makes a great leap of association to a richly nostalgic romantic memory. His sudden insight into the little girls' minds has reminded the poet of "a tale" a young woman once, in an intimate moment, told him about an unhappy childhood experience at school. The opening of this stanza—"I dream of a Ledaean body, bent / Above a sinking fire"—parallels the poem's first line ("I walk through the long schoolroom questioning") grammatically but hardly emotionally. Their impacts are as different from each other as chalk dust and blackboards are from a "sinking fire" beside which two lovers exchange confidences.

And yet the subjective connection is clear. In that cherished moment of rapport, the poem tells us, "it seemed that our two natures blent / Into a sphere from youthful sympathy." The poet's quick empathy with the little schoolgirls' view of him is a similar psychological identification. He not only remembers the romantic occasion in the long-ago past but also imagines his beloved as one of the children staring at him in the classroom. He imagines it so vividly that "thereupon my heart is driven wild: / She stands before me as a living child."

This vision brings the third stanza to an end, and afterwards the poem takes a new turn. But it is interesting to note the double sexual identity the poem has striven toward: first, in the poet's seeing himself as the schoolgirls see him; and second, in his "blending" with his beloved's nature and making her memories his own. Without pressing a thesis, one may observe a like striving to understand, and empathize with, female sensibility in such other work as "Leda and

Yeats and Maud Gonne in the 1930s

the Swan" in *The Tower* and the Crazy Jane poems and "A Woman Young and Old" in *The Winding Stair*.

It may be going too far to see a relationship between the "staring virgin" of "Two Songs from a Play" and the little virgins who "stare in wonder" in "Among School Children"; or between that "fierce" personage in the former poem, whom the poet saw "tear the heart out" of Dionysus and "bear that beating heart away," and the poet's "phoenix," who has broken his heart and dominated him in the "Memory" poems and elsewhere. One can, indeed, allow such associations to tease one's reading out of reasonable limits. But it is also true that we have seen an evolution from early poems of lost love (perhaps related to the lost mother), through an interim poetry of frustration and inability to comprehend the beloved, to later efforts—detached, on the surface at least, from personal confession of love-difficulties—at empathic insight into feminine mentality. The second stanza of "Among School Children," which reflects this evolution perfectly, is worth quoting here. Its beginning is charged with romantic feeling, while its ending—vastly distant from the sort of confession it might have fallen into—plays whimsically both on the egg that Leda's swan-sired children emerged from and on Aristophanes' witty account, in Plato's *Symposium,* of the origin of the sexes:

> I dream of a Ledaean body, bent
> Above a sinking fire, a tale that she
> Told of a harsh reproof, or trivial event
> That changed some childish day to tragedy—
> Told, and it seemed that our two natures blent
> Into a sphere from youthful sympathy,
> Or else, to alter Plato's parable,
> Into the yolk and white of the one shell.

The next four stanzas re-enter the world of irrevocable aging and disillusion explored in "Sailing to Byzantium" and "The Tower." The beloved's "present image floats into the mind"— "hollow of cheek as though it drank the wind / And took a mess of shadows for its meat." And the poet himself, he reminds us self-derisively, is at best "a comfortable kind of old scarecrow." But he does not linger, as he did in the volume's first poems, on his own miseries. Rather, he again tries to reach outward, into the minds of women. Would any young mother, he asks, think the pain of giving birth, and her fears for her baby's survival, worthwhile if she could foresee her child "with sixty or more winters on its head"? Even such glorious figures as Plato, Aristotle, and Pythagoras have inevitably dwindled at last, like the poet, into "old clothes upon old sticks to scare a bird."

So, then, the seventh stanza tells us, "both nuns and mothers worship images" that deceive them. The images mothers worship are glorified visions of their children. The nuns' images "keep a marble or a bronze repose. / And yet they too break hearts." The poem has shifted its focus here to an old complaint of Yeats's: the waste and betrayal of life's possibilities through singleminded devotion to ideals—those tormenting "Presences" that are the "self-born mockers of man's enterprise."

The closing stanza, as we have seen, pushes hard to counteract the gathering despair flooding down from the previous stanzas. It is interesting that, just as Yeats chose female exemplars—"nuns and mothers"—to symbolize our human predicament in the preceding stanza, so now he presents the counter-effort as a kind of "labour" that is all joy and does not "bruise" the body but instead gives birth to a mystically transcendent state.

It was his sonnet "Leda and the Swan," of course, that sensationally introduced his effort in *The Tower* to see into female sensibility and sexuality. The octave and the first line of the sestet have several obvious levels. The most elemental is that a violent act of ravishment is graphically presented, but without the infliction of pain or any sense of humiliation or trauma after the girl's first "terrified" resistance. Rather, her "loosening thighs" respond to the caresses of the "feathered glory" as she feels its"strange heart beating" against her heart. The orgasmic "shudder in the loins" is presumably a shared one. At this level the scene enacts a common daydream, doubtless more an expression of male curiosity about how women experience intercourse than the reverse—although we must remember that the supposed point of view is Leda's. Despite the literal subject, we are far from a police-blotter report of criminal rape.

Pictorially, this elemental level is essential to the tactile muscularity of the poem, as in the various paintings or bas-reliefs that have been suggested as its inspiration. But in addition—again as with the paintings—what is being illustrated is a mythical event. The "rapist" is not a man but a god—the most powerful of the Greek gods—in the form of a swan. And the sexual act here is an apocalyptic event, parallel in Yeats's view to the conception of Christ. Yeats printed "Leda and the Swan" as the epigraph to Book V of *A Vision,* commenting:

> I imagine the annunciation that founded Greece as made to Leda, remembering that they showed in a Spartan temple, strung up to the roof as a holy relic, an unhatched egg of hers; and that from one of her

eggs came Love and from the other War. But all things are from antithesis, and when in my ignorance I try to imagine what older civilisation that annunciation rejected I can but see bird and woman blotting out some corner of the Babylonian mathematical starlight.

The phrasing here points up some of the connections linking this poem with both "Two Songs from a Play" and "Among School Children." The new civilization created by the mating of Zeus and Leda that "founded Greece" is linked with the Trojan War and the epic and tragic literature around it. But was Leda, the human participant, merely the passive carrier of the future thus engendered by the god's "power," or did she—i.e., *we*—take on his "knowledge" as well as his seed? The sestet puts the issue:

> A shudder in the loins engenders there
> The broken wall, the burning roof and tower
> And Agamemnon dead.
>   Being so caught up,
> So mastered by the brute blood of the air,
> Did she put on his knowledge with his power
> Before the indifferent beak could let her drop?

The forceful sexual phrasing of the octave is matched here, but the sestet breaks away from the language of female erotism after its transitional first line. Leda's private sensations no longer dominate the poem. Instead, the emphasis has shifted to her symbolic embodiment of the puzzle of human history. This kind of shift of emphasis—from an intense intimacy to a less personal but still passionate poetic rhetoric—is characteristic of the whole volume and certainly anticipates "Among School Children."

The eleven short numbered pieces called "A Man Young and Old" make for a fairly uneven sequence in which four pieces, however, do stand out. These are the first ("First Love"), the fourth ("The Death of the Hare"), the eighth ("Summer and Spring"), and the ninth ("The Secrets of the Old"). All four are very simple in form. They are made up of extended ballad stanzas with six lines or more each. The sequence begins bravely with "First Love," which reprises Yeats's earlier poems of love-suffering—but with a difference. The suffering is poignantly conveyed, yet in an odd way made almost impersonal by the prevailing lunar and astronomical imagery:

> Though nurtured like the sailing moon
> In beauty's murderous brood,
> She walked awhile and blushed awhile
> And on my pathway stood
> Until I thought her body bore
> A heart of flesh and blood.
>
> But since I laid a hand thereon
> And found a heart of stone
> I have attempted many things
> And not a thing is done,
> For every hand is lunatic
> That travels on the moon.
>
> She smiled and that transfigured me
> And left me but a lout,
> Maundering here, and maundering there,
> Emptier of thought
> Than the heavenly circuit of its stars
> When the moon sails out.

The *strangeness* of this plaint is what gives it its power. It goes the story of Endymion one better and somehow leaves the moon-girl's brain-stricken lover, "maundering" somewhere in darkened space, with the dignity of having touched the beautiful but "murderous" realm of the totally non-human. It is an uncertain glory, a triumph of an odd sort, to become comparable in any way to "the heavenly circuit" and to have turned "lunatic" because one has had the advantage of great opportunities and has "laid a hand" on the moon. If "touched," the cold, stony reality of outer space and the galaxies, indifferent to our needs and reveries, must chill us into a sense of madness—but only because we are facing the "desolate heaven" without self-deception.

It was this kind of depressive transcendence that led to one of the key lines in "The Tower": "For if I triumph I must make men mad." The perspective the whole volume has been unfolding is that we must, in the face of hard knowledge, give up illusory romantic hopes while, nevertheless, we insist "madly" that all reality is the creation of human will. "First Love" helps clear the way to "All Souls' Night," the eerie, witty, tragic concluding poem of *The Tower,* in which a typical passage reads:

> I have a marvellous thing to say,
> A certain marvellous thing
> None but the living mock,
> Though not for sober ear;
> It may be all that hear
> Should laugh and weep an hour upon the clock.

But to return now to "A Man Young and Old." Another remarkable piece in it is "The Death of the Hare." Like "Among School Children," this self-reproachful lyric continues the advance into greater empathy with women that began soon after Yeats's marriage in late 1917. (As we have seen, strong evidence of this turn appeared in two poems of 1918 to 1919: "An Image from a Past Life," perhaps the first poem he wrote after the couple moved into Thoor Ballylee, and "Towards Break of Day.") "The Death of the Hare" connects in a new way, too, with "Memory" and "Two Songs of a Fool":

> I have pointed out the yelling pack,
> The hare leap to the wood,
> And when I pass a compliment
> Rejoice as lover should
> At the drooping of an eye,
> At the mantling of the blood.
>
> Then suddenly my heart is wrung
> By her distracted air

And I remember wildness lost
And after, swept from there,
Am set down standing in the wood
At the death of the hare.

A perfectly simple story, at least in stanza one. Two parallel
hunts are going on simultaneously. In full chase, both the "yelling
pack" and the rejoicing gallant feel that victory is at hand, while the
fleeing hare and blushing woman are beset by their imminent danger. But the second stanza utterly reverses the poem's emotional
direction. Its first line is a surge of pity and remorse for the distress
"I" have caused "her." Its closing line slams things shut with the
brutal letdown of seeing the hare torn apart by the dogs—a reminder
as well of the squalor of sexual pursuit for the sake of victory in the
chase. The sight of her "distracted air" has dissipated the "wildness"
of the lover's unthinking sensual arousal. And so he is "swept from
there"—an effective touch of surreal ambiguity—and "set down"
elsewhere "in the wood," where the hare is being slain. Together
with the psychological shock of the man's suddenly awakened sympathy, the poem also projects his genuine confusion and loss of bearings.

"The Death of the Hare" has subtle affinities with the two
poems mentioned earlier. With the gradual sloughing off of domination by the woman celebrated in the "Memory" group, the symbolic
associations of the word "hare" changed somewhat. In "Two Songs
of a Fool," the hare's wildness remains. The poor Fool has thought of
her as his "tame hare" and has feared for her; but once she "drank the
wind" through the open door, she chose to "drum with her heel and
to leap" away and make her escape. The Fool is left with remorse and
concern. So is the lover in "The Death of the Hare." But his feelings
now are a matter neither of undying passion nor of lost possibilities
but of guilt because of his callous role as a hunter. In the movement of
The Tower as a whole, this poem contributes to the sense of bleakness
the book struggles against.

The other two more telling poems in "A Man Young and Old"

celebrate the possession of memories of love relationship, whether happy or unhappy. "Summer and Spring" begins as a simpler variation on the passage in "Among School Children" in which the two lovers blend into one "from youthful sympathy" after a moving confidence. But then it introduces a third character: "Peter," who has a jealously "murdering look" because, it turns out, "he and she / Had spoken of their childish days" with exactly the same results. The irony and self-parody here sound more like Hardy than like Yeats— but the point is not the irony but the gift of intense experience:

> O what a bursting out there was,
> And what a blossoming,
> When we had all the summer-time
> And she had all the spring!

The other poem of memory-celebration, "The Secrets of the Old," is the gentlest and most endearing, yet in its quiet way the most objective, piece in the sequence. It is about passion when all passion is treasured only as old songs and stories are treasured. One might almost forget that its feeling is the sort that comes in the wake of total loss—what the poem calls "solitude." The earlier poem by Yeats closest to it in tone is probably "Broken Dreams," but "The Secrets of the Old" is neither nostalgic nor self-pitying, despite its touching subject-matter:

> I have old women's secrets now
> That had those of the young;
> Madge tells me what I dared not think
> When my blood was strong,
> And what had drowned a lover once
> Sounds like an old song.
>
> Though Margery is stricken dumb
> If thrown in Madge's way,
> We three make up a solitude;
> For none alive today

Can know the stories that we know
Or say the things we say:

How such a man pleased women most
Of all that are gone,
How such a pair loved many years
And such a pair but one,
Stories of the bed of straw
Or the bed of down.

These poems, the most realized ones in the sequence, define its scope and dynamic progression. I should mention, though without going into detail, that its atmosphere of being in a state of "madness" resulting from total loss and isolation is reinforced in several of the lesser poems—most explicitly in "The Empty Cup" but also in "The Friends of His Youth" and "His Wildness." The sequence thus anticipates the book's closing poem," "All Souls' Night," in which Yeats lets himself go further than anywhere else in acting out the role of deranged seer.

To do so, he sets up an imaginary séance with the ghosts of former companions in mystical and occultist studies. He summons them, not to answer his questions as in "The Tower" or in an actual séance held by a medium, but to listen to his thoughts—"mummy truths" that sober living folk would naturally mock. The three ghosts will be an understanding audience. They will know that "mummy truths" are of their world, spoken by someone who—like them when they were alive—has long pressed to see beyond the barrier of death. All had been his friends, although one had become "of late estranged," and all had died recently, between 1917 and 1919. Yeats wrote "All Souls' Night" in 1920, long before most of the other poems in *The Tower*. But he placed it, appropriately, at the book's end, where its fused elegiac and darkly visionary character gives it special weight. For the same reason, he made it the epilogue to *A Vision*.

All Souls' Day, usually November second, is a time for prayers for the dead. All Souls' Night, then, after "midnight has come," is an especially fitting occasion to conjure up dead friends in an atmosphere both religious and spectral. To this mixture Yeats adds a certain macabre drollness in his opening stanza:

> Midnight has come, and the great Christ Church Bell
> And many a lesser bell sound through the room;
> And it is All Souls' Night,
> And two long glasses brimmed with muscatel
> Bubble upon the table. A ghost may come;
> For it is a ghost's right,
> His element is so fine
> Being sharpened by his death,
> To drink from the wine-breath
> While our gross palates drink from the whole wine.

In the ghostly world, this is a congenial setting for a banquet. The three friends—the mystical artist William Thomas Horton, the actress Florence Farr Emery, and MacGregor Mathers (an occultist and fellow member of the Order of the Golden Dawn whom Yeats came to disagree with sharply despite their long friendship)—are therefore called upon to join the poet. On this night the circumstances are such that perhaps he, who like them is "wound in mind's pondering/As mummies in the mummy-cloth are wound," can connect with them.

Two stanzas of elegiac description are given to each guest. Taken together, the six long stanzas are the heart of the poem. They embody the communion with the dead that Yeats had dreamt of for many years and that he imagines even more movingly in this poem than in the later, more dazzling "Byzantium." The depth of sympathetic recollection that comes through has the force of bringing the essential natures of the three old friends directly before us. The purity of Horton and of his love for his deceased wife, the pity of Florence's Emery's disfiguring cancer that led her to leave her country and friends and become a teacher in India, and the confusing contrariness of the brilliant and generous but "crazed" MacGregor are evoked beautifully. And each evocation has, by its very nature,

the quality of mystical communion. The first—and most beautiful—
is of Horton's visionary reveries about his wife:

> Two thoughts were so mixed up I could not tell
> Whether of her or God he thought the most,
> But think that his mind's eye,
> When upward turned, on one sole image fell;
> And that a slight companionable ghost,
> Wild with divinity,
> Had so lit up the whole
> Immense miraculous house
> The Bible promised us,
> It seemed a goldfish swimming in a bowl.

In the second, Florence Emery's discovery about "the soul's
journey," learned during the "foul years" she endured "hidden from
eyesight to the unnoticed end," is lovingly recalled:

> How it is whirled about
> Wherever the orbit of the moon can reach,
> Until it plunge into the sun;
> And there, free and yet fast,
> Being both Chance and Choice,
> Forget its broken toys
> And sink into its own delight at last.

And finally, the eccentric MacGregor, whose loneliness had
"driven him crazed," is characterized with acerbic empathy:

> For meditations upon unknown thought
> Make human intercourse grow less and less;
> They are neither paid nor praised.
> But he'd object to the host,
> The glass because my glass;
> A ghost-lover he was
> And may have grown more arrogant being a ghost.

The hard-wrung spirituality that colors these portraits, however affectionate, is the final direction of *The Tower*. It is a resultant of all the assertions in previous poems of the will's power to countervene fatality. Four lines in the closing stanza carry this insistence to its limit:

Nothing can stay my glance
Until that glance run in the world's despite
To where the damned have howled away their hearts,
And where the blessed dance. . . .

VII

Drama of the 1930s

Yeats's last plays reflect his deepening preoccupation with what—in a letter of 2 or 4 October 1927—he had called the only worthwhile topics: "sex and the dead." The boldest and most experimental of the seven plays of his final decade are the twin pieces *A Full Moon in March* and *The King of the Great Clock Tower* (both published in 1935) and *The Herne's Egg* (1938), which link these topics directly and sometimes crudely. *The Resurrection* (1931), *The Words upon the Window-Pane* (1934), *The Death of Cuchulain* (1939), and *Purgatory* (1939) do so far more subtly yet with greater force.

It is of some importance, also, to take note of Yeats's adaptations of Sophocles' *Oedipus Tyrannos*—anglicized as *Sophocles' King Oedipus*—and *Oedipus at Colonus*. These versions, prose renderings except for the choral songs, were first produced in 1926 and 1927 respectively. They are not, of course, original works in the same sense as Yeats's other plays, and he was properly modest about his qualifications as a translator. Nevertheless, on a very practical level, they gave him a chance to try his hand at rendering Sophoclean dialogue into simple, natural English accessible to a wide audience. The larger success of this effort lay in the experience he gained by "rewriting" some of the greatest plays ever written: highly concentrated tragic drama of enormous significance for European mythical memory. His finest original work of the period profits from what he learned from Sophocles' economy, rhythms of dialogue, and cumulative intensity.

He felt a kinship, as well, with the plays' exalted sense of Oedipus' sex-and-death-linked tragic burden. Their sexual directness—particularly the theme of incest, though treated with shocked horror by all the characters—had led to their banning in the British Isles. Yeats, whose struggle with parochial prejudices in his own country had a long history, was especially pleased when official censorship ended in Ireland. As he wrote in the *New York Times* of 15 January 1933: "Ireland had no censorship, and a successful performance might make her proud of her freedom, say even, perhaps, 'I have an old historical religion moulded to the body of man like an old suit of clothes, and am therefore free.'" And he saw affinities with Irish cultural traditions in these works. For instance:

> . . . being an ignorant man, I may not have gone to Greece through a Latin mist. Greek literature, like old Irish literature, was founded upon beliefs, not like Latin literature upon documents. No man has ever prayed to or dreaded one of Vergil's nymphs, but when Oedipus at Colonus went into the Wood of the Furies he felt the same creeping in his flesh that an Irish countryman feels in certain haunted woods in Galway and in Sligo. At the Abbey Theatre we play both *Oedipus the King* and *Oedipus at Colonus,* and they seem at home there.

Obviously, the primal *frisson* at the sensed presence of the supernatural, which Yeats thought Sophocles' world shared with rural Ireland, connects with feelings about sex and death. In *Oedipus the King,* after the hero has finally seen the whole dreadful truth about himself, a choral song nakedly presents the ancient world's shudder of horror at violation of the incest taboo:

> But, looking for a marriage-bed, he found the bed of his
> birth,
> Tilled the field his father had tilled, cast seed into
> the same abounding earth;
> Entered through the door that had sent him wailing forth.

The final pages of *Oedipus at Colonus* link death and the unseen powers with the same awe. Oedipus, now the sacred guardian of Athens because of the very curse on his name, takes his leave of life, and the Chorus sings:

> I call upon Persephone, queen of the dead,
> And upon Hades, king of night, I call;
> Chain all the Furies up that he may tread
> The perilous pathway to the Stygian hall
> And rest among his mighty peers at last,
> For the entanglements of God are past.
>
> Nor may the hundred-headed dog give tongue
> Until the daughters of Earth and Tartarus
> That even bloodless shades call Death has sung
> The travel-broken shade of Oedipus
> Through triumph of completed destiny
> Into eternal sleep, if such there be.

Accompanied by his daughters, King Theseus of Athens, and a messenger, and guided by invisible divinities—Hermes and "The Goddess of the Dead"—Oedipus finds his way to a destined place where he will be drawn into the realm of death. There, the messenger reports, "a voice spoke and summoned Oedipus, and the hair stood up upon our heads, for it was a God that spoke." At Oedipus' command, all but Theseus turned away. When, shortly afterwards, they looked back, "Oedipus had gone and the King stood there, a hand raised to shade his eyes as from some dreadful sight."

His renderings of Sophocles seem to have helped free Yeats to deal even more directly than before with sex and death. At the same time, too, he saw more clearly how to project—not comically but in serious dramatic fashion—that "creeping of his flesh" he says a typical superstitious countryman feels when he senses uncanny presences nearby "in certain haunted woods."

What Yeats's note on the play calls "the terror of the supernatural" is precisely the feeling evoked in the most effective moments of *The Resurrection,* whose composition overlapped his work on the Oedipus plays. Certainly the opening and closing Musicians' songs—called "Two Songs from a Play" in *The Tower* and discussed in the preceding chapter—provide a model of depressive transcendence somehow engendered by that very terror. One other song, placed strategically at the center, is a variation—really a primitivistic chant—on the motif of Dionysus' death and rebirth introduced at the play's start.

This motif merges with the larger dramatic motif of *The Resurrection*: the mystery of the risen Christ. The two major songs, which assume a cyclical relationship in the virgin births as well as the deaths and resurrections of Dionysus and Jesus, show all these sacred events as harbingers of cataclysmic changes in human history. Their emotional and intellectual sweep, and the outburst of barbaric wildness and promiscuity in the eerie chant of Dionysus' female followers midway through the piece, are the most powerful achievements in the play. Yeats, incidentally, once gave high praise to Vachel Lindsay's work, and the chant does sound like a duet by those very unlike poets:

> Astrea's holy child!
> A rattle in the wood
> Where a Titan strode!
> His rattle drew the child
> Into that solitude.
Barrum, barrum, barrum
> *[Drum-taps accompany and follow the words]*
> We wandering women,
> Wives for all that come,
> Tried to draw him home;
> And every wandering woman
> Beat upon a drum.
Barrum, barrum, barrum
> *[Drum-taps as before]*
> But the murderous Titans
> Where the woods grow dim

> Stood and waited him.
> The great hands of those Titans
> Tore limb from limb.
> Barrum, barrum, barrum
> > *[Drum-taps as before]*
> > On virgin Astrea
> > That can succour all
> > Wandering women call;
> > Call out to Astrea
> > That the moon stood at the full.
> Barrum, barrum, barrum
> > *[Drum-taps as before]*

The women's song accompanies the description, by a Greek follower of Christ, of a scene in which worshippers of Dionysus have taken over Jerusalem's streets after the Crucifixion. Some of them are "men dressed as women that they may attain in worship a woman's self-abandonment"; others are dancers who "have gashed themselves with knives, imagining themselves . . . at once the god and the Titans that murdered him." And "a little further off," he says, "a man and a woman are coupling in the street. She thinks the surrender to some man the dance threw into her arms may bring her god back to life." The ecstasy of violence and abandonment thus described invites, but does not quite embody, the thrill of terror Yeats sought to create in this play. It comes off more as a listing by a bemused Shavian observer of naughty things going on in the street. (At one point he says, "My God! What a spectacle!") Yet at the same time, the scene marks a further step in Yeats's progress toward shedding self-censorship in his art—a fact that does not, however, in this instance strengthen its impact.

Indeed, except for one brief, important scene toward the very end, there is little in the play's prose body to approach the genuine intensity of its three songs. Much of it is simply heightened discussion, admittedly interesting in itself and because of the pressured circumstances in which it takes place. At the start we see two young followers of Christ: "the Greek" (just quoted) and "the Hebrew."

They are watching the Dionysians' riotous frenzy below and awaiting a third companion, "the Syrian." Christ has been crucified, Peter
has denied him, and the fugitive apostles are in hiding in a further
room.

A very promising dramatic situation, but it soon turns didactic.
While waiting, the Hebrew and the Greek debate whether or not
Jesus was truly the Messiah. *No,* says the Hebrew; he was just flesh
and blood—"the best man who ever lived." *Yes,* says the Greek; he
assumed a human image but was actually all spirit, a phantom. For a
while they are distracted by the Dionysian revels on the street. Then
the Syrian arrives, breathless with great tidings: the two Marys, with
other women, have been to Jesus' tomb at daybreak and found it
empty! This exciting news soon becomes part of the debate. The
Hebrew says that the Romans must have stolen the body, the Greek
that a phantom would have had no problem escaping the tomb, and
the Syrian (here Yeats's surrogate) that miracles are beyond logic:
"What matter if it contradicts all human knowledge?—another Argo
seeks another fleece, another Troy is sacked."

After these words the emotional tempo speeds up. The Syrian's
laughter adds a pitch of ironic wildness to his "irrational" cyclical
explanation. His thoughts, echoing the Musicians' visionary first
song, break up the play's hitherto balanced debate-rhythm. Meanwhile, the Dionysus worshipers' drumming and rattle-shaking
outdoors counterpoint his contempt for logic. The Grecian age
of love for objective knowledge and "beautiful humane cities" is
over. A new barbarism, like it or not, is in the ascendancy. And the
Syrian asks fundamental modern questions about history that recall
the endings of both "The Second Coming" and "Leda and the
Swan":

> What if there is always something that lies outside knowledge,
> outside order? What if at the moment when knowledge and order
> seem complete that something appears?

Then, at the very end, the play reaches the eerie level it has not
so far quite attained outside the songs.

[*The figure of Christ wearing a recognizable but stylistic mask enters through the curtain. The Syrian slowly draws back the curtain that shuts off the inner room where the apostles are. The three young men are towards the left of the stage, the figure of Christ is at the back towards the right.*]

The Greek. It is the phantom of our master. Why are you afraid? He has been crucified and buried, but only in semblance, and is among us once more. [*The Hebrew kneels.*] There is nothing here but a phantom, it has no flesh and blood. Because I know the truth I am not afraid. Look, I will touch it. It may be hard under my hand like a statue—I have heard of such things—or my hand may pass through it—but there is no flesh and blood. [*He goes slowly up to the figure and passes his hand over its side.*] The heart of a phantom is beating! The heart of a phantom is beating!

[*He screams. The figure of Christ crosses the stage and passes into the inner room.*]

The Syrian. He is standing in the midst of them. Some are afraid. He looks at Peter and James and John. He smiles. He has parted the clothes at his side. He shows them his side. There is a great wound there. Thomas has put his hand into the wound. He has put his hand where the heart is.

The Greek. O Athens, Alexandria, Rome, something has come to destroy you. The heart of a phantom is beating. Man has begun to die. Your words are clear at last, O Heraclitus. God and man die each other's life, live each other's death.

At this climactic moment the Musicians take over, singing their final song of the "Galilean turbulence" and "odour of blood when Christ was slain," of the death of the clear, bright era of Grecian civilization, and of the self-consuming character of all human accomplishment. The "beating" heart of Christ, like that of Dionysus in its time, drums in the next stage of human dreams and suffering.

The ending of *The Resurrection* is brilliant, and its relevance to the turbulence of our end-of-the-twentieth-century world remarkable. And yet its celebration, its wild laughter and awed wonder at the prospective triumph of bloodstained irrationality, had its dark counterpart in Yeats's psyche. Breaking loose into the freedom of genuine transport can be a sign of genius but may also bring one close to madness. Yeats flirts with that precarious condition in the play's "proof" that the Syrian is right: namely, the epiphany in its final scene. We have seen this flirtation before—in "The Tower," for instance ("For if I triumph I must make men mad"), and in "All Souls' Night." But after *The Resurrection* he showed his fascination with clinical madness in his last prose play, *The Words upon the Window-Pane,* and almost seemed to be suffering from it himself in the three plays after that: *A Full Moon in March, The King of the Great Clock Tower,* and *The Herne's Egg.*

Yeats finished work on *The Words upon the Window-Pane* late in 1930, two or three years before a certain unbalanced excitement—however one would diagnose it—showed itself in his writings and his general activities. He had not yet quite reached his mid-1930's phase of extremely arbitrary assertiveness, feverish sexuality (including a Steinach operation to restore potency), and obsession with eugenics, fascism, and a fiercely idiosyncratic nationalism. The central figure in *The Words upon the Window-Pane* is the ghost of Jonathan Swift in the depths of insane degradation. The play thus foreshadows the period to come. Nevertheless, Yeats easily kept Swift's character at a strategic remove from his own.

The play, though too short to be divided into acts or scenes, moves through five stages. In the first, John Corbet, an Irish doctoral candidate at Cambridge writing on Swift and Stella, visits a séance of the Dublin Spiritualists' Association in a house that once belonged to friends of Stella. Skeptical yet receptive, he is like Yeats but without commitment to "psychic research." He sounds more like Yeats when he explains what he hopes his dissertation will accomplish. It will dwell on Swift as representative of the greatness of Irish thought in the eighteenth century:

I hope to prove that in Swift's day men of intellect reached the height of their power—the greatest position they ever attained in society and the State, that everything great in Ireland and in our character, in what remains of our architecture, comes from that day; that we have kept its seal longer than England.

And it will show that Swift's vision was prophetic and tragic:

His ideal order was the Roman Senate, his ideal men Brutus and Cato. Such an order and such men had seemed possible once more, but the movement passed and he foresaw the ruin to come. Democracy, Rousseau, the French Revolution; that is why he hated the common run of men,—"I hate lawyers, I hate doctors," he said, "though I love Doctor So-and-so and Judge So-and-so"—that is why he wrote *Gulliver,* that is why he wore out his brain, that is why he felt *saeva indignatio,* that is why he sleeps under the greatest epitaph in history. You remember how it goes? It is almost finer in English than in Latin: "He has gone where fierce indignation can lacerate his heart no more."

Fortunately, John Corbet does not continue to hold forth at such length. But these observations are an important part of the play's exposition and, moreover, succeed in reflecting Yeats's views while being spoken by Corbet. Their reactionary impact is softened by the odd scene onstage, where a fictitious young scholar is describing a famous eighteenth-century satirist's ideas to a little group gathered for a séance. Also, his remarks soon shift attention to Swift's eccentricities and to the intensity of his "fierce indignation" ("*saeva indignatio*"). The Latin epitaph that Corbet refers to had struck a deeply responsive chord in Yeats and had provided a model of vehement precision. Within the play itself, it is an important point of reference for the character of Swift as it emerges later on in the action. The original epitaph reads:

Ubi saeva indignatio
Ulterius cor lacerare nequit.
Abi viator
Et imitare, si poteris,
Strenuum pro virili libertatis vindicem.

"Swift's Epitaph," written in 1930, was Yeats's elegant and only slightly free translation:

> Swift has sailed into his rest;
> Savage indignation there
> Cannot lacerate his breast.
> Imitate him if you dare,
> World besotted traveller; he
> Served human liberty.

The dialogue takes on a livelier human interest in the play's second phase, which introduces the various personalities attending the séance. Mrs. Henderson, the medium, gets things under way with the help of her "control": "a dear little girl named Lulu who died when she was five or six years old." Yeats knew séances well, and the play shows the usual mixed purposes—often flatly practical or naïvely comical or both—of the people taking part. One of them, for instance, seeks financial advice from her dead husband. Another wants to learn whether, in heaven, he can still eat and drink and walk about with his dog. But the expectations both of such wonderfully literal-minded folk and of more sophisticated spiritualists in the group are marred by a disturbing fear: that the "horrible spirit" who has spoiled their séances in the past will do so again this time. Here and there in the work there is deft interplay—not overdone, however—among lightly amusing, matter-of-fact, and darkly serious elements. At the very end the interplay hardens into a very tough-minded irony.

That ending is foreshadowed in the third phase of the play, in which we see the séance in progress. A violent emotional outburst explodes within it. It is a desperate exchange between two voices of the dead: the "horrible" Jonathan Swift and his beloved "Vanessa" (Hester Vanhomrigh). They are re-enacting the painful issue of their relationship. He upbraids her for writing to his other beloved female friend, Stella (Esther Johnson), whom Swift addresses with affectionate gratitude further along. Unable to understand why, after their long but chaste intimacy, Swift is still unwilling to marry her, Vanessa had written to find out whether Stella and Swift are secretly married. Pressed to the extreme, Swift grants that he has "wronged" both women by refusing them the normal marital love and mother- hood they desire. His reason is that although, as Vanessa puts it, "no man in Ireland is so passionate," he has "something in my blood that no child must inherit."

In his brilliant essay on the play, printed as "Notes" in *Wheels and Butterflies* (1934), Yeats discussed the speculations of Sir Walter Scott and various scholars concerning Swift's celibacy and his rela- tions with Vanessa and Stella. "There is no satisfactory solution," Yeats wrote; "Swift . . . hid two things which constituted perhaps all that he had of private life: his loves and his religious beliefs." For the play's purposes, however, he accepted the theory that Swift's "dread of madness" was the cause, for madness seemed to be "already present in [his] constant eccentricity." The whole essay is a revealing exploration of the connection between Swift's mentality and modern history, with a certain emphasis on Irish concerns as well.

Two thoughts among many in the "Notes" (which offer a gener- alizing commentary on key phrases in the play without attention to artistic considerations) are useful to quote here. The first is: "I seek an image of the modern mind's discovery of itself, of its own perma- nent form, in that one Irish century that escaped from darkness and confusion." The second comes in the form of a question: "Was Swift mad? Or was it the intellect itself that was mad?" Add these thoughts to those advanced by John Corbet in the early part of the play, and it becomes increasingly clear that *The Words upon the Window-Pane* is that rare work in which ideas are flashes of vital awareness and feeling just as poetic images are.

This play is poetic (or at least prose-poetic) drama of a special sort. It does not have the Musicians' songs familiar in so many of Yeats's plays although there are verse quotations scattered here and there: two quatrains from Hymn 564 of the *Irish Church Hymnal* and fourteen lines from a poem Stella wrote for Swift's fifty-fourth birth- day. "Tradition says" she scratched some of the lines on the window-pane of the play's title. The poignancy of her poem, which honors his moral tutelage, hardly derives from the didactic tribute its octo-syllabic couplets trudge through. It lies, rather, in the contrast be-tween its unreserved homage and the tormented ghost-dialogue pre-ceding it.

The urgent, sometimes stichomythic rhythm of that dialogue overrides everything else in the utterances of Mrs. Henderson, the medium, from whose mouth all the spirit voices issue forth. In her trance, she simply transmits whatever is being said by the most forceful spirit-presences, no matter which others are eager to be heard. As for the living participants, they have been adjured by Dr. Trent, president of the Dublin Spiritualists' Association, to treat all spirits with respect, never as evil beings to be exorcised. As a result, Swift's raging and Vanessa's desperate questions dominate the play's emotional life:

Mrs. Henderson [in a child's voice]. That bad old man,
  that bad old man in the corner, they have let him come
  back. Lulu is going to scream. O. . . . O. . . . [In a
  man's voice]. How dare you write to her? How dare you ask
  if we were married? How dare you question her?
Dr. Trench. A soul in its agony—it cannot see us or hear
  us.
Mrs. Henderson [upright and rigid, only her lips moving,
  and still in a man's voice]. You sit crouching there. Did
  you not hear what I said? How dared you question her? I
  found you an ignorant little girl without intellect,
  without moral ambition. How many times did I not stay
  away from great men's houses, how many times forsake the
  Lord Treasurer, how many times neglect the business of
  the State that we might read Plutarch together? . . . [In
  Vanessa's voice]. I questioned her, Jonathan, because I
  love. Why have you let me spend hours in your company if
  you do not want me to love you? [In Swift's voice]. When
  I rebuilt Rome in your mind it was as though I walked its
  streets. [In Vanessa's voice]. Was that all, Jonathan?
  Was I nothing but a painter's canvas? [In Swift's voice].

My God, do you think it was easy? I was a man of strong passions and I had sworn never to marry. [*In Vanessa's voice*]. If you and she are not married, why should we not marry like other men and women? . . .

Earlier, Dr. Trench has explained the endless misery of certain souls: "Some spirits . . . think they are still living and go over and over some action of their past lives, just as we go over and over some painful thought, except that where they are thought is reality." After Swift and Vanessa have once again come up against their old impasse, the play relaxes briefly into relative detachment as the participants discuss their reactions to what they have just been hearing. Then, suddenly, Swift's voice is heard again, this time speaking tenderly and ruefully—not to Vanessa but to Stella. The dynamics here, in the play's shift from the vehement pitch of the previous exchange to this gentler fourth phase, resemble those of a poem in which, without transition, there is a leap into a new realm of feeling. It is in this context that Swift happily quotes from Stella's poem to him, startling Corbet into an excited cry of recognition: "The words upon the window-pane!" We have been brought far enough into Swift's anguish to see why he thinks her forced rhymes and commonplace if heartfelt sentiments "noble" and "touching." They make no demands, not even through the kind of affection they reveal:

> You taught how I might youth prolong
> By knowing what is right and wrong;
> How from my heart to bring supplies
> Of lustre to my fading eyes;
> How soon a beauteous mind repairs
> The loss of chang'd or falling hairs;
> How wit and virtue from within
> Can spread a smoothness o'er the skin.

Just before the play ends, there is one more turn. Mrs. Henderson, exhausted by her concentrated effort and disappointed because yet another séance has been "spoilt" by the "bad old man," awakes from her psychically induced trance. After the others have paid her and left, only the grateful Corbet—who pays her twice her usual small fee—remains. She has confirmed his views on Swift's celibacy, and he is convinced that she is "an accomplished actress and scholar" who can help him deal with other problems. "Swift," he says to her,

> was the chief representative of the intellect of his epoch, that arrogant intellect free at last from superstition. He foresaw its collapse. He foresaw Democracy, he must have dreaded the future. Did he refuse to beget children because of that dread? Was Swift mad? Or was it the intellect itself that was mad?

Mrs. Henderson has not a clue what Corbet is talking about. She ignores what he is saying about that rough beast, Democracy, and is surprised to learn that the nasty séance-spoiler, "that dirty old man," is a famous figure named Jonathan Swift. All she knows is that "I saw him very clearly just as I woke up. His clothes were dirty, his face covered with boils. Some disease had made one of his eyes swell up, it stood out from his face like a hen's egg." That, Corbet tells her, was how Swift looked in his old age: "His brain had gone, his friends had deserted him. The man appointed to take care of him beat him to keep him quiet." Her reply is a detached amalgam of Hindu philosophy and Christian piety: "It is sometimes a terrible thing to be out of the body, God help us all." But after Corbet leaves, and she has counted her money and made herself tea, Swift takes possession of her and operates her as if she were his puppet. He has her count her fingers while his voice tells over the great ministers of state who "were my friends and are gone." And he moves her aimlessly about the stage, emptied of any will of her own, until she drops a saucer she is carrying and says, again in his voice but speaking to the whole human condition: "Perish the day on which I was born!"

Thus the play, which began so coolly, has grown into a vision of the intrinsic cruelty of existence. Yeats's feeling for the erratically assertive, madness-fearing, sexually baffled, yet caring and honorable Swift of his play comes close to terrified identification. And the play's thrill of horror in dwelling on death and the kind of existence one might confront beyond it is of a piece with much of Yeats's later work that we have been contemplating. It is a triumph of prose-poetic drama, psychologically acute and with realistic elements unique in his writing.

Yeats completed *The Words upon the Window-Pane* in time to include it in the 1934 edition of his *Collected Plays*. For the reasons just mentioned, it made for a most suitable conclusion to the volume. Almost flatly rational in tone at one level, vehemently tendentious at another, and charged with the undying passions of Swift and Vanessa at still a third, it projects Yeats's characteristic tensions of double awareness: empirical and visionary. Although in fact a fantasy, it *seems* the least fantasizing of his plays. For one thing, the colloquies of the dead take place within the realistic setting of a conventional séance and are themselves psychologically realistic. The ferocity of the key passages, in which Swift's voice rises out of the mental hell he still inhabits after death, has the intrinsic realism an Ibsen or a Strindberg would have no trouble recognizing. And the lines from the hymnbook and by Stella, all decidedly prosaic rather than imaginatively lyrical, serve to sustain the illusion of ordinary events on an ordinary day.

Shortly afterwards Yeats wrote the twin plays *A Full Moon in March* and *The King of the Great Clock Tower*: pure fantasies based on traditional legendry and somewhat indebted to Oscar Wilde's *Salome*. In the former play an unmarried queen has offered herself and her kingdom to the man who "best sings his passion" to her, provided he otherwise pleases her as well. A candidate, "the Swineherd," appears. He is so insulting and "foul in his rags, his origin, his speech" that she has him beheaded, although he has in fact stirred her desire. She then sings a tender song to the severed head, which sings a grim parody of "Jack and Jill" in reply; and afterwards she performs a sexually symbolic dance with the head in her arms.

The plot of *The King of the Great Clock Tower* has a similar pattern, despite such differences of detail as that here the queen is already married and remains silent for most of the play. She appeared mysteriously before the king a year earlier and he chose to marry her;

but she has never spoken and he still does not know her name or origin. Suddenly a stranger, a poet who calls himself "the Stroller," arrives and asks to see her. He has heard of her beauty and written songs about her that are sung throughout the world. Then he demands that she dance for him and says that Aengus, the god of love, has prophesied that "the Queen shall kiss my mouth." The king has him beheaded for his insolence, after which—as in *A Full Moon in March*—we have an exchange of songs by the queen and the head, followed by an erotic dance by the queen.

Both plays experiment with motifs of traditional legendry. For instance, the hero in each boldly risks and loses his life in an attempt to win the beautiful queen. Heads are severed, arbitrarily and with a touch of sadistic feeling. Especially in *A Full Moon in March,* morbid grossness competes with attractively free improvisation and there is a constant association of love with filth and cruelty. Thus the opening stanza of the play's first chorus:

> Every loutish lad in love
> Thinks his wisdom great enough,
> *What cares love for this and that?*
> To make all his parish stare,
> As though Pythagoras wandered there.
> *Crown of gold or dung of swine.*

And toward the end, the song of the swineherd's bleeding head begins

> I sing a song of Jack and Jill.
> Jill has murdered Jack . . .

These are but two instances of the play's freewheeling and even lighthearted cynicism. Its efforts at stylistic brutality are not altogether unlike the bourgeois-shocking effects of Alfred Jarry (1873–1907), who, though younger than Yeats, had produced his *Ubu Roi* many years before *A Full Moon in March*. The climax of this tendency comes in the key exchange between the swineherd and the queen. Their dialogue mixes ardor, sophisticated thought, and vulgarity in a strange combination:

> *The Swineherd.* My mind is running on our marriage night,
>   Imagining all from the first touch and kiss.
> *The Queen.* What gives you that strange confidence? What
>   makes
>   You think that you can move my heart and me?
> *The Swineherd.* Because I look upon you without fear.
> *The Queen.* A lover in railing or in flattery said
>   God only looks upon me without fear.
> *The Swineherd.* Desiring cruelty, he made you cruel.
>   I shall embrace body and cruelty,
>   Desiring both as though I had made both.
> *The Queen.* One question more. You bring like all the rest
>   Some novel simile, some wild hyperbole
>   Praising my beauty?
> *The Swineherd.*   My memory has returned.
>   I tended swine, when I first heard your name.
>   I rolled among the dung of swine and laughed.
>   What do I know of beauty?
> *The Queen.*   Sing the best
>   And you are not a swineherd but a king.
> *The Swineherd.* What do I know of kingdoms?
>   [*Snapping his fingers*] That for kingdoms!
> *The Queen.* If trembling of my limbs or sudden tears
>   Proclaim your song beyond denial best,
>   I leave these corridors, this ancient house,
>   A famous throne, the reverence of servants—
>   What do I gain?
> *The Swineherd.* A song—the night of love,
>   An ignorant forest and the dung of swine.
>   [*Queen leaves throne and comes downstage.*]
> *The Queen.* All here have heard the man and all have
>   judged.
>   I led him, that I might not seem unjust,
>   From point to point, established in all eyes
>   That he came hither not to sing but to heap

Complexities of insult upon my head.
The Swineherd. She shall bring forth her farrow in the
     dung.
But first my song—what nonsense shall I sing?
The Queen. Send for the headsman, Captain of the Guard.

As a whole, *A Full Moon in March* has a lyrical structure that accompanies the literal plot but is independent of it. The play's first impression is of a whimsical letting-go. Two "Attendants"—an elderly woman and a young man who will do all the singing—stand on the stage before the inner curtain rises. Their conversation is utterly lackadaisical. It suggests that the author ("he") is so indifferent to what he is writing that he has told his characters to say and do whatever and however they choose:

First Attendant. What do we do?
     What part do we take?
     What did he say?
Second Attendant. Join when we like,
     Singing or speaking.
First Attendant. Before the curtain rises on the play?
Second Attendant. Before it rises.
First Attendant. What do we sing?
Second Attendant. "Sing anything, sing any old thing," he
     said.
First Attendant. Come then and sing about the dung of
     swine.

The Second Attendant then sings the opening choral song quoted earlier on, with its double refrain expressing love's self-centredness (*"What cares love for this and that?"*) and the play's disdain for the world's usual standards of relative value (*"Crown of gold or dung of swine"*). Thus a tonal context is established that the swineherd's attitude, in his colloquy with the queen, reinforces but gives an increasingly darker coloration to as the play progresses. The process reaches its grisliest moment after the queen informs him that his head will be brought to her after the execution. He responds with a prophetic "story" about a woman "in my country" who "stood all bathed in blood"—as the queen will stand when given his newly severed, bleeding head: "A drop of blood / Entered her womb and there begat a child."

The queen is revolted by this story ("O foul, foul, foul!"); yet before she dismisses him to his death, *"She turns towards him, her back to the audience, and slowly drops her veil."* It is an act of submission, but a dangerous one. In Yeats's late plays, love is treacherous. The beheadings in them are punishments of male desire, even if reciprocated: a motif re-echoed at the end of *A Full Moon in March* in a series of poetic, visual, and musical effects.

The first of these effects is a song by the First Attendant, about "an ancient Irish Queen / That stuck a head"—her lover's—"upon a stake" and "heard the dead lips sing." The second effect is the sight of the blood-splotched queen holding the head in the air and singing to it, tenderly and ruefully, a song that addresses it as "child and darling." The head then responds with its chillingly eerie song about Jill's murder of Jack. (The songs are actually sung by the attendants, who voice the roles of queen and swineherd for the moment.) The queen's Salome-like dance follows, to the accompaniment of drum-taps that grow ever quicker as her movements approach an imitation of orgasmic climax. The final effect in this whirling series is the attendants' closing song on the mystery underlying all the preceding action.

What they sing is a variation on "the uncontrollable mystery on the bestial floor" of "The Magi," in which the holy, idealized images created by human yearning stare down at the teeming physical world below to find guidance to their own meaning. The attendants' song is made up of three stanzas, in each of which one singer raises questions and the other presents an answering refrain. The first stanza will illustrate:

> *Second Attendant.* Why must those holy, haughty feet
>   descend
> From emblematic niches, and what hand
> Ran that delicate raddle through their white?
> My heart is broken, yet must understand.

What do they seek for? Why must they descend?
First Attendant. For desecration and the lover's night.

"Desecration and the lover's night," embodied in the filthy but articulate swineherd, is what the queen, in all the cold, cruel perfection of her beauty and her virginity, desires despite herself. Yet the inevitable result is disillusionment with cherished ideals, as in "Among School Children," and disappointment in love itself. (Hence "My heart is broken, yet must understand.") There is an echo, too, in this play of "First Love" and other poems in which a loved woman is compared to the changing moon passing impersonally through uncontrollable phases. The second stanza, which also speaks of the shudder of terror in the presence of mystery—as in *The Resurrection*—introduces this complex of feeling powerfully:

Second Attendant. I cannot face that emblem of the moon
  Nor eyelids that the unmixed heavens dart,
  Nor stand upon my feet, so great a fright
  Descends upon my savage, sunlit heart.
  What can she lack whose emblem is the moon?
First Attendant. But desecration and the lover's night.

Formally, *A Full Moon in March* is an original experiment in dramatically loose but lyrically unified theater. To use Yeats's phrase for something else entirely, the play is a "crazy salad" that mixes ingredients from many sources: folk tales, Romantic self-mockery, sexual curiosity, fascination with squalor and bald lust, modern disillusion, and wonder at the self-contradictoriness of the human condition. Its twin play, *The King of the Great Clock Tower,* seems a paler variant despite certain differences: its silent, already married queen, its obsession with literal death, and its hero who is a poet rather than a swineherd who talks like one. It is also something of a potpourri of passages that read like drafts of poems Yeats casually lifted from his notebooks. These differences aside, the two plays are parallel in structure and bearing; and together they reflect Yeats's heightened interest, in the 1930's, in the mystery of female sexuality. That interest is richly humane in the Crazy Jane poems of *The Winding Stair*

(1933) especially, grows randy in his next play, *The Herne's Egg* (written in 1936), and deepens into tragic vision in his last plays, *Purgatory* and *The Death of Cuchulain* (written, respectively, in spring and autumn of 1938).

The Herne's Egg, an unusually long play for Yeats, is divided into six numbered scenes. It is set in Ireland's timeless mythical past, and its "historical" context is a war between Congal, king of Connacht, and Aedh, king of Tara. The leading female character is the priestess Attracta, whose sensuality rivals that of Decima in *The Player Queen* and the queens in the twin plays just discussed. She is betrothed to a bird-god, The Great Herne (i.e., Heron), and one may speculate on the unusual interest Yeats shows in imagining the sexual union of women with birds ("Leda and the Swan," for instance) or with beasts (Europa and the bull in "A Woman Young and Old"; the queen and the unicorn in *The Player Queen*). Attracta's servant, Corney, has a donkey whose copulations affect human destiny. Among the other characters are three young women eager for Attracta to teach them about sexual love, especially with a herne; two men named Pat and Mike (Mike's comical one-word utterances are taken as guru-wisdom); and characters with biblical names but no holy missions: Peter, John, Matthias, Malachi. Yeats let himself go so far toward lighthearted blasphemy and rollicking obscenity in this play that the Abbey refused to produce it.

Summing up the kaleidoscopic plot, with its rotating patterns of burlesque, bawdiness, pathos, and shivering awe, would make for an impossible clutter of detail. But the play moves along two intertwined lines: the pointless struggle between the two kings, both killed by the play's end; and the sexual life and apotheosis of Attracta. As handled here, the war between Congal and Aedh is a comic parody of heroic war-sagas that becomes, finally, an ironic treatment of the human dream of outwitting destiny. When, in a fit of rationality, the kings arrange a peace banquet, it becomes a scene of bloody slaughter in the traditional way of such affairs. In this play, though, the whole business is handled as the Marx Brothers might do it. Congal insists that the banquet food must be herne's eggs only,

despite being warned that herne's eggs are taboo for anyone but the
Great Herne and "women of these rocks, / Betrothed or married" to
him. Put under a spell by the vengeful Herne so that she becomes a
mechanical instrument of his will, she places a hen's egg instead of a
herne's before Congal at the banquet table. He is enraged, blames
Aedh and kills him with a table-leg during the fracas that breaks out,
and later decrees that Attracta must be punished as well on her
wedding night. He and his six companions will all "handle, penetrate, and possess" her—not only in retribution but also to free her
from her "virgin snow" and her bondage to "that snow image, the
Great Herne."

   All this nonsense culminates in a fatal curse laid upon Congal by
the Herne, and in a mystically ambiguous aura around the events of
the wedding night. Congal is doomed to die next day, in a manner
sung to him by the omniscient Corney:

> "This they nailed upon a post,
> On the night my leg was lost,"
> *Said the old, old herne that had but one leg."*

> "He that a herne's egg dare steal
> Shall be changed into a fool,"
> *Said the old, old herne that had but one leg."*

> "And to end his fool breath
> At a fool's hand meet his death."
> *Said the old, old herne that had but one leg."*

In the final scene, one Tom Fool, eager for the reward of an un-
specified number of pennies, does indeed kill Congal. His action and
motive, of course, anticipate those of the Blind Man in *The Death of
Cuchulain*.

   Such are the main aspects of the plot, though hardly described
in full detail. It would take a director of genius to carry it through on
the stage in all its mad ingenuity: its simultaneous hilarity and pathos, and its pursuit—at the risk of whatever absurd grotesqueries—

of that *frisson* in the presence of the uncanny that Yeats sought more and more to evoke in his last decade. Two sections of the play, Scene I and a passage in Scene IV, may stand as instances of the range of tones and styles brought into a cacophonous harmony in *The Herne's Egg*.

Scene I is beautiful and funny. It begins with a symmetrically choreographed battle-ballet, without dialogue, of opposing armies. Next, there follows a matching verbal ballet by the two warrior-kings. And then Aedh's joke about two rich fleas, seasoned by Congal's brief, unexpectedly acid comment on the wars the two rulers have devoted their lives to, ends the scene. It is a preliminary twirl of the kaleidoscope, opening us to the capricious spirit of the whole play:

> *Mist and rocks; high up on backcloth a rock, its base hidden in mist; on this rock stands a great herne. All should be suggested, not painted realistically. Many men fighting with swords and shields, but sword and sword, shield and shield, never meet. The men move rhythmically as if in a dance; when swords approach one another cymbals clash; when swords and shields approach drums boom. The battle flows out at one side; two Kings are left fighting in the centre of the stage; the battle returns and flows out at the other side. The two Kings remain, but are now face to face and motionless. They are Congal, King of Connacht, and Aedh, King of Tara.*
>
> *Congal.* How many men have you lost?
> *Aedh.* Some five-and-twenty men.
> *Congal.* No need to ask my losses.
> *Aedh.* Your losses equal mine.
> *Congal.* They always have and must.
> *Aedh.* Skill, strength, arms matched.
> *Congal.* Where is the wound this time?
> *Aedh.* There, left shoulder-blade.
> *Congal.* Here, right shoulder-blade.
> *Aedh.* Yet we have fought all day.
> *Congal.* This is our fiftieth battle.

Aedh. And all were perfect battles.
Congal. Come, sit upon this stone.
  Come and take breath awhile.
Aedh. From daybreak until noon,
  Hopping among these rocks.
Congal. Nothing to eat or drink.
Aedh. A story is running around
  Concerning two rich fleas.
Congal. We hop like fleas, but war
  Has taken all our riches.
Aedh. Rich, and rich, so rich that they
  Retired and bought a dog.
Congal. Finish the tale and say
  What kind of dog they bought.
Aedh. Heaven knows.
Congal.   Unless you say
  I'll up and fight all day.
Aedh. A fat, square, lazy dog,
  No sort of scratching dog.

The second of the instances of the play's range I have referred to comes in Scene IV. It is Attracta's spellbound song about her coming bridal night: a song of exaltation but also of overwhelming fear. She sings it as Congal and his men are deciding the order in which they will possess her. In Scene V (the next morning) Attracta will be sure she has consummated her marriage with the Herne, while Congal's crew will believe she has been with each of them—but the "truth" will not be revealed. At the close of Scene IV, however, the emphasis, painfully serious, is on Attracta's feelings about mating with a divine "beast" of "bird and claw":

> When I take a beast to my joyful breast,
> Though beak and claw I must endure,
> *Sang the bride of the Herne, and the Great Herne's bride,*
> No lesser life, man, bird or beast,
> Can make unblessed what a bird made blessed,
> Can make impure what a beast made pure.

Where is he gone, where is that other,
He that shall take my maidenhead?
Sang the bride of the Herne, and the Great Herne's bride,
Out of the moon came my pale brother,
The blue-black midnight is my mother.
Who will turn down the sheets of the bed?

When beak and claw their work begin
Shall horror stir in the roots of my hair?
Sang the bride of the Herne, and the Great Herne's bride,
And who lie there in the cold dawn
When all the terror has come and gone?
Shall I be the woman lying there?

In the two scenes after Attracta's song, there is none of the lighthearted whimsy we saw earlier on. There is grotesquely absurd fancy in the way Congal is killed by Tom Fool, and in the twist given to the role of Corney's donkey—in its previous existence a "rapscallion Clareman." But a grim seriousness underlies the style nevertheless. Everything in the play has converged on the themes of death and of the power and mystery, rather than the delight, of sex. A whole complex of fertility symbolism linked to mythic and religious tradition is suggested by the business of the eggs, the situation of the virgin Attracta's betrothal to the bird-god, and Congal's idea of purifying her through ritual intercourse. It is also related to a tragic motif: that we can observe but cannot control our destinies.

At the very end of the play the sexual emphasis takes over. Attracta and Corney come upon the dying Congal, who fears lest, when he is dead, that vengeful deity the Great Herne "may put me / Into the shape of a brute beast." At once the compassionate Attracta commands Corney to lie down with her—"lie and beget"—"before his body has had time to cool." The idea is that Congal will be reincarnated in the form of whatever creatures happen to be copulating at the moment of his death. But it turns out that the donkey has broken loose and is already coupling with another donkey. And so Congal must be reborn as a "brute beast" after all. Or, as Corney puts

it in the play's closing speech, with its wryly humorous implication of
the futility of human effort:

> I have heard that a donkey carries its young
> Longer than any other beast,
> Thirteen months it must carry it.
> All that trouble and nothing to show for it,
> Nothing but just another donkey.

The Herne's Egg is Yeats's last great plunge into letting his
fantasy go wild yet somehow maintaining control of its direction.
The direction is tragic despite the endless high jinks. Indeed, Corney's "All that trouble and nothing to show for it" anticipates the Old
Man's dismayed "Twice a murderer and all for nothing" just before
the classically compressed *Purgatory* ends. It even bears a real
though distant resemblance to the hero's surprised recognition in
The Death of Cuchulain that all his prowess will count for nothing in
his future existence:

> There floats out there
> The shape that I shall take when I am dead,
> My soul's first shape, a soft feathery shape,
> And is not that a strange shape for the soul
> Of a great fighting-man?

Yeats completed *Purgatory* in the spring of 1938 and *The Death
of Cuchulain* in late December. The interval of about nine months
saw a marked shift, reflected in the lines just quoted, away from a
drama usually centered on characters who, as in *King Oedipus,* resist
their fates. Cuchulain's gentle if astounded acquiescence in his beheading is a great departure from the challenging bravado of the
Swineherd and the Stroller, the intransigence of Swift even after
death, Congal's dying cry to remain a human being in his next life,
and the effort of the Old Man in *Purgatory* to end the cycle of family
tragedy he was born into.

The shift represented in *The Death of Cuchulain,* Yeats's last play, may seem natural enough: a gracious acceptance of the inevitable by the dying poet who has decided to "go gentle into that good night" rather than raging against it. The play is not quite that simple, and is certainly far from cheerfully sentimental, but it does suggest a complex mood of fatalistic acceptance of what must be, and even of melancholy cooperation with it. We have seen the evolution of Cuchulain's character, and something of its intermeshing with that of Yeats, in the section on the Cuchulain cycle in Chapter Four, where *The Death of Cuchulain* is discussed in some detail. But it is interesting to note that in planning the posthumously published volume that others were to name *Last Poems and Two Plays* (Cuala Press, 1939), Yeats decided to end the book with *Purgatory* and not with the play he wrote still later.

Although no one would have quarreled had he reversed the order, it was a reasonable decision. *The Death of Cuchulain,* an invocation of motifs and figures involved in the cycle over the years, is a symbolic confrontation of death that sloughs off its protagonist's—and, by implication, its author's—heroic self-image. It projects the transformation of that romantic image into something timid and humble and anonymous. And it ends with three elegiac after-effects: the Morrigu's explanation to "the dead" of how Cuchulain received his six mortal wounds; Emer's dance of rage and adoration around the black parallelogram symbolizing his head; and the Street-Singer's lament for the lost glory of the ancient myth-making vision that created Cuchulain and his fellows and brought them briefly to life again in the events of 1916.

But *Purgatory,* though hardly naturalistic, takes place in a version of the real world: a tormented realm of inescapably recurrent suffering, in its way resembling that of *The Words upon the Window-Pane.* In it the protagonist—the Old Man—must again and again reenact the consequences of modern history and of his family's and his own actions and existential situation. There is no Cuchulain here, nobly readying himself for the obliteration of the "great fighting-man" that he has been and for his re-creation as a "soft feathery thing" (a birdlike singing shroud, if we may add that image from

"Cuchulain Comforted"). It is easy to see in Cuchulain's steadfast calm before death a beautiful model Yeats has created for himself. But it is far more drastic emotionally to see the unresolved pressures of the poet's life reflected in the Old Man's predicament. These include, at the least, the lost mother and, associated with that loss, the social triumph of wanton and murderous grossness at the expense of the "many ingenious lovely things" mourned in "Nineteen Hundred and Nineteen."

The "purgatory" of the play—most of us would choose to call it a mental hell—is a projection of fears that even after death those pressures will continue. As Yeats explains in *A Vision,*

> the *Spirit* is compelled to live over and over again the events that had most moved it; there can be nothing new, but the old events stand forth in a light which is dim or bright according to the intensity of the passion that accompanied them. They occur in the order of their intensity or luminosity, the more intense first, and the painful are commonly the more intense, and repeat themselves again and again. . . . All that keeps the *Spirit* from its freedom may be compared to a knot that has to be untied or to an oscillation or a violence that must end in a return to equilibrium. **(from Section VI)**

And again:

> We all to some extent meet again and again the same people and certainly in some cases form a kind of family of two or three or more persons who come together life after life until all passionate relationships are exhausted, the child of one life the husband, wife, brother or sister of the next. Sometimes, however, a single relationship will repeat itself, turning its revolving wheel again and again, especially, my instructors say, where there has been strong sexual passion. All such passions, they say, contain "cruelty and deceit"—I think of similar statements in D. H. Lawrence's *Rainbow* and in his *Women in Love*— and this *antithetical* cruelty and deceit must be expiated in *primary* suffering and submission, or the old tragedy will be repeated. **(from Section XI)**

I have no wish to shift attention to *A Vision* here, or even to digress into defining its special vocabulary. But—*pace* some of the vocabulary and the assumption of the spirit's continuing identity

after death—these passages happen to be commonsense psychological observations about our subconscious lives and family histories. At
the same time, they are directly relevant to the dramatic situation in
Purgatory. I hope I may be forgiven if I devote a few paragraphs to a
summary that illustrates the point.

The plot of this brief play, barely over six pages long, could
hardly be simpler. Two characters, the "Old Man" and his surly son
the "Boy," arrive at the site of a now-ruined house, with a now-bare
tree in the background, where the father was born. It was formerly,
he explains, one of Ireland's great houses, inhabited by "great people": government officials, military and political leaders, cultivated
persons who loved learning and beauty. All this property—the house
and "this scenery and this countryside, / Kennel and stable, horse and
hound"—had formerly belonged to the Old Man's mother. But she,
infatuated with an ignorant and vicious training-stable groom, had
"looked at him and married him, / And he squandered everything she
had." In the context of the play she has sinned in two ways: one by
self-betrayal and the other by betraying the rich old traditions she
was bred to. Thus the Old Man's line, "She died in giving birth to
me," has more than one meaning.

The groom, "that he might keep me at his level," refused to send
the child to school (although people loyal to the family educated
him), and finally "burned down the house when drunk." The Old
Man, then sixteen, stabbed him to death, took to the roads as an
itinerant peddlar, and some years later begot his bastard son "upon a
tinker's daughter in a ditch." And now, on "the anniversary / Of my
mother's wedding night, / Or of the night when I was begotten," he
has returned to the source of it all with the Boy, who at sixteen is
primed for the next violent turn of the family "wheel."

As the two stand there, the Old Man sees the figure of his
mother, which the Boy is blind to, in a suddenly lighted window. He
hears hoofbeats—"My father is riding from the public-house, / A
whiskey-bottle under his arm"—and begs his mother: "Do not let
him touch you!" Thinking the Old Man has gone mad, the Boy tries

to steal his money and after a struggle is killed by the same knife that his grandfather died by. (He has finally seen a figure, his murdered grandfather's, in the window, and in his horrified distraction does not defend himself.) The Old Man is content to think that he has now "finished all that consequence" and freed his mother from reliving, again and again, the violation her folly had subjected her to:

> Dear mother, the window is dark again,
> But you are in the light because
> I finished all that consequence.
> I killed that lad because had he grown up
> He would have struck a woman's fancy,
> Begot, and passed pollution on.

Alas, it is not over after all. As he cleans his knife and begins to gather his scattered money, he hears the hoofbeats once again. The play ends with his outcry:

> Hoof-beats! Dear God,
> How quickly it returns—beat—beat—!
>
> Her mind cannot hold up that dream.
> Twice a murderer and all for nothing,
> And she must animate that dead night
> Not once but many times!
>
> O God,
> Release my mother's soul from its dream!
> Mankind can do no more. Appease
> The misery of the living and the remorse of the dead.

The play leaves it a trifle unclear whether or not both pairs— mother and groom, and Old Man and Boy—are in the purgatory of unresolved and therefore repeated outrage. Are they all revenants, like Swift and Vanessa, or is it just the mismated couple who must relive the scene again and again? Almost certainly, the former alternative is the intended one. If "all that consequence" has not ended, then presumably the Old Man will always be returning, experiencing the Oedipal trauma in retrospect, killing his son, and coming to the same hopeless conclusion.

And if that reading is at least possible, then we may see the whole play in a different light from the one it appears in at first. At the very start, we are aware only that father and son have been making a long journey. The Boy's complaint opens the dialogue. Its heavy initial stresses, repetitions, alliteration, and internal rhymes emphasize his dragging resistance to the whole enterprise. This opening note, which certainly foretokens the Old Man's failure at the end, may also reflect a sunken memory of having made the same journey many times in the past:

> *Boy.* Half-door, hall door,
> Hither and thither day and night,
> Hill or hollow, shouldering this pack,
> Hearing you talk.

How many times has all this, and what follows, happened before? At any rate, this speech is the beginning of an exchange at cross-purposes. Where the Old Man recalls the once-vivid life of a Great House and a richly green tree, the Boy sees only the dreary remains of both. Nor does he respect his father's acute mystical or visionary observations:

> *Old Man.* The moonlight falls upon the path,
> The shadow of a cloud upon the house,
> And that's symbolical; study that tree,
> What is it like?
> *Boy.*   A silly old man.
> *Old Man.* It's like—no matter what it's like
> I saw it a year ago stripped bare as now,
> I saw it fifty years ago
> Before the thunderbolt had riven it,
> Green leaves, ripe leaves, leaves thick as butter,
> Fat, greasy life. Stand there and look,
> Because there is somebody in that house.

[*The Boy puts down pack and stands in the doorway.*]
Boy. There's nobody there.
Old Man.   There's somebody there.
Boy. The floor is gone, the windows gone,
    And where there should be roof there's sky,
    And here's a bit of an egg-shell thrown
    Out of a jackdaw's nest.
Old Man.   But there are some
    That do not care what's gone, what's left:
    The souls in Purgatory that come back
    To habitations and familiar spots.
Boy. Your wits are out again.
Old Man.   Re-live
    Their transgressions, and that not once
    But many times; they know at last
    The consequences of those transgressions
    Whether upon others or upon themselves;
    Upon others, others may bring help,
    For when that consequence is at an end
    The dream must end; if upon themselves,
    There is no help but in themselves
    And in the mercy of God.

This passage carries the play beyond anything like literal realism. Poetically speaking, it has placed the characters in that purgatorial realm that the Old Man has such intimate knowledge of— and this play does move by poetic leaps. In the world of the play, the figure in the window is really there. And more significantly, the "dream" the Old Man has of ending "the consequence" is *his* dream of preventing his mother's sexual gratification in the arms of a despoiler of love's meaning and life's higher values. It is in *his* purgatory, as well as hers, that the irreversible event occurs repeatedly. He describes the event so graphically and with such revulsion that his words bring the play to its highest pitch of intensity except for his outburst at the very end. The description begins when he hears hoofbeats and tries to tell the Boy what they are. I have already referred to this revelatory moment, but it merits fuller quotation:

Old Man. Listen to the hoof-beats! Listen, listen!
Boy. I cannot hear a sound.
Old Man.   Beat! Beat!
   This night is the anniversary
   Of my mother's wedding-night,
   Or of the night wherein I was begotten.
   My father is riding from the public-house,
   A whiskey-bottle under his arm.
                [*A window is lit showing a young girl.*]
   Look at the window; she stands there
   Listening, the servants are all in bed,
   She is alone, he has stayed late
   Bragging and drinking in the public-house.
Boy. There's nothing but an empty gap in the wall.
   You have made it up. No, you are mad!
   You are getting madder every day.
Old Man. It's louder now because he rides
   Upon a gravelled avenue
   All grass to-day. The hoof-beat stops,
   He has gone to the other side of the house,
   Gone to the stable, put the horse up.
   She has gone down to open the door.
   This night she is no better than her man
   And does not mind that he is half drunk,
   She is mad about him. They mount the stairs,
   She brings him into her own chamber.
   And that is the marriage-chamber now.
   The window is dimly lit again.

   Do not let him touch you! It is not true
   That drunken men cannot beget,
   And if he touch you he must beget
   And you must bear his murderer. . . .

The climactic horror here, as in the even higher-pitched ending, is obviously, yet doubtless subconsciously, Oedipal. Yeats's translations of Sophocles had allowed him to bring this buried dimension of his psychic life to the surface, so that it became a motif he had already dealt with—although even in *Purgatory* there is no reason to believe he thought the play personally confessional in this particular sense. When the Old Man has finished his vicious, repeated stabbing of his son, he glows with a short-lived, unjustifiable rapture to think he has freed his mother's spirit from the passionate subjection that has trapped her. The play's surface emphasis is not on its compelling "Freudian" pressures. Rather, it is on the pain and the pity of doomed human efforts to "appease / The misery of the living and the remorse of the dead." Nevertheless, these two streams of onrushing feeling converge irresistibly. As a result, *Purgatory* is a powerful embodiment both of Yeats's driven visionary imagination and of the unresolved fears and self-questioning that mark the final phase of his work.

VIII

Poetry after *The Tower*

1. *The Winding Stair and Other Poems*

The Winding Stair and Other Poems (1933) climbed its own winding stair over a period of four years to find its final shape: an untitled opening section of twenty-seven poems, followed by the two sequences "Words for Music Perhaps" and "A Woman Young and Old." The brief history of its growth is worth noting because Yeats was slowly discovering the organic relationships implicit in it.

To sum up quickly: The book's initial printing, as *The Winding Stair* (1929), contained only the five pieces that start off the present volume and the eleven-poem sequence "A Woman Young and Old." Then, in 1932, Yeats published *Words for Music Perhaps,* consisting of the twenty-one poems later added to the opening *Winding Stair* group and a twenty-five poem title-sequence. Finally, in 1933, both previous books were combined, in the order already mentioned, in *The Winding Stair and Other Poems.*

It seems clear that Yeats, while still preoccupied with "sex and the dead," was searching for fresh orientations. In "A Woman Young and Old" and in the first seven poems—the "Crazy Jane" group—of "Words for Music Perhaps," he attempted the difficult experiment of

298

trying to see the motifs that had so possessed him through female eyes. Meanwhile, among the exceedingly uneven twenty-seven poems that precede the sequences, a few stand out so powerfully or idiosyncratically that they have a life completely their own despite their continuum with the work in *The Tower*. These include "In Memory of Eva Gore-Booth and Con Markievicz" (the first poem), "A Dialogue of Self and Soul," "Coole Park and Ballylee, 1931," "Byzantium," "Vacillation," and—at a lesser pitch—"Death," "The Crazed Moon," "The Mother of God," "Quarrel in Old Age," "Swift's Epitaph," "The Choice" (originally the next-to-last stanza of "Coole Park and Ballylee 1932 [*sic*]," in *The Winding Stair*), and "Remorse for Intemperate Speech." The dozen poems just named give the volume its center of continuity with past work, while the Crazy Jane group and "A Woman Young and Old" provide a new surround of female sensibility as Yeats imagined it.

As transitional poems trailing clouds of glory from *The Tower,* the original five opening pieces might well have been part of that book. "In Memory of Eva Gore-Booth and Con Markievicz" is one of Yeats's most telling elegiac poems. Dated October 1927, it commemorates two sisters who had died recently, in 1926 and 1927 respectively. Both these women, members of the Gore-Booth family in Sligo, had been committed political activists. Constance Markievicz, a leader of the Easter Rising, had been sentenced to death but then given a prison term instead. Yeats begins by recalling them—in four exquisite, nostalgic lines—as young beauties in Lissadell, their family estate, and then shifts abruptly to a darker, horrified tone that echoes the notes of revulsion and disillusionment in the civil-war poems and elsewhere. The long first verse-unit begins:

> The light of evening, Lissadell,
> Great windows open to the south,
> Two girls in silk kimonos, both
> Beautiful, one a gazelle.
> But a raving autumn shears
> Blossom from the summer's wreath;

> The older is condemned to death,
> Pardoned, drags out lonely years
> Conspiring among the ignorant.
> I know not what the younger dreams—
> Some vague Utopia—and she seems
> When withered old and skeleton-gaunt,
> An image of such politics . . .

After this painful torque the poem returns to its initial evocation of charmed memory. Now, though, the language is tinged with sadness. The poet expresses his longing to seek out "one or the other" sister among the shades and "mix pictures of the mind" with her. Together, they would recall "that old Georgian house" and "the talk of youth" around the table there. And then in the second unit, which closes the poem, he addresses them in a new tone entirely. Whatever his criticism has been, he and they are fellow veterans of the same idealistic if disillusioning struggles. The new tone is reminiscent of that of "Easter, 1916"—or would be, except that here the poet proudly joins the ranks of those he has criticized. Their effort was to transcend time; and he wishes, presumably through his art, to strike a match whose flame will set time itself on fire and thus win transcendence after all. The image connects directly with the defiant assertions in Part III of "The Tower":

> Dear shadows, now you know it all,
> All the folly of a fight
> With a common wrong or right.
> The innocent and the beautiful
> Have no enemy but time;
> Arise and bid me strike a match
> And strike another till time catch;
> Should the conflagration climb,
> Run till all the sages know.
> We the great gazebo built,
> They convicted us of guilt;
> Bid me strike a match and blow.

Both verse-units in this elegy begin with passages of extraordinary lyric purity. Each of the poem's first four lines resonates with a single effect of remembered beauty, and the five lines that open the second unit are charged with affectionate sympathy. The harsher phrasing in between, though seeming to quarrel with that sympathy, actually heightens it by bringing forward the grim predicaments the sisters—and their country—have had to face. The piece as a whole picks up from much of Yeats's previous writing, and yet its combination of nostalgia, relentless candor, and rueful bravado makes for a new tonal turn in his style. For that reason, and because it quietly anticipates the woman-centered sequences to come, it seems a perfect overture for this new volume.

After this humanely expressive beginning, the brief, more abstract poem called "Death" follows. It starts by offering a childlike, really banal thought that nevertheless touches a nerve: that a "dying animal" is unaware of either dread or hope, while a dying man feels both. It ends by asserting—another echo of Part III of "The Tower"—that "man has created death." The state of awareness that enables us to imagine death, name it, and think beyond it is felt to be our key to transcendence. Its supreme instance is the heroism of some archetypal "great man in his pride / Confronting murderous men" and contemptuous of the danger. Such men have died and risen again "many times"—either as resurrected hero-gods or as re-embodiments of one another's unique force and mission.

It is interesting that this poem, which refuses to yield to death, should directly follow the elegy for the Gore-Booth sisters. In some tenuous, indirect sense, the poet would seem to be linking them, and himself, and all who help build a "great gazebo" of noble though delusory aspiration, with the type of death-despising hero celebrated in "Death." Yeats's dedicatory note to the book's American edition names one such person: "I think that I was roused to write 'Death' . . . by the assassination of Kevin O'Higgins, the finest intellect in Irish life." All this foreshadows the parallel Yeats was later to imply between his own readying for death and the hero's in *The Death of Cuchulain.*

More immediately, these poems anticipate his confrontation
with the subject in the next piece, one of the most compelling in the
collection. "A Dialogue of Self and Soul" has the basic form of a
medieval *débat*. In it the Soul tries to frighten the Self into surrendering entirely to the thought of death, so as to prepare itself for salvation, while the Self refuses to abandon its cherished emblems of
sexual and aesthetic life at the full. These are an ancient samurai
sword in a wooden scabbard, around which is wound a scrap of
"flowering, silken, old embroidery, torn / From some court-lady's
dress."

The poem is made up of elegantly patterned eight-line stanzas
rhyming *abbacddc* (but with many off-rhymes) and with line-
lengths (five- or four-stress) that vary at regular intervals. I would
not wish to press the point too literally, but it does seem that this
patterning is like the "silken, old embroidery" wrapped around the
sword, and that the poem's gravely serious *débat*-form, with its exultant thrust at the end, is like the "razor-keen" sword itself. More
technically, the longer lines and ample stanzas allow for intellectual
and associative expansion, while the shorter lines and the shiftings of
rhyme-pattern control and quicken the movement.

At the start of the *débat,* the Soul's sepulchral instructions might
be expected to overwhelm the poor Self's reliance on frivolous,
worldly symbols. The Soul speaks first, its summons fraught with
age-old wisdom and authority:

My Soul. I summon to the ancient winding stair;
    Set all your mind upon the steep ascent,
    Upon the broken, crumbling battlement,
    Upon the breathless starlit air,
    Upon the star that marks the hidden pole;
    Fix every wandering thought upon
    That quarter where all thought is done:
    Who can distinguish darkness from the soul?

"The steep ascent" the Self is asked to ponder is the body's long
climb toward decrepitude and death. In addition, the mind is told to

fix its attention on whatever "star," invisible now, may be found at "the hidden pole" that lies beyond death's intervening darkness, in "that quarter where all thought is done." This last phrase has a delphic ambiguity, simultaneously denoting two contrary states after death: that of the extinction of thought along with the body, and that of pure, eternal Platonic thought. The same phrase, then, acts as both a warning and a threat.

In two other stanzas of Part I of the poem, the Soul holds forth in the same manner, urging the Self to forsake profane concerns and focus on "ancestral night." Thus it can free itself of the life-cycle—"the crime of death and birth." (We are close here to the notion of the existential trap that dominates the play *Purgatory*.) The Soul's final speech, at the end of Part I, is a masterpiece of dire prophetic argument and of the kind of "delphic ambiguity" mentioned earlier. "Ancestral night" may be read either as the eternal darkness of the grave or as the Erebus-like passageway to eternal life that mortal eyes cannot penetrate.

Against the Soul's terrifying arsenal of pronouncements, and its scorn for a man who, though "long past his prime," can still let his imagination dwell on "things . . . / Emblematical of love and war," the Self holds its ground doughtily. The "consecrated blade" and the silk embroidery with its "heart's purple" figures of flowers are defended without regard to theological profundities:

> all these I set
> For emblems of the day against the tower
> Emblematical of the night,
> And claim as by a soldier's right
> A charter to commit the crime once more.

This is more swashbuckling defiance than argument. The Soul, given the last word in Part I, seems to have "won" by virtue of its intense and subtle seriousness and by implying a knowledge impossible to convey in human terms. Its closing lines—"Only the dead can be forgiven; / But when I think of that my tongue's a stone"—have an impact far weightier than the attractively gaudy language so far offered by the Self. But then, in Part II, the Self alone holds the stage. Embroidery and sword do not figure here. Instead, we have a stirring acknowledgment, which becomes a personal confession, that life—the one life, in *this* world, that we know we have—is indeed mainly humiliating and squalid. The confession, and its buoyant after-effect, liberate the poem's spirit from the heavy burden of the Soul's crushing admonition that "only the dead can be forgiven" for the "crime" of being part of the natural life-cycle.

The reciprocity between this poem and the two that precede it is striking. In the elegy for the Gore-Booth sisters, the emphasis at first was on their loveliness in a happy setting and on the sheer delight of having shared the zest of youth with them. Then darker memories and notes of disapproval and grief cut ruthlessly into the mood. But finally, and especially with the line "They convicted us of guilt," the poem accepts the necessary consequences of one's beliefs and actions and becomes nobly carefree. The next poem, "Death," has no thought of guilt in proclaiming human courage and creative purpose triumphant over mortality.

The feeling of a need to be "forgiven" for the very nature of human existence lies deep in many religious and moral traditions. It is doubtless rooted, as well, in a primal groping to account for death and other catastrophes as punishment for personal or tribal sins. Yeats coped with this oppressive feeling in various works, most pessimistically perhaps in *Purgatory*. He had touched upon it very obliquely, yet with enormous psychological reverberation, in his 1908 poem "His Dream," which can be read as a denial of the ancient concepts the Soul advances. He handles it most joyously at the end of "A Dialogue of Self and Soul." It is as if he had risen from the psychoanalyst's couch cleansed of any sense of having to atone for being the person he was:

> I am content to live it all again
> And yet again, if it be life to pitch

Into the frog-spawn of a blind man's ditch,
A blind man battering blind men;
Or into that most fecund ditch of all,
The folly that man does
Or must suffer, if he woos
A proud woman not kindred of his soul.
I am content to follow to its source
Every event in action or in thought;
Measure the lot; forgive myself the lot!
When such as I cast out remorse
So great a sweetness flows into the breast
We must laugh and we must sing,
We are blest by everything,
Everything we look upon is blest.

Part of the ecstasy here comes from the Self's appropriating the language of benediction. The Soul, sure of its exclusive right to such language, had said, "But when I think of that my tongue's a stone." But the secular Self has won out after all and become the true authority on salvation. It can speak out and say "forgive" and "cast out remorse" and "blest," and no longer be tyrannized over and shamed like the mother in "The Dolls."

"Blood and the Moon," the fourth of the opening poems retained from the original *The Winding Stair,* takes this priestly privilege for granted from the start: "Blessed be this place, / More blessed still this tower." But its dominant tone is not of private internal struggle and emergent joy but rather of mostly bitter prophetic utterance. Despite passages of compelling quality, it is marred poetically by its awkward four-part progression and, in Part II, by the sort of tendentiousness and special allusions we often find in Pound's *Cantos.*

The poem begins in a spirit of pugnacious, sardonic affirmation. Part I, a brief half-incantation in three-stress lines, is tersely critical of Irish history and of the present age and asserts that "In mockery I have set / A powerful emblem up" against the "bloody arrogant power" that has arisen. The "emblem" is the poet's tower, and Part

II—in jagged rhyming tercets each made up of a six-stress, an eight-stress, and a seven-stress line and often echoing Whitman or Blake—strenuously pushes this idea forward.

In this section, the longest in the poem, Yeats insists that his tower, with its winding stair, is as significant as the "beacon tower" of Alexandria, the astronomical tower of Babylon, and Shelley's imagined towers that he called "thought's crowned powers." Yeats conceives of it as the embodiment of his own struggle, which he merges with the efforts of the eighteenth-century Anglo-Irish figures Goldsmith, Swift, Burke, and Berkeley:

> I declare this tower is my symbol; I declare
> This winding, gyring, spiring treadmill of a stair is my
>   ancestral stair;
> That Goldsmith and the Dean, Berkeley and Burke have
>   travelled there.

Their vision is precisely the kind Yeats has his spokesman John Corbet attribute to Swift in *The Words upon the Window-Pane*. The final tercet, though rather abstract, foreshadows Corbet's words:

> *Saeva indignatio* and the labourer's hire,
> The strength that gives our blood and state magnanimity
>   of its own desire;
> Everything that is not God consumed with intellectual
>   fire.

Parts III and IV return to the literal scene of "this tower." Each, although written in a five-stress pattern, is like Part I in being twelve lines long and echoing its rhyme scheme—but with subtle variations hardly noticeable because of Yeats's virtuosic mastery of off-rhymes. But in reality the two sections should be combined as a single unit.

Emotionally interlinked, the pair—which have the effect of slightly unconventional, truncated sonnets—are at their best when they provide isolated sensuous impressions created by the full moon shining on the tower. The simple immediacy of the opening lines in each is startling after all the abstractions. Part I begins:

The purity of the unclouded moon
Has flung its arrowy shaft upon the floor.

And Part II:

Upon the dusty, glittering windows cling,
And seem to cling upon the moonlit skies,
Tortoiseshell butterflies, peacock butterflies.
A couple of night-moths are on the wing.

These impressions stand in ironic contrast to the dark associations of the tower's history. "There," Part III tells us—"There, on
blood-saturated ground, have stood / Soldier, assassin, executioner."
And inside the tower: "Odour of blood on the ancestral stair!" Part
IV, more theoretical, picks up a thought advanced "in mockery" at
the end of Part I. The thought was that the top of the tower, where
the butterflies cling to "the dusty, glittering windows," symbolizes a
murderous time "half dead at the top." But now the poem de-
spairingly repudiates the right of the living to say such things, for
"wisdom is the property of the dead" alone. What the living possess is
merely "power" and whatever else "has the stain of blood." There is
no getting around that predicament. The clear, pointed "arrowy
shaft" of moonlight mocks our "drunken frenzy" for both power and
reassurance. So does the glow of the "unclouded moon," unstained
but—at least in the pre-astronaut year 1927—far distant from human
struggle:

but no stain
Can come upon the visage of the moon
When it has looked in glory from a cloud.

In this uneven but impressive and heartfelt poem, Yeats has
allied the prophetic role of a Jeremiah or the author of Ecclesiastes to
some private burden (whatever its causes) of depression and free-
floating guilt. The shadow of this complex mood hangs, with only a
few exceptions, over the rest of the volume's opening section. Thus,

the nine pieces succeeding "Blood and the Moon" are mostly tiny and trivial; but taken together, they do underpin that mood.

The first two, in fact, intensify that poem's contrast between "blood and the moon": that is, between gross human reality and the vision of holiness or heavenly light. "Oil and Blood" does so with pathological relish. It sets two kinds of death images against each other: the miraculously preserved "bodies of holy men and women" and the buried "bodies of the vampires full of blood." ("Their shrouds are bloody and their lips are wet.") "Veronica's Napkin" follows, opposing a magnificently devout sense of the universe— "The Heavenly Circuit; Berenice's Hair; / Tent-pole of Eden," with "the Father and His angelic hierarchy" at the center—against the sordid misery below:

> Some found a different pole, and where it stood
> A pattern on a napkin dipped in blood.

We are back here to the "odour of blood when Christ was slain." The allusion is to the cloth said to have taken the imprint of Jesus' bleeding face when St. Veronica wiped it for him. But the mysteriously riddling "Some found a different pole," and the emphatic detachment of the couplet just quoted from the rest of the poem, have a sinister or squalid connotation, vaguely sexual and perhaps referring to menstrual blood. This phrasing accords well with the extremely unpleasant vampire-blood imagery of the previous poem and points ahead to the "mad" quality of a play like *A Full Moon in March*.

The volume restores its balance with "Coole and Ballylee, 1931," a poem of sad resignation but also of enormous dignity. The setting is almost the same as that of "The Wild Swans at Coole," but some fifteen years later—and this time the poem begins at the tower, "under my window-ledge," and follows the "racing" water flowing below to the lake at Coole. There, once again, the "sudden thunder of the mounting swan" is compared, as in "Nineteen Hundred and Nineteen," to the human soul. The moment of revelation, when the soul is glimpsed in its brave flight toward the unknown, disappears, "no man knows why," like the soaring swans. Nevertheless, the sight is "so lovely that it sets to right / What knowledge or its lack had set awry."

Here, halfway through, the poem shifts attention to Lady Gregory in her home at Coole Park, in her seventy-ninth or eightieth year—"sound of a stick upon the floor, a sound / From somebody that toils from chair to chair"—among her beloved books and marble busts and paintings and other reminders of her family's cultivation and accomplishments. Now, with "all that great glory spent" in this disregardful age, the sudden focus on this cherished woman in her world becomes a revelatory moment, like sighting the glory of the flying swans. The poem ends in a lament that, as in "The Tower," is also filled with pride. The rank humiliation souring "Blood and the Moon," and the morbidity of the two poems following it, have been left behind. The sense of tragic loss remains, but immeasurably ennobled:

> We were the last romantics—chose for theme
> Traditional sanctity and loveliness;
> Whatever's written in what poets name
> The book of the people; whatever most can bless
> The mind of man or elevate a rhyme;
> But all is changed, that high horse riderless,
> Though mounted in that saddle Homer rode
> Where the swan drifts upon a darkening flood.

Two more poems define the highest accomplishment of this section of the volume. "Byzantium," written a year or so before "Coole and Ballylee, 1931," is the essence of a different kind of romanticism than Yeats was thinking of when he wrote that "we were the last romantics." In it he acts out the effort of creative imagination to transcend time and death and asserts its success—though at the expense of life, "the fury and the mire of human veins," as we know it. He has overcome the sheer revulsion at our blood-drenched destiny of "Blood and the Moon" and, at an even higher pitch of intensity,

Portrait of Lady Gregory, by John Butler Yeats

has made acceptance of ourselves as we actually are something more strenuously generative than in "A Dialogue of Self and Soul."

Each of the first three stanzas provides a different symbol of human self-transcendence: the "great cathedral" of Santa Sophia and its "starlit or . . . moonlit dome" at the start, then the "image, man or shade" of one's "superhuman" self beyond life's boundary, and

then the golden bird first encountered—but in a context of personal
yearning—in "Sailing to Byzantium." The first stanza gives the
imagined setting. It is the "Emperor's" whole domain. Literally, that
would be ancient Byzantium, now Istanbul. More widely, it includes
all of Heaven and Hades and earth. In this first stanza especially,
Yeats's phrasing breaks new imaginative ground:

> The unpurged images of day recede;
> The Emperor's drunken soldiery are abed;
> Night resonance recedes, night-walkers' song
> After great cathedral gong;
> A starlit or a moonlit dome disdains
> All that man is,
> All mere complexities,
> The fury and the mire of human veins.

The vision is immense with awe and tension: the whole empirical world of daily life "receding" from view and growing silent, while
the great spiritual artifact takes dominion under the moon and stars.
But despite the dome's "disdain" for them, life's "complexities" remain. The "soldiery" are only sleeping; the "night-walkers' song"
and other street noises will return. So also in the second stanza, the
mirror image from the world of the shades that "floats" before the
poet does not replace him. It "may" be an intermediary to that other
world—"Hades' bobbin bound in mummy-cloth / May unwind the
winding path"—but the living man is what that image reflects. Similarly, the golden bird of the third stanza may look with "scorn" on
"common" birds, yet it too is but an intermediary. "Planted on the
star-lit golden bough" and able to mimic "the cocks of Hades," it
may, like the "shade" of the previous stanza, help unwind the path
between the worlds.

In the two closing stanzas, the teeming world of flesh and blood,
in the throes of creation, comes into its own. "At midnight" pure
forms are forged in the "golden smithies of the Emperor." There
"blood-begotten spirits come / And all complexities of fury leave."
The process is endless:

> Astraddle on the dolphin's mire and blood,
> Spirit after spirit! The smithies break the flood,
> The golden smithies of the Emperor!
> Marbles of the dancing floor
> Break bitter furies of complexity,
> Those images that yet
> Fresh images beget,
> That dolphin-torn, that gong-tormented sea.

The "sea" is the common life itself, "tormented" by the cathedral gong's summons from above to rise beyond itself into pure form. Meanwhile, from the sea's depths, the leaping dolphins carry the spirits of the dead toward the Isles of the Blest—an image from mythology that parallels the first stanzas' dome and shade and miraculous bird. Out of the gross physical world, incessantly begetting new life yet incessantly condemned to contempt and death, comes every energy and element that makes for the creation of immortal forms. The vision of immortality at the expense of life is a tragic one, like that in Keats's "Ode on a Grecian Urn," but strangely vital at the same time.

The remaining work of special interest in the long opening section is "Vacillation," a sequence of eight short, untitled poems. Its simple personal center appears in the two middle poems, Parts IV and V. The first of these describes a memory of having once sat at a table in "a crowded London shop" where, inexplicably, "my body of a sudden blazed" and for some twenty minutes "it seemed, so great my happiness, / That I was blessèd and could bless." In the second, the poet confesses to a spiritual heaviness so great, when he recalls "things said or done"—or not said or done—"long years ago," that he can give due attention to nothing else. Around these opposed states "Vacillation" swirls.

Thus, Part I begins with the lines: "Between extremities / Man runs his course." The thought clearly anticipates the contrasting emotional states in the two middle poems. But the rest of the poem is tipped toward the darker side. We are reminded that remorse and death inevitably triumph, destroying all the "antinomies" that drive any life. If that is so, the poem asks abruptly at its close without staying for answer, then "What is joy?"

The next poem comes closer than any other in the sequence to giving a reply more general than the memory of a single momentary surge of bliss. Its glamorous and complex central symbol gives it prophetic authority (slightly weakened, though, by two or three lines of incantatory mumbling that verge on the comic):

> A tree there is that from its topmost bough
> Is half all glittering flame and half all green
> Abounding foliage moistened with the dew;
> And half is half and yet is all the scene;
> And half and half consume what they renew,
> And he that Attis' image hangs between
> That staring fury and the blind lush leaf
> May know not what he knows, but knows not grief.

"A tree there is" has the ring of sacred legendry, and this effect is well sustained. The imagined tree juxtaposes nature's prolific richness and the fires of creative change, as do the successive images in "Byzantium." The major difference is that the emphasis on their interaction is far less dynamic here than in the lines on the Emperor's "golden smithies" and their "dancing floor." At the end, the riddling lines on the god Attis, whose worshippers castrated themselves at his annual festival, provide an unexpected turn. Those men, by a kind of death, have gained release from sexual torment and, in that sense, attained a negative joy like that connected with bodily weakness in "Demon and Beast." The poem has given us an eccentric turn on the theme of self-transcendence at the cost of life.

Part III provides another variation, a warning in two stages. In the first stage, the thought is practical: that a life crammed with profit and the satisfying of ambition will not reward our most natural desires. ("All women dote upon an idle man.") In the second, it is Nietzschean: that the highest "work of intellect or faith" must also be a sacrificial "preparation for your death." It must be suitable only for those who "come / Proud, open-eyed and laughing to the tomb" and put aside whatever will hinder their aim of perfection.

The final three poems of "Vacillation" stress freedom from caring about consequences and from rigid dogma. Part VI, one of Yeats's most taking ballad-like poems, has its heroes—great rulers and conquerors—crying out the refrain that is "the meaning of all song"; namely, "Let all things pass away!" Parts VII and VIII follow through by presenting two uncowed defenses, one by "The Heart" against the preaching of "The Soul," the other by the poet against the Catholic philosopher Von Hügel. The position, in both cases presented genially but firmly, is that one advances farther toward creative transcendence by the pagan and half-secular way of myth and art than by the ascetic path of orthodox Christianity: "Homer is my example and his unchristened heart." Friedrich von Hügel's *The Mystical Element of Religion* (1908) had contrasted Homeric with Christian thought, and Yeats in this line takes the opposite tack from his. He is attractively lighthearted in his disagreement, and ends the poem most amiably: "So get you gone, Von Hügel, though with blessings on your head."

In its opening section, we have seen, *The Winding Stair and Other Poems* gives major attention to passionate life as it affects creative or spiritual self-transcendence. The sequence of seven Crazy Jane poems that follows, at the start of the "Words for Music Perhaps" section, carries this emphasis forward and dramatizes it in the character of the woman supposedly speaking. There is no question that Yeats's curiosity about the erotic side of female sensibility, as in "Leda and the Swan," colors these poems. But it soon becomes apparent that certain of his basic poetic obsessions—religious tyranny (in the perspective of William Blake, but with an Irish turn), the mysteries of personal destiny and death and the sense of the supernatural, and the relation of all this to one's art—are very much a part of them.

The first poem, "Crazy Jane and the Bishop," is an immediate instance. Its love theme is no more striking than either its eerily matter-of-fact assumption of communion with the dead or its anger at the Church and its influence. Jane's "dear Jack that's dead" was, and remains, her lover. Long ago, when alive, he was excommunicated and banished by the man, later made Bishop, who "cried that we lived like beast and beast." Now, at midnight, she will stand under "the blasted oak" to curse the Bishop and have a tryst with Jack's ghost:

> Jack had my virginity,
> And bids me to the oak, for he
> (*All find safety in the tomb.*)
> Wanders out into the night
> And there is shelter under it,
> But should that other come, I spit:
> *The solid man and the coxcomb.*

The Bishop had once called Jack a "coxcomb" (it was "the least he said" about him), and the refrain returns the insult. In fact, it was Jack who was "the solid man," for—while the Bishop resembled an ugly, composite bird, with skin "wrinkled like the foot of a goose" and a "heron's hunch upon his back"—Jack stood straight: "a birch-tree." The poem is self-contained enough to be read just as a violently bitter monologue by a woman whose life has been wrecked by the Church's decree and either is actually "crazy" or has broken past the barrier of Jack's death and is still close to him in a state of eerie transport. The further resonances relating to the country's lost ancient freedoms and extending to all sorts of troubles such as the memory of Parnell's downfall and parochial distrust of the unfamiliar in art should be obvious.

These motifs are echoed later in "Crazy Jane Talks with the Bishop," in which the Bishop urges Jane to repent her sins before it is too late. His argument is thoroughly insulting: "Those breasts are flat and fallen now, / Those veins must soon be dry; / Live in a heavenly mansion, / Not in some foul sty." She replies with a barrage of wisdom that brings the poem to a pitch of realization even keener than that in "Byzantium." The key lines not only stress the physical realities of sexual love; they also take over from the Bishop the privilege of citing the New Testament to support a moral position:

> For Love has pitched his mansion in
> The place of excrement.

In this poem a stand is explicitly taken against the notion that sexual freedom is especially degrading to women. Yeats's earlier work, such as his Solomon-and-Sheba poems and the "Memory" sequence, often shows his understanding of women as full equals and, often, his mentors. But "Crazy Jane Talks with the Bishop" goes farther in pursuing its special point, not as ideological argument but as Jane's natural, dignified response to the Bishop's cruel and ignorant bias. She has had lovers, yes—but "a woman can be proud and stiff / When on love intent."

In an earlier poem of the sequence, Jane has been warned—by whom?—against her dear Jack: "So never hang your heart upon / A roaring, ranting journeyman." But that poem, "Crazy Jane Reproved," is a happy, elusive dance of feeling. Does Crazy Jane have serious doubts about Jack? Is she pretending to "reprove" herself in mockery of such an idea? Is the "I" of the poem Crazy Jane at all? No matter. In any case, the poem steps lightly away from acceptance of brute sexuality as the sole force behind choice and destiny: "Great Europa played the fool / That changed a lover for a bull." God the artist is given to more intricately demanding tasks:

> To round that shell's elaborate whorl,
> Adorning every secret track
> With the delicate mother-of-pearl,
> Made the joints of Heaven crack.

"That shell" is as ambiguous as the rest of this delightful poem. Very likely the lines have to do with the infinite labor of evolving even a tiny seashell. Or "that shell" may be the intricately designed universe. Or it may be an image for Jane's complex psychosexual nature, or her whole self—or all these things, since the referent for the shell symbol is not made altogether clear. Whatever the "answer," we are again in the realm of the connection between swarming mundane physicality and miraculous creations that seem totally apart from it. This is so even though the refrain, *"Fol de rol, fol de rol,"* leavens the serious implications of the shell's "elaborate whorl" and "secret tracks" by seeming to laugh it all off.

It is interesting that, while Jack is somehow an ardently desired presence in most of these poems, there are no directly erotic passages. In "Crazy Jane on the Day of Judgment," the two are presumably side by side—or so we must gather from the alternating refrains: *"And that is what Jane said"* and *"'That's certainly the case,' said he."* Apart from "his" two refrains, Jane does all the talking. Her subject, except in the third stanza, is "true love." It remains "unsatisfied," she says, unless it can "take the whole/Body and soul." Her example is herself: "Take the sour/If you take me,/I can scoff and lour/And scold for an hour"—an announcement that he heartily seconds as "certainly the case." After this touch of comic realism, the third stanza drops into a depressive abyss that wrenches the poem to a new level of intensity:

> "Naked I lay,
> The grass my bed;
> Naked and hidden away,
> That black day";
> *And that is what Jane said.*

The final stanza will return to the subject of true love, and will end with the ironic reply *"That's certainly the case"* when Jane says we can never understand it in this life. But the unexplained picture of Jane lying "naked and hidden" in the grass on "that black day" (presumably when Jack died) has become the poem's emotional center. Despite its ambiguity, that picture is now a strong elegiac force in the sequence. Also, it ushers in a sense of existential loneliness and despair that the next two poems cope with. The depth of that sense suddenly makes the title "Crazy Jane on the Day of Judgment" seem more relevant than before. Emotionally, the lines anticipate Jane's own death as well as recalling Jack's. In that altered light, then, the closing stanza's talk of learning love's true meaning when "Time" has been left behind may refer to Plato's idea of entering the realm of pure being. In this little sequence, Yeats uses his ability to suggest multiple *just possible* meanings—all carried in concrete yet ambiguous phrasing—to superb effect.

The next two poems are the most complex, emotionally, in the group. The first, "Crazy Jane and Jack the Journeyman," begins with a reflection on the relation of lovers that is at once pointedly realistic and mystical:

> I know, although when looks meet
> I tremble to the bone,
> The more I leave the door unlatched
> The sooner love is gone,
> For love is but a skein unwound
> Between the dark and dawn.

In the next stanza, attention swings from Jane's passion to thoughts of her death. It occurs to her that, should she die and be properly buried, her "ghost" (or spirit) must leave "love's skein" behind and come "to God" in loneliness. It would leap from the tomb "into the light" of Heaven that her birth had made her forget. But the final stanza then gives earthly passion the last word. If Jane had her choice, and could simply be left to "lie alone / In an empty bed," her ghost would wait for her dead lover's ghost to come by at night, and would join and walk along with it thereafter.

"Crazy Jane on God," the most provocative piece in the group, continues the elegiac strain, combined with the sense of spiritual isolation, that marks the two previous poems. Different in structure from the other Crazy Jane poems, it conjures up four separate situations or scenes, linked mainly, with one exception, by a common tone of passive, stoical resignation. In the first stanza, we learn that Jane's various "lovers of a night" would come and go as they wished, "whether I would or no." In the second, we are told of banners and men-at-arms and armored horses crowding "the narrow pass" where "the great battle was." The third describes a house like that in the play *Purgatory*. It is "uninhabited, ruinous," but is "suddenly lit up / From door to top"—a pattern-changing vision of possible promise, slightly echoed in the last stanza's unabated singing in the wake of loss:

> I had wild Jack for a lover;
> Though like a road
> That men pass over
> My body makes no moan
> But sings on;
> *All things remain in God.*

As we have seen, vehement affirmation comes into its own in the next poem, "Crazy Jane Talks with the Bishop." And yet, as in "Crazy Jane on God," Jane's view of her life—as opposed to the Bishop's—also involves a melancholy acceptance of how things are:

> My friends are gone, but that's a truth
> Nor grave nor bed denied,
> Learned in bodily lowliness
> And in the heart's pride.

The final turn in the little sequence comes in "Crazy Jane Grown Old Looks at the Dancers." Jane sees the dancers' immersion in the passion their ritual movements express as the one permanent value we can wring out of chaotic experience. Here all is concentrated in their dance of murderous love. *"Love is like the lion's tooth"* is the apt refrain; and the "chosen youth" dancing with "that ivory image" seems to want to strangle her, while she "drew a knife to strike him dead." Jane envies the uninhibited display of sexual fury: "They had all that had their hate." (We should recall Yeats's old use of "hatred" to mean passionate intensity.)

The remaining poems in "Words for Music Perhaps" do not on the whole, despite the appeal of a number of them, match the originality and impact of the Crazy Jane group. "Her Anxiety" would have made a lovely incidental piece on love's precariousness within that group, "Lullaby" would have added a tender dimension, and "After Long Silence" a time-mellowed note of regret—but all three would have been alien to the deeper pulse of the first seven poems. "'I Am of Ireland,'" of course, is an irresistible improvisation on an old song and has some of the same feeling of solitude and bitter courage as "Crazy Jane on the Day of Judgment," but could hardly have been fitted into Jane's world.

All but one of the eleven poems in "A Woman Young and Old" were composed between 1923 and 1929, before any in the Crazy Jane group. (The exception is the fourth poem, "Her Triumph," a happy but awkward poem of implied sexual liberation.) As a more coherent sequence than the overloaded "Words for Music Perhaps," it gives *The Winding Stair and Other Poems* a tight-knit final section, but it seems clear that about half the work in it overlaps with the Crazy Jane poems. The rest does not because of differences of dramatic character or situation.

For instance, the first poem, "Father and Child," assumes that the "Woman" of the sequence, when young, lives in a respectable, protected world. Her father does the speaking in this poem. He is helplessly distressed by her infatuation with "a man / that has the worst of all bad names" but whose hair, she says, "is beautiful," and whose eyes are "cold as the March wind." Perhaps Crazy Jane was once like her, but the poems associated with her name all present a full-grown woman in an isolated world of profoundly contemplated passion and death. She does not quarrel with her natural desires— she is past all that—but puts them at the center of her philosophizing.

But to return to the developing "Woman" (as we must call her). In the next two poems, "Before the World Was Made" and "A First-Confession," she struggles to repress desire and live up to a Platonic ideal of perfect beauty that was created "before the world was made."

The charm (which may seem factitious to many modern readers) of
"A First Confession" resides largely in her old-fashioned sense of
maidenly propriety in conflict with the "satisfaction" that "a man's
attention / Brings." The amusing, somewhat coy beginning is like a
music-hall song:

> I admit the briar
> Entangled in my hair
> Did not injure me;
> My blenching and trembling,
> Nothing but dissembling,
> Nothing but coquetry.

Neither this tone nor the overwhelming imagery of guilt and
fear that abruptly replaces it in the closing stanza would be true to
Jane's sensibility. But another feeling, of being under the spell of a
force of destiny ("the Zodiac"), is there as well and brings the poem
an unexpected depth closer to Jane's ponderings:

> Brightness that I pull back
> From the Zodiac,
> Why those questioning eyes
> That are fixed upon me?
> What can they do but shun me
> If empty night replies?

Yeats wrote and inserted the fourth poem, "Her Triumph," after
beginning the "Crazy Jane" series. The Woman's "triumph" is to
have been rescued from the "dragon" of moral repression by a lover:
her personal "Saint George or else a pagan Perseus." Hitherto she
had not realized the wondrous change that gratified desire, as part of
true love, brings about. But it has happened, and now she and her
rescuer "stare astonished at the sea," while "a miraculous strange
bird shrieks at us." This primal shriek hardly makes for a perfect final
line, but it does annunciate the point where the "she" of "A Woman

Young and Old" puts her old cares behind her and becomes a twin to Jane. It is a pity that "Her Triumph" is not a more vital poem instead of the facile, truncated Shakespearean sonnet that it is. But the transition has been made.

Certain lines and passages in the remaining poems underscore the convergence of the two characters. Only one such instance, in the aubade called "Parting," is lighthearted. It comes at the end: "I offer to love's play / My dark declivities." Another poem, "A Last Confession," begins lightly, as if to parody A. E. Housman: "What lively lad most pleasured me / Of all that with me lay?" But its tone alters dramatically, and at the end the speaker might well be Jane. Explaining her experiences of pleasure in love, she finds it ironic that, when she "gave her soul," she "loved in misery," but that she "had great pleasure with a lad / That I loved bodily." This is not quite Jane yet, but the climactic passage certainly is:

> I gave what other women gave
> That stepped out of their clothes,
> But when this soul, its body off,
> Naked to naked goes,
> He it has found shall find therein
> What none other knows . . .

Together with this passage, the poem "Chosen" comes closest to the Crazy Jane poems in seriousness and in self-abandonment to fated love. Its opening is the high point of the sequence:

> The lot of love is chosen. I learnt that much
> Struggling for an image on the track
> Of the whirling Zodiac.
> Scarce did he my body touch,
> Scarce sank he from the west
> Or found a subterranean rest
> On the maternal midnight of my breast
> Before I had marked him on his northern way,
> And seemed to stand although in bed I lay.

One other poem, "Her Vision in the Wood," stands besides "Chosen" as outstanding in original force. Questions of ideology aside, it is the closest Yeats ever came to a poem anticipating modern feminism. It begins with the Woman remembering herself, now aged, at the center of a mythical world:

> Dry timber under that rich foliage,
> At wine-dark midnight in the sacred wood,
> Too old for a man's love I stood in rage
> Imagining men. Imagining that I could
> A greater with a lesser pang assuage
> Or but to find if withered vein ran blood,
> I tore my body that its wine might cover
> Whatever could recall the lip of lover.

As she stands there bleeding, a torchlight procession, with "deafening music," enters, bearing wounded Adonis on a litter and singing of "the beast that gave the fatal wound." A company of "stately women" arrives as well, singing and appearing to be "grief-distraught" members of "a Quattrocento painter's throng." But then an ambiguous term enters the Woman's account:

> Till suddenly in grief's contagion caught,
> I stared upon his blood-bedabbled breast
> And sang my malediction with the rest.

The word "malediction" comes as a huge surprise. Are they cursing the wild boar that was Adonis' killer? Or is their song one of hatred against the beautiful god himself, while the appearance of grief was merely an illusion? The Woman does not explain directly, but in the final stanza the "grief"/"malediction" ambivalence clarifies itself as part of the traumatic revelation that comes to her:

> That thing all blood and mire, that beast-torn wreck,
> Half turned and fixed a glazing eye on mine,
> And, though love's bitter-sweet had all come back,

Those bodies from a picture or a coin
Nor saw my body fall nor heard it shriek,
Nor knew, drunken with singing as with wine,
That they had brought no fabulous symbol there
But my heart's victim and its torturer.

Yeats ends the sequence with one of his best translations from the Oedipus cycle: a chorus from the *Antigone* that, like "Her Vision in the Wood" but more simply and ironically, mourns the irreversibility of fate, ending: "Oedipus' child / Descends into the loveless dust." It is a gentle afterbeat to the fierce "vision" that teaches the painful private bearing of tragic myth. The inescapable double sacrifice and bittersweetness of all that love entails are set side by side in the Woman's "vision" with the existential betrayal she feels as she stands "in rage / Imagining men." And Yeats has discovered, in reaching this far in trying to imagine female subjectivity, a key to his own helplessness in the face of tragic knowledge of all kinds.

2. From "Parnell's Funeral and Other Poems" *through* Last Poems

It seems useful to treat Yeats's later poems—all written during 1933 to 1939—together, almost as if they had appeared in a single volume. The final sweep of his work is represented in two volumes published during his lifetime, *A Full Moon in March* (1935) and *New Poems* (1938), and in the posthumous *Last Poems and Two Plays* and *On the Boiler* (both 1939).

The first of these collections contains, in addition to the "mad" plays *A Full Moon in March* and *The King of the Great Clock Tower,* a quite small selection of verse under the title "Parnell's Funeral and Other Poems." It is notable for two strong political pieces and for the sequence "Supernatural Songs." In the sequence, one Ribh, a skeptical "hermit" who rejects Christianity with sympathetic good humor, holds forth very much as though he were William Butler Yeats. *New*

Poems is a wide-ranging volume focusing largely on sexual and political motifs and on growing old, as do the few poems in the one-
issue periodical *On the Boiler*. *Last Poems and Two Plays,* which
closes with *The Death of Cuchulain* and *Purgatory,* reflects a most
remarkable mustering of creative energy up to the very end of the
poet's life.

A succession of political poems, sometimes violently nationalis-
tic, sometimes revolted by violence, and sometimes toughmindedly
satirical, appears in these volumes. For instance, the title poem in
"Parnell's Funeral and Other Poems" is a vehement attack on what
Yeats saw as the betrayal of Parnell by a craven, bigoted, and misled
Irish public. The poem opens with a mythical scene of ritual sacrifice,
comparable in its rich detail to the one in "Her Vision in the Wood."
In it a miraculous boy who might have wrought wonders is killed
and his heart cut out. Thus it was with Parnell, whose downfall is
seen as the everlasting shame of the nation:

> An age is the reversal of an age:
> When strangers murdered Emmet, Fitzgerald, Tone,
> We lived like men that watch a painted stage.
> What matter for the scene, the scene once gone:
> It had not touched our lives. But popular rage,
> *Hysterica passio* dragged this quarry down.
> None shared our guilt; nor did we play a part
> Upon a painted stage when we devoured his heart.

This is the best passage in the poem, which goes on to say that
political leaders of a later age would have been able to prevent civil
war and to act more nobly if only they could have "eaten Parnell's
heart" and thus partaken of his courage and wisdom. There is a mad
edge to the rage in this poem, reminiscent of the two plays in the
volume. It is echoed in the Roger Casement verses in *New Poems* and
in the sometimes incoherent "Three Marching Songs" in *Last Poems
and Two Plays*. On the other hand, the "Parnell's Funeral" collection
also contains "Church and State," a pointedly enlightened poem of
fine simplicity that shows a totally other side of Yeats's politics:

Here is fresh matter, poet,
Matter for old age meet;
Might of the Church and the State,
Their mobs put under their feet.
O but heart's wine shall run pure,
Mind's bread grow sweet.

That were a cowardly song,
Wander in dreams no more;
What if the Church and the State
Are the mob that howls at the door!
Wine shall run thick to the end,
Bread taste sour.

"Supernatural Songs," the main offering of the "Parnell's Funeral" section of *A Full Moon in March,* is a sequence of ten poems divided between a sexually saturated mystical philosophizing and a more straightforward lyricism. The first and last—and also the best—poems in the group are "Ribh at the Tomb of Baile and Ailinn" and "Meru." In the former poem, Ribh, the definitely unorthodox prophet-guru of the sequence, reads from his "holy book" at the tomb of the legendary Irish lovers Baile and Ailinn. Erotic love, for them, has been transformed into "the intercourse of angels": "a light / Where for the moment both seem lost, consumed." The poem, a triumph of gently envisioned ecstasy, opens the way to two sorts of pieces to follow. One is the poetry of revelatory but non-Christian incantation—sometimes a bit polemical—in succeeding work like "Ribh Denounces Patrick" and "Ribh Considers Christian Love Insufficient." The other sort celebrates the sexual origin and nature of the universe in poems like "Ribh in Ecstasy" ("Godhead on Godhead in sexual spasm begot / Godhead") and "Whence Had They Come?" The sexual frankness of a number of poems in later volumes is prefigured here.

The closing poem, "Meru," is of a depressive cast hardly related to the rest of "Supernatural Songs," except possibly the fatalistic "The Four Ages of Man." In that respect, it is more akin to "Man and the Echo" and "The Circus Animals' Desertion" in *Last Poems and Two Plays* than to anything in "Supernatural Songs." But at the same time it does in its way belong in that sequence, which often goes counter to conventional "positive" religious and moral postures. "Meru" is simply a forthright statement of what the other poems have been implying:

> Civilisation is hooped together, brought
> Under a rule, under the semblance of peace
> By manifold illusion; but man's life is thought,
> And he, despite his terror, cannot cease
> Ravening through century after century,
> Ravening, raging, and uprooting that he may come
> Into the desolation of reality . . .

The relentlessness of these lines seems natural in the wake of certain passages in the poems preceding "Meru." Ribh's detestation of dogma—a form of "manifold illusion" deliberately cultivated by theological rhetoric—surfaces here as it did at the end of "Vacillation." In "Ribh Denounces Patrick," it leads him to scorn the doctrine of the all-male Trinity, so contrary to the sex-centered vision of his own "holy book," as "an abstract Greek absurdity." And in "Ribh Considers Christian Love Insufficient," he chooses to "study hatred" rather than "love," which "is of God and surpasses human wit." In so doing, he will free himself of doctrinally imposed "terror and deception"—so that

> Then my delivered soul herself shall learn
> A darker knowledge and in hatred turn
> From every thought of God mankind has had.
> Thought is a garment and the soul's a bride
> That cannot in that trash and tinsel hide:
> Hatred of God may bring the soul to God.

The closing line of the stanza makes this poem, probably written in 1934, a sophisticated afterbeat of "Running to Paradise," written in 1913. In the earlier piece, the beggar who is "hurrying" to Paradise follows the model of "the wind / That nobody can buy or bind." He has no faith to reassure him, and he asks for none, and yet—because it is the great dream or gamble—he is, in his own way, making for some unlikely "Paradise." Similarly, Ribh has used the "besom" of his hatred to "clear the soul" of the "trash and tinsel" of doctrinal faith. Doing so, he says, *may* "bring the soul to God." It is another gamble; Ribh, too, is "running to Paradise."

Where "Meru" sees human thought inevitably closing in on "the desolation of reality," these two poems bespeak our instinct to behave as though an undefinable hope hovered beyond the limits of our knowledge. "Meru," placed at the end of the sequence, resists even that faint urge but does not obliterate it. A shadow of hope persists in a poem like "Ribh Considers Christian Love Insufficient," even while carrying with it the terror of the unknown. We see the same paradoxical sub-affirmation in "The Four Ages of Man." There, in succession, the soul loses its crucial struggles: first, to remain unborn and free of bodily existence; then to stay clear of the heart's turmoil and forbidden desires; then to resist abandoning the heart in favor of intellectual objectivity; and then to stave off self-immersion in the unknown force called "God":

> He with body waged a fight,
> But body won; it walks upright.
>
> Then he struggled with the heart;
> Innocence and peace depart.
>
> Then he struggled with the mind;
> His proud heart he left behind.
>
> Now his wars with God begin;
> At stroke of midnight God shall win.

"Supernatural Songs" as a whole balances mystical riddling of this sort, which allows for use of the language of religiosity (however uncommitted), against naked despair. The scattered pieces that in-

sist on a sexual principle driving all of being—"As man, as beast, as
an ephemeral fly begets, Godhead begets Godhead"—mediate, as it
were, between an eccentric spiritualism and a pessimistic secularism.
They can be pedantically assertive, as in the line just quoted from
"Ribh Denounces Patrick." But they can also create, beautifully, a
reverie world of love and transfiguration such as we have seen in
"Ribh at the Tomb of Baile and Ailinn." Again, in "Ribh in Ecstasy,"
the soul has for a moment found "all happiness" at hearing "those
amorous cries" that arise from the orgasmic joy of "Godhead" with
"Godhead." And in the entranced "He and She," the moon, symbolizing female sexuality, dances toward and away from the sun, and "all
creation shivers" with her "sweet cry." Like an inspired but deconse-
crated oracle, Yeats rides the interactions of opposites and of dispa-
rate moods in these poems. Thus, the challenging verse-riddle called
"What Magic Drum?" seems to be evoking an Edenic world and yet
making it pre-paradisal. Its tone conveys a state of transport at once
blissful and barbarous:

> He holds him from desire, all but stops his breathing lest
> Primordial Motherhood forsake his limbs, the child no
>   longer rest,
> Drinking joy as it were milk upon his breast.
>
> Through light-obliterating garden foliage what magic
>   drum?
> Down limb and breast or down that glimmering belly move
>   his mouth and sinewy tongue.
> What from the forest came? What beast has licked its
>   young?

The poem's phrasing, especially the image of a "magic drum"
beating ritually from somewhere above, suggests a sacred birth. "Pri-
mordial Motherhood" is contained within the imagined primeval
male being seen licking his young. Separation of the sexes, which he
fears because his intimate, joy-giving contact with the newborn child

will be taken from him, has not yet occurred. The scene throbs like a
Van Gogh painting, a fantasy of the origin of life or perhaps a har-
binger of changes yet to come.

Admittedly, this brilliantly original fantasy is demanding to an
extreme. But "Supernatural Songs" was composed, and created a
certain order within Yeats's riotous imagination, during the period in
the 1930's when his writing for the stage was in its wildest phase.
The more interesting side of all this is the imaginative vitality of the
poem regardless of how we paraphrase it. It projects an atmosphere
of compelling but controlled desire, of tenderness, and of mysterious
animal force. The next poem, "Whence Had They Come?" carries
on from there by proclaiming that "Eternity is passion." The utterance—followed by thoughts about the "passion-driven" sources of
art and of history's "sacred drama"—is also true to the feeling that
saturates "What Magic Drum?"

Several outstanding pieces in *New Poems* (1938) and the posthumous *Last Poems and Two Plays* (1939) carry on in the erotic
spirit of "Supernatural Songs." In *New Poems,* the sequence of seven
poems beginning with "The Three Bushes" does so in relatively
simple form, as does "The Wild Old Wicked Man." In the *Last
Poems* volume, the primary instance is "News for the Delphic Oracle." ("Politics," the brief closing poem, is certainly in harmony with
that spirit.)

"The Three Bushes," a narrative poem using an expanded and
modified ballad stanza, with refrain, tells the story of a lady torn
between her chastity and her sympathy for her poet-lover. It is notable for its deft handling of the form and for its happily insouciant
amorality. The poem begins:

> Said lady once to lover,
> "None can rely upon
> A love that lacks its proper food;
> And if your love were gone
> How could you sing those songs of love?
> I should be blamed, young man."
>   *O my dear, O my dear.*

She would, she says, "drop down dead / If I lost my chastity," but also do so "if he stop loving me." Her solution is to have her chambermaid take her place at night, unbeknownst to the lover:

> "So you must lie beside him
> And let him think me there,
> And maybe we are all the same
> Where no candles are,
> And maybe we are all the same
> That strip the body bare."
> *O my dear, O my dear.*

All goes well in this division between love of the soul and love of the body. But one day the lover's horse has a mishap, the lover falls to his death, and the lady—who has witnessed the accident—"dropped and died" on the spot, "for she / Loved him with her soul." The chambermaid has them buried side by side and plants two rose-bushes over their graves, to which a third will be added when she too dies and is buried next to them: "And now none living can, / When they have plucked a rose there, / Know where its roots began." Meanwhile, everything has been set right by a priest at the chamber-maid's deathbed, a man very unlike the strait St. Patrick of "Super-natural Songs" and much more like Ribh. His sympathetic attitude makes "The Three Bushes" the pleasantest tragic "leching song" (to quote the poem) e'er sung:

> When she was old and dying,
> The priest came where she was;
> She made a full confession.
> Long looked he in her face,
> And O, he was a good man
> And understood her case.
> *O my dear, O my dear.*

The six "songs" that follow orbit about this ballad. In effect, they are arias—the first three by the lady, the fourth by the lover, and the next two by the chambermaid. They are less flip than the ballad, and they go beyond even Yeats's plays of the mid-1930's in their sexual directness. "The Lady's First Song" shows the agony of her repressed physical desire painfully: "I turn round / Like a dumb beast in a show." Her second song, a response to the chambermaid's questioning, begins:

> What sort of man is coming
> To lie between your feet?
> What matter, we are but women.
> Wash; make your body sweet . . .

And in her third song, she explains the reciprocity of soul and body, and of the sense of sin and that of ecstasy. She and the chambermaid will "split his love,"

> That I may hear if we should kiss
> A contrapuntal serpent hiss,
> You, should hand explore a thigh,
> All the labouring heaven sigh.

"The Lover's Song" and "The Chambermaid's First Song" match this frank language of love-relationship. "The Chambermaid's Second Song," which concludes the sequence, goes it one better, putting both the spiritual and the sensual aspects of love into the same phallic imagery:

> From pleasure of the bed,
> Dull as a worm,
> His rod and its butting head
> Limp as a worm,
> His spirit that has fled
> Blind as a worm.

In this sequence, and in the other erotically centered later poems I have mentioned—"The Wild Old Wicked Man" and "News for the

Delphic Oracle"—Yeats's lyrical skill and dramatic imagination take on a bright clarity like that we have noted in *The Words upon the Window-Pane* and *Purgatory*. Also, he has cast off inhibiting caution and now seems to care less than ever whether or not conventional readers will be offended. "The Wild Old Wicked Man," written in the first person, is implicitly a confession of sexual longings, perhaps unfulfillable, combined with some sexual boasting and with forebodings of death. In the two final stanzas, tragic recognitions add needed ballast to the poem.

Except for one stanza, "The Wild Old Wicked Man" is entirely a monologue by the old man of the title. In part it is a plea to a young woman to console him in his last days by accepting him as her lover. Her reply, in the third stanza, is that of someone whose piety and chastity—her language, except for one phrase, might well be a nun's—make her immune to his appeal. But his monologue, which from the start casts a wide net of free association, swirls forward around this rock of resistance. Certain images and turns of thought in it give it a range of complexity beyond the literal dramatic situation. The very first stanza implies this range. Even the refrain, "*Daybreak and a candle-end*," suggests both a morning song and the coming of death:

> "Because I am mad about women
> I am mad about the hills,"
> Said that wild old wicked man
> Who travels where God wills.
> "Not to die on the straw at home,
> Those hands to close these eyes,
> That is all I ask, my dear,
> From the old man in the skies."
> *Daybreak and a candle-end.*

The first four lines are a curious mixture. Almost—but not quite—joking, they add a sense of guidance by a whimsical God to the old man's confession that he is "mad" about women and therefore about "the hills." The link, which obviously lies in the contours of both and also in the ancient view of the earth as female, helps give him a vague, untenured supernatural role. He roams the earth, a twentieth-century diminished satyr, yearning and insecure.

In the fifth line the focus shifts from his adoration of the female principle in general to his appeal for a particular young woman's compassionate company. It is interesting that he appeals simultaneously to her and to God, whom he mentions familiarly as "the old man in the skies." And it is even more interesting that she should later repeat the same epithet. Although this is a serious poem, Yeats sometimes lets a sudden eccentric or comic impulse run away with it for a moment. The same thing happens again when the old man is described as holding "his stout stick under his hand"—a priapic nudge out of Aristophanes even while the woman is avowing her love for God alone.

Such contradictory effects are present throughout the poem. Another instance can be seen in the old man's two ways of speaking of love. On the one hand, he boasts of his superiority to "warty lads" who have only their bodies to offer, while he can offer a woman "words . . . that can pierce the heart" or "that can make a cat laugh." But on the other hand he might be a "warty lad" himself when he speaks of finding what he really wants among willing "girls down on the seashore / Who understand the dark"—for "a young man in the dark am I," though "a wild old man in the light."

The stream of contradictory feeling disappears in the final two stanzas, in which the poem reaches its lyrical resolution. The first of these stanzas is Yeats at his purest, expressing the deepest kind of tragic recognition through the old man:

> "All men live in suffering,
> I know as few can know,
> Whether they take the upper road
> Or stay content on the low,
> Rower bent in his row-boat
> Or weaver bent at his loom,
> Horseman erect upon horseback
> Or child hid in the womb."

In the final stanza, the old man sees only one way to cope with this existential trap, short of some miraculous "stream of lightning" from above that would change everything. Waiting piously and praying for "the old man in the skies" to make that happen might be a saint's solution, but there is something to be said for the temporary consolations—however pathetic—of ordinary life:

> "But a coarse old man am I,
> I choose the second-best,
> I forget it all awhile
> Upon a woman's breast."

The scattered series of erotically centered pieces I have just been discussing reach their climax in the powerfully dynamic "News for the Delphic Oracle." This poem envisions a world beyond death where only souls and divinities exist, though in bodily form. Its three graphic stanzas each present a separate scene within that world. The first scene reveals an Isle of the Blessed on which philosophers, poets, and legendary lovers reside languidly in a lotus-eater state of total gratification:

> There all the golden codgers lay,
> There the silver dew,
> And the great water sighed for love
> And the wind sighed too.

A comic irreverence reminiscent of "The Wild Old Wicked Man" colors this rapturous account of a narcotic dream world. Even the reference to God as "the old man in the skies" in that poem is echoed here, when the grand figures in the scene are called "golden codgers." In the same way, the legendary heroine Niamh, who took the initiative in wooing the poet Oisin, is jokingly called "man-picker Niamh." Everything is pure pleasure, the glamorous ease of the chosen. On their island of endlessly amorous joy, the "golden codgers" have gone beyond human cares and sympathy.

But of course they are in the realm beyond death, and the second

stanza takes us directly to a more forbidding scene in that realm.
Souls of the dead were said, in ancient Greece, to be borne to the Isles
of the Blessed on the backs of dolphins. The new stanza shifts attention to the surrounding waters, where a recurrent, impersonal cruelty attends the arrival of newcomers. The sudden reorientation is
like that in "The Wild Old Wicked Man," when the stanza beginning "All men live in suffering" darkens the poem's major emotional
bearing. But in "News for the Delphic Oracle," the turn is far more
drastic. It starts with the arrival of the Holy Innocents slaughtered by
Herod:

> Straddling each a dolphin's back
> And steadied by a fin,
> Those Innocents re-live their death,
> Their wounds open again.
> The ecstatic waters laugh because
> Their cries are sweet and strange,
> Through their ancestral patterns dance,
> And the brute dolphins plunge
> Until, in some cliff-sheltered bay
> Where wades the choir of love
> Proffering its sacred laurel crowns,
> They pitch their burdens off.

In this context, the reminder of death and suffering is in sharp
contrast to the images of "the ecstatic waters" and "the choir of love."
The "waters"—the universal surround of life and death, fed by all the
rhythms of existence—are indifferent to our individual needs and
feelings. It is enough for them that the cries of the Innocents "are
sweet and strange."

This impersonality of "ecstatic" universal process is the tragic
dimension of human destiny allegorized here. It leads us to the third
stanza: a different scene again, throwing a harsh light on the opening
dream of total love-gratification. This final stanza presents a teeming
panorama of incessant, driven sexual activity. It begins exquisitely

enough, but then becomes anything but exquisite. Peleus and
Thetis, who will become the parents of Achilles, are seen facing one
another. He is human, she a nereid, and for the moment he takes on
her finer sensibility and she his human physicality:

> Slim adolescence that a nymph has stripped,
> Peleus upon Thetis stares,
> Her limbs are delicate as an eyelid,
> Love has blinded him with tears;
> But Thetis' belly listens . . .

What her "belly" hears is an "intolerable music" from the mountain cavern above, where Pan the goatish fertility god dwells. All
around them, sheer grossness prevails while "nymphs and satyrs /
Copulate in the foam." The meeting of the human and the divine has
been embodied in three juxtaposed scenes that also show the over-
weening power of sex in shaping our construction of paradise as well
as life here on earth.

The high-voltage intensity of "News for the Delphic Oracle"
brings the series of poems in this erotically driven vein to its climax,
bridging *A Full Moon in March, New Poems,* and *Last Poems and
Two Plays.* In this context, I should mention "Politics," the piece that
closes the *Last Poems* volume. On its surface it is a flip little reply to a
comment made by Thomas Mann during the Spanish Civil War and
shortly before World War II: "In our time the destiny of man presents its meanings in political terms." Yeats's cavalier rejoinder begins:

> How can I, that girl standing there,
> My attention fix
> On Roman or on Russian
> Or on Spanish politics?

He then grants that there are knowledgeable persons whose
grave warnings deserve respect. Nevertheless, the clear implication
is, politics are hardly the whole of life. The author of "News for the

Delphic Oracle" ends this poem much as his alter ego, the wild old
wicked man, might have done:

> And maybe what they say is true
> Of war and war's alarms,
> But O that I were young again
> And held her in my arms.

Yeats, we know, had long been aware of the political dimension
of "destiny." His poems of the late 1930's give added testimony.
Some have to do primarily with Ireland. These are not usually his
best work, for he was often tempted to write a swashbuckling variety
of militant verse suitable for recitation to a mob. Thus, the beginning
of "Three Marching Songs" in the *Last Poems* volume:

> Remember all those renowned generations,
> They left their bodies to fatten the wolves,
> They left their homestead to fatten the foxes,
> Fled to far countries, or sheltered themselves
> In cavern, crevice or hole,
> Defending Ireland's soul.
>
> Be still, be still, what can be said?
> My father sang that song,
> But time amends old wrong,
> All that is finished, let it fade.

Mob-oriented or not, it is still Yeats; its swinging cadence and
bitter tone, and a few stirring lines like the first one, can be addictive.
In substance, "Three Marching Songs" echoes many of his earlier
poems bemoaning the philistine or cowardly betrayal of the ideals so
many patriots and leaders had sacrificed so much for. But in his
political poems of the 1930's, he often seems to have forgotten his
distress at the violence and bloodshed of revolution in earlier work.
As for his other serious poetry of the period, a disillusioned tone and

an anti-egalitarian bias often ride it. Even "Man and the Echo," one
of the most moving pieces in *Last Poems and Two Plays,* reflects
second thoughts—and clearly justifiable—about his earlier idealism,
although its major concern lies elsewhere. Two rueful lines in it—
"Did that play of mine send out / Certain men the English shot?"—
recall the humane spirit of Yeats's "Easter, 1916" but omit any positive note concerning the poet's or the political movement's original
motives.

The crabbed couplet in *New Poems* called "Parnell" can serve as
an introduction to Yeats's poetry of political letdown—especially
since its grim prophecy, as we now know, hardly applies to Ireland
alone:

> Parnell came down the road, he said to a cheering man:
> "Ireland shall get her freedom and you still break
>   stone."

A more narrowly Irish bearing does, however, enter and give a
special turn to a number of poems that are not in the main political.
One has only to read "The Curse of Cromwell" or "The Municipal
Gallery Revisited," both in *New Poems,* to grasp the complexity of
Yeats's sometimes self-contradictory political thought in this period.
These are poems of 1937. The Easter Rising, the later struggles for
independence, and the civil war are in the past. But "The Curse of
Cromwell" shows that even Yeats could harbor a lingering resentment against past English wrongs as though the situation had not
really changed. "Cromwell's house and Cromwell's murderous
crew" are still symbolically present, the poem asserts, in the British-
influenced business mentality now infecting Ireland. The old popular dream of a land of love and dancing, gallant swordsmen and
horsemen, feudal loyalty, and "neighborly content and easy talk" is
forever driven out by "money's rant." (Shades of Tennyson's *Maud*
and Ezra Pound's harangues!) The final stanza begins with four lines
that anticipate the scene and import of *Purgatory*:

> I came on a great house in the middle of the night,
> Its open lighted doorway and its windows all alight,
> And all my friends were there and made me welcome too;
> But I woke in an old ruin that the winds howled through.

"The Municipal Gallery Revisited," a far more introspective and accomplished poem, is equally nostalgic for a lost Irish past. This time, though, it is a very recent past encompassing the poet's own earlier years, summoned up for him by paintings on view in Dublin's Municipal Gallery. The first stanza is filled with "the images of thirty years," mostly having to do with political figures and situations he is vividly reminded of:

> Around me the images of thirty years:
> An ambush; pilgrims at the water-side;
> Casement upon trial, half hidden by the bars,
> Guarded; Griffith staring in hysterical pride;
> Kevin O'Higgins' countenance that wears
> A gentle questioning look that cannot hide
> A soul incapable of remorse or rest;
> A revolutionary soldier kneeling to be blessed . . .

The scenes and portraits recall a time of excitement and crucial events of the greatest concern to Yeats. Yet what is remarkable here is the absence of polemical comment of any sort. The poem combines intimate interest with distancing in the perspective of time. Sir Roger David Casement, an Irish Nationalist, had tried to obtain arms for the Rising from the German government. He was hanged as a traitor by the British in 1916, largely on the basis of diaries that may have been forged. Arthur Griffith, who negotiated the treaty with England establishing the Irish Free State, was among the people hostile to any literature, especially by John Synge, that showed their country in a light they considered unbecoming. Kevin O'Higgins, an important figure in the Free State government whom Yeats admired and regarded as a friend, was assassinated in 1922. Yeats had strong words, in private life and in other poems, about all these figures, and it is significant that he focuses on their portraits so revealingly at the start of his poem. But the frame he puts them in is not political. They appear as vivid memories of a time gone by, and soon blend in with other portrait-evoked memories: a "beautiful and gentle" woman met "fifty years ago / For twenty minutes in some studio"; members of Lady Gregory's family; and then Lady Gregory herself and John Synge, figures especially close to Yeats who, together with him, he says,

> thought
> All that we did, all that we said or sang
> Must come from contact with the soil, from that
> Contact everything Antaeus-like grew strong.
> We three alone in modern times had brought
> Everything down to that sole test again,
> Dream of the noble and the beggar-man.

These two comrades-in-arms, neither of them anything like a political activist, are seen as representing the whole rich body of Ireland's history. By its end the poem has become a tribute to them: "My glory was I had such friends." (Politicians often quote these words, altogether out of context, simply to praise people who have helped them in their campaigns.)

The first stanza's descriptions of Casement and the others keeps them keenly alive in memory, yet distanced by their deaths and by time. This double effect is reinforced by the extended memorializing of Synge and Lady Gregory, who had died in 1909 and 1932 respectively. We see, finally, that "The Municipal Gallery Revisited" is in fact an elegy for them. In general, Yeats's late poetry tends to be elegiac, mourning dead friends and ideals forgotten in a "leveling" age and—more subtly—continuing to confront his own old age and coming death. We have already observed something of the self-elegiac symbolism of "Cuchulain Comforted" and *The Death of Cuchulain,* as well as of "The Wild Old Wicked Man" in *New Poems*.

New Poems also has the kindred but more immediately confes-

sional pieces "An Acre of Grass," "What Then?" and "Are You
Content?" The first of these begins in apparently quiet acceptance of
an old man's lot:

> Picture and book remain,
> An acre of green grass
> For air and exercise,
> Now strength of body goes . . .

"My temptation," the poem goes on, is just to drift in quiet
despair, for "here at life's end" imagination and intellect lack their old
energy. Then, suddenly, comes a prayer for renewed inspiration,
even at the cost of madness, to break out of this enforced passivity.
And thereupon the poem soars:

> Grant me an old man's frenzy.
> Myself must I remake
> Till I am Timon or Lear
> Or that William Blake
> Who beat upon the wall
> Till truth obeyed his call;
>
> A mind Michael Angelo knew
> That can pierce the clouds
> Or inspired by frenzy
> Shake the dead in their shrouds;
> Forgotten else by mankind
> An old man's eagle mind.

"An old man's frenzy" like that of mad William Blake or Shakespeare's Timon and Lear would hardly be pure joy. But the poem's
lift into visionary power gives it far more zest than the plaintive
"What Then?" and "Are You Content?" There is also an unrepressed
note of continuing restless ambition in the line "forgotten else by
mankind," which suggests a reluctance to lose public attention. In
"What Then?" all ambition has been fulfilled—fame as a writer,

"sufficient money for his needs," true friends, marriage, children: in short, all of Yeats's successes—and yet the nagging, negating question of what it all adds up to remains. The refrain ("'What then?' sang Plato's ghost, 'What then?'") is an unanswerable and poignant challenge to complacency. So is the refrain "But I am not content" that answers the title's question in "Are You Content?"—another attempt by the poet to cope with the issue of what his life has really amounted to. This poem of considerable charm calls upon his ancestors "to judge what I have done" and decide whether or not he has lived up to his heritage in his writings—as if to help his descendants say the right things about him at his obsequies.

The poems just discussed are only indirectly self-elegiac. They cope, as it were, with what might conceivably be said about the poet after his death, when even their self-doubting or self-denigrating introspection could be praised as superb humility despite overwhelming achievements. But in "Under Ben Bulben," the opening poem of *Last Poems and Two Plays*, Yeats forestalls anyone else who might try to compose his epitaph. The inscription on his tombstone he "commands" in the poem was used when he was buried in "Drumcliff churchyard," County Sligo, near the mountain named in the title. Cast in the astringent mode of the *Greek Anthology*, it consists of the three short lines at the end of the poem's brief closing section:

> Under bare Ben Bulben's head
> In Drumcliff churchyard Yeats is laid,
> An ancestor was rector there
> Long years ago; a church stands near,
> By the road an ancient Cross.
> No marble, no conventional phrase,
> On limestone quarried near the spot
> By his command these words are cut:

> Cast a cold eye
> On life, on death.
> Horseman, pass by!

The whole of "Under Ben Bulben" is a preface to this lapidary close. Originally given the title "His Convictions," it takes the form, in the five sections preceding the one just quoted, of a series of pronouncements giving the "gist" of what certain supernatural beings wish to make known. The supernatural beings are the wondrous heroine of Shelley's "The Witch of Atlas" (as interpreted, Yeats casually implies, by mystical Egyptian devotees he calls the "Sages") and the immortal Sidhe of Irish tradition. The poem thus acts as a voice from Yeats's grave, as though he had learned the wisdom he is passing on to us by swearing fealty to those beings. The beginning of "Under Ben Bulben" invokes their spell that will lead to the poem's later utterances:

> Swear by what the Sages spoke
> Round the Mareotic Lake
> That the Witch of Atlas knew,
> Spoke and set the cocks a-crow.
>
> Swear by those horsemen, by those women,
> Complexion and form prove superhuman,
> That pale, long-visaged company . . .

Shelley's "Witch," a spirit of supernal beauty and wisdom, could see into ultimate meaning beyond the superficies of death and suffering. Shelley imagined her undoing and reversing those apparent evils, thus foreshadowing Yeats's own musings in the face of his burdens of age and frailty. The connection with Section II of the poem—the first of the poem's supposedly inspired utterances—is obvious. There is no finality in death, we are told, for "many times man lives and dies / Between his two eternities, / That of race and that of soul."

Without transition, but taking the long view of Section II that death does not really matter, the next section seems at first to introduce entirely political concerns. It centers its pronouncement on the nineteenth-century nationalist leader John Mitchel's prayer: "Send

war in our time, O Lord." But soon we see that Yeats is not quoting
Mitchel to incite revolutionary warfare. Rather, he uses the "prayer"
as a startling reminder that, at crucial moments, "even the wisest
man" must abandon words and choose "some sort of violence," not
necessarily physical, "before he can accomplish fate." When he has
become "fighting mad" enough to give himself unreservedly to a
drastic decision, his vision grows clear and he "laughs aloud, his
heart at peace." To judge from Sections IV and V, the direct bearing
of Mitchel's prayer for the poet seems to lie in its relevance to the
work of artists: those choices of commitment that determine the
quality of a lifetime of creative labor.

Section IV then plunges into instructing artists in the direction
they must take. Although it begins by addressing "poet and sculp-
tor," it has to do mainly with painters and their need to learn from
their "great forefathers": the inventors of the "stark" Egyptian and
the "gentler" Greek forms, Michelangelo and his sexually vital figures that can shock tourists into excited arousal, and other Renaissance painters whose background scenes from nature

> Resemble forms that are, or seem
> When sleepers wake and yet still dream,
> And when it's vanished still declare,
> With only bed and bedstead there
> That heavens had opened.

Yeats's brief, highly selective history of art corresponds with his
general conservatism and nostalgia for a lost past. He goes on to say
that painters of later times, after "that greater dream had gone," have
gradually lost the clear vision of their bolder predecessors, which
came with the discovery of "measurement" that "began our might"
and enabled them to become masters of form. But as the modern age
approached, "confusion fell upon our thought."

Section V then turns to poetry, urging Irish poets to pick up the
slack in their art and in the arts generally: "Irish poets, learn your

trade, / Sing whatever is well made." This means re-learning and regaining the power of form and—a considerable letdown in the momentum of this poem—singing the old feudal values accumulated over "seven heroic centuries." Suddenly, for a few lines at the end of V, all that has gone before is reduced to the retrograde, parochial battle-cry: "Cast your mind on other days / That we in coming days may be / Still the indomitable Irishry." Then comes Section VI, gratefully detached from this lapse into narrowness. There is certainly an air of aristocratic disdain for common concerns in the words "Cast a cold eye / On life, on death." But they hark back to the noble refusal to be cowed by death in Section II. They also reinforce the challenge to humanity, in III and IV, to create self-images "violent" enough to "bring the soul of man to God" and "make him fill the cradles right" in the future, so that there will be no further decline. A slightly suspect trace of propaganda for the eugenics movement lingers in that last quoted phrase, but it is sunken in the larger thought of the heaven-storming potentialities of artistic imagination.

One other piece in *Last Poems and Two Plays,* "The Statues," attempts the curious linking of the triumph of "measurement" in the forms of Western art over "Asiatic vague immensities" to Yeats's program for the creation of a triumphant Irish culture. Both "The Statues" and "Under Ben Bulben" have this unwieldy orientation, although the latter poem reveals so much more of the varied motives—personal, artistic, and national—underlying the linkage. "Under Ben Bulben" makes it clear that, in confronting his coming death, Yeats regarded himself as the bearer of ancient artistic and social values that were also dead or dying. He mourned them and himself together, and at the same time hoped that future Irish artists would grasp what he stood for, revive those values in their individual ways, and thus bring him back to life after all. Just as he saw Cuchulain reborn in the leaders of the Rising, he would be the Cuchulain reborn of Irish culture. This particular identification did not appear in the already overloaded "Under Ben Bulben," but the ending of "The Statues" at least implies it:

When Pearse summoned Cuchulain to his side,
Who stalked through the Post Office? What intellect,
What calculation, number, measurement, replied?
We Irish, born into that ancient sect
But thrown upon this filthy modern tide
And by its formless spawning fury wrecked,
Climb to our proper dark, that we may trace
The lineaments of a plummet-measured face.

Despite the many points of interest in Yeats's late poems, their elegiac and aesthetic-centered strains are the predominant ones. In *New Poems,* for instance, "Lapis Lazuli" appears at first to be about attitudes toward the unstable military situation in Europe. The year the poem was written was 1936. The Spanish Civil War was under way and Hitler's purposes were growing more and more apparent. The poem begins by speaking sardonically about persons who think artists merely frivolous if they do not abandon their work and devote themselves to heading off the looming war:

I have heard that hysterical women say
They are sick of the palette and fiddle-bow,
Of poets that are always gay,
For everybody knows or else should know
That if nothing drastic is done
Aeroplane and Zeppelin will come out,
Pitch like King Billy bomb-balls in
Until the town lie beaten flat.

The rest of the poem drops the little matter of the war crisis and turns to a defense of art as the whole point of civilization. The ironies of the opening verse-unit have their justification but are far too facile; they demean people who, rightly, took the threat very seriously and for the most part made no special demands on artists. That said, the succeeding verse-units show superbly the meaning of the artist's "gaiety": an ecstatic devotion to the demands of one's art, even if it means recurrent defeats and new starts: "All things fall and are built again, / And those that build them again are gay."

The second verse-unit sees us all as characters in a tragic play, with roles we must sustain to the end. The basic perception, summed up in the line "All perform their tragic play," grounds the poem in dark elegiac feeling. Gaiety in this context is the courage and integrity to play one's role to the hilt, like the characters in *Hamlet* and *King Lear* who never "break up their lines to weep." Whole civilizations have been forced to accept being "put to the sword." Their sustaining strength and that which guides the artist are inseparable.

The closing unit is given entirely to the image of a carving in lapis lazuli of two Chinamen climbing a hill toward a "little half-way house," where the poet imagines they will rest, "staring on all the tragic scene" and listening to "mournful melodies." As they do so, he thinks, "their eyes, / Their ancient glittering eyes, are gay." Their calm is in diametric contrast to the "hysterical" persons described in the poem's opening lines. It is an open question whether or not the stoical quietism the poem seems to advocate in the face of gathering horror is justifiable. But its sense of the relationship of art to "all the tragic scene" is another matter altogether.

The detached sense of aesthetic encompassment of those two Chinese figures whom Yeats says he "delights to imagine" is matched in "Long-legged Fly." Or perhaps it is outdone, because the latter poem does not entangle itself initially in a waspishly sarcastic sort of polemic. It simply presents three scenes in which, in silence, three different sorts of human creative power are in process of formation while outside influences are held at bay.

The first stanza of "Long-legged Fly" imagines Caesar in his tent planning a decisive campaign: "His eye fixed upon nothing, / A hand under his head." In the second a young girl, "part woman, three parts a child," secretly lets her feet "practise a tinker shuffle / Picked up on a street." She must be left to develop undisturbed; perhaps she is a Helen of Troy in the making. The third stanza imagines Michelangelo painting the creation of Adam in the Sistine Chapel. Once

it is done, "girls at puberty" can study the ideal male form and so
"find / The first Adam in their thought." In each case the mystery of
the mind's silent workings is stressed by the refrain: "Like a long-
legged fly upon the stream / His [or her] mind moves upon silence."

To return now to the major affective coloration of Yeats's late
work: many more poems in *Last Poems and Two Plays* and *On the
Boiler,* in addition to those already discussed, play richly on elegiac
motifs. Sometimes they press into recesses of sheer dread. The two-
pronged "The Black Tower" is one instance. In its main body it
seems a last-ditch echo of "Lapis Lazuli," mourning the doom of
cherished old values and loyalties but refusing to surrender them:

> Say that the men of the old black tower,
> Though they but feed as the goatherd feeds,
> Their money spent, their wine gone sour,
> Lack nothing that a soldier needs,
> That all are earth-bound men;
> Those banners come not in.

The poem's shifting refrain, on the other hand, faces literal
death with a macabre graveyard imagery that parodies the work's
primary stance of defiance. The first of the four-line refrains begins:
"There in the tomb stand the dead upright." All of them end: "Old
bones upon the mountain shake." In effects like these, the elegiac or
self-elegiac strain I have mentioned takes on a grisly intensity.

We find a similar shiver of horror in "The Apparitions" and
again in "A Bronze Head." The former poem is a naked personal
confession of need for strength "because of the increasing Night /
That opens her mystery and fright." It has a pathetic and chilling
refrain: "Fifteen apparitions have I seen; / The worst a coat upon a
coat-hanger." "A Bronze Head" is a nightmarish response to a bust of
Maud Gonne placed in the Dublin Municipal Gallery. Its resemblance to a stylized death's-head apparently took Yeats by surprise
and shocked him. The first lines will show how extraordinarily different this poem's tone is from the overwhelming nostalgia of "The
Municipal Gallery Re-visited":

Here at right of the entrance this bronze head,
Human, super-human, a bird's round eye,
Everything else withered and mummy-dead.
What great tomb-hunter sweeps the distant sky
(Something may linger there though all else die)
And finds there nothing to make its terror less
Hysterica passio of its own emptiness?

By comparison with poems like these, "John Kinsella's Lament for Mrs. Mary Moore" is downright jolly. It is like "The Wild Old Wicked Man" in its hearty affirmation, *faute de mieux,* of the "second-best" existence has to offer. Poor John Kinsella is distraught because his "dear Mary Moore" is no longer alive to supply him with everything he loves most. His comically anguished refrain—"What shall I do for pretty girls / Now my old bawd is dead?"—means first of all what it says literally. But by the end of the poem it has come to mean far more than physical pleasure. For one thing, Mary Moore represents the native Irish gift for witty, colorful speech and racy humor that the poem implies is now disappearing:

> And O! but she had stories
>   Though not for the priest's ear,
> To keep the soul of man alive,
>   Banish age and care,
> And being old she put a skin
>   On everything she said.
> What shall I do for pretty girls
>   Now my old bawd is dead?

For another thing, there is the matter of losing the old, innocent faith in the Church and the priesthood. The turn-over of their sacred authority to the likes of Mary Moore, whose "stories" can nourish the soul but are "not for the priest's ear," is a familiar rhetorical device in Yeats. ("Crazy Jane Talks with the Bishop" and "A Dialogue of Self and Soul" are the most striking examples.) John Kinsella carries the secular emphasis farther than other poems, though, in adding the vision of an earthly paradise to the joys the dead "old bawd" (by now symbolizing religious faith) once had to offer him but that now are lost:

> The priests have got a book that says
> > But for Adam's sin
> Eden's garden would be there
> > And I there within.
> No expectation fails there,
> > No pleasing habit ends,
> No man grows old, no girl grows cold,
> > But friends walk by friends.
> Who quarrels over halfpennies
> > That plucks the trees for bread?
> What shall I do for pretty girls
> > Now my old bawd is dead?

The music-hall bounce of the poem continues to the end, always underlined by the refrain. But meanwhile, the changing context of the refrain in each stanza makes the piece increasingly serious in its grief over what is lost: first sexual and other bodily pleasures, then a heart-delighting habit of rich and vivid speech, and then the hope of eternal bliss. John Kinsella's "lament" may well recall the much earlier "Running to Paradise," with its implication that humanity, in racing toward an irretrievable Eden, lives at best in the footloose condition of a fool or a beggar.

The two poems, both confessional and self-elegiac, that come just before "Politics" in *Last Poems and Two Plays* are "Man and the Echo" and "The Circus Animals' Desertion." They are the most personally immediate pieces in the volume—a far cry from the prophetically ambitious "Under Ben Bulben" at its beginning—so that after them "Politics" seems the last brave little hurrah of its would-be wild old wicked author. These two poems, in their depressive mood but sustained emotional force, give the sort of ballast to the volume that "Cuchulain Comforted" does near the beginning. They thus contribute greatly to its structure as a brave and honest se-

quence of poems and plays in which the poet wrestles with the twin
spectres of death and the breakdown of traditions he has tried to
live by.

"Man and the Echo" sets the stage at once for its uncanny,
remorseful dialogue of "Man" with his own "Echo." Or rather, the
dialogue sets its own stage as Man reveals that he has wandered into
an ancient rocky chasm ("a cleft that's christened Alt") and finds
himself at the bottom of a gloomy pit. There he is beset by guilty self-
doubts that he feels compelled to "shout . . . to the stone" in this
secret place. Did an early play (*Cathleen ni Houlihan*) inspire any
young men to sacrifice their lives? Did something he said cause a
young woman to go mad? Could he have prevented disaster to a
certain family?—"And all seems evil until I / Sleepless would lie
down and die." And Echo answers, "Lie down and die."

Man's second speech, a reply to Echo's mimic injunction, is
more abstract. No, suicide or mortal illness is no solution. The work
of sorting out the meaning of past actions must go on, delayed
though it may be by the body's needs. Once the body is dead, his
"intellect" will find its way to "one clear view" and can "sink at last
into the night." And Echo, that delphic "Rocky Voice," answers,
"Into the night." Man has not reached that ultimate point, however.
He is here in this pit, unsure of his moral bearings, and immensely
troubled by fears concerning sufferings he may have caused, the
suffering in the world around him, and his own death:

> O rocky voice,
> Shall we in that great night rejoice?
> What do we know but that we face
> One another in this place?
> But hush, for I have lost the theme,
> Its joy or night seem but a dream;
> Up there some owl or hawk has struck,
> Dropping out of sky or rock,
> A stricken rabbit is crying out
> And its cry distracts my thought.

"The Circus Animals' Desertion" presents a related sort of dismay, though one in which guilt does not figure. Its first line—"I sought a theme but sought for it in vain"—connects with the words "I have lost the theme" in the foregoing passage. All the poet has ever wanted in the past, he says, was to project and give himself to dream visions that were emblems of the neglected needs of his "embittered heart." The underlying desires they came out of were pushed aside, for "players and painted stage took all my love, / And not those things that they were emblems of." Now, in old age, those visionary figures (the "masterful images" that were his "circus animals": the Countess Cathleen, Cuchulain, and the others) have deserted him. He is left, as in "Man and the Echo," with himself in the ambiguous depths of unresolved life. The despair and sense of loss are the keenest here of any of Yeats's poems. His description of the elements of his inner self, as opposed to the ideals he has constructed over the years, adds up to sheer squalor (and perhaps, even, reflects terror at the thought of the body's fate after death):

> Those masterful images because complete
> Grew in pure mind but out of what began?
> A mound of refuse or the sweepings of a street,
> Old kettles, old bottles, and a broken can,
> Old iron, old bones, old rags, that raving slut
> Who keeps the till. Now that my ladder's gone
> I must lie down where all the ladders start
> In the foul rag and bone shop of the heart.

Doubtless the three poems that appeared posthumously, along with *Purgatory,* in *On the Boiler* might have been added to the *Last Poems* group. "Why Should Not Old Men Be Mad" is a lively complaint about the injustices and disappointments one inevitably observes if one lives to old age. "Crazy Jane on the Mountain" turns Crazy Jane into a social critic weeping over the murders of the Russian royal family and the symbolic diminution of "great-bladdered Emer" and "her violent man / Cuchulain," whom she glimpses being carried along in a "two-horsed carriage." "The

Index

I. Individual Poems, Sequences, and Plays by Yeats
(Note: play-titles in italics)

355

II. Prose Pieces and Complete Volumes by Yeats Cited

III. General Index